LIFE ON THE LINE

Jeremy Bullard was born in 1958. Following a degree in Economic History, he decided to become a chartered accountant but quickly found that the ride to work – on his 50cc Puch moped – was by far the most exciting part of his day. He is a Fellow of the Royal Geographical Society and this is his first book.

LIFE ON THE LINE

Jeremy Bullard

Blue-Footed

First published in the United Kingdom in 2012
by Blue-Footed Publishing

info@blue-footed.com

www.blue-footed.com

All the events described happened. The names of some people and places have been changed to protect identities.

A CIP record for this work is available from the British Library.

ISBN 978–0–9569683–0–2

Typeset by Bookcraft Ltd, 18 Kendrick Street, Stroud, GL5 1AA.

Printed and bound by Henry Ling Ltd, The Dorset Press, Dorchester

Copyright acknowledgements:

The author gratefully acknowledges permission to reprint the following copyright material:

This book is for my father

A journey, after all, neither begins the instant we set out, nor ends when we have reached our doorstep once again. It starts much earlier and is never really over, because the film of memory continues running on inside us long after we have come to a physical standstill.

Ryszard Kapuściński, Travels with Herodotus

I know that I'm a prisoner
To all my father held so dear
I know that I'm a hostage
To all his hopes and fears
I just wish I could have told him in the living years.

Mike Rutherford, 'The Living Years'

FRED

It was a beautiful day for a blessing. The priest, dressed in a brown cassock and blue hat, smiled at me and nodded at my motorbike. The scent of flowers filled the air. He had two cars and a green truck covered in rosettes to bless before he'd be ready for me. Copacabana Cathedral, beside Lake Titicaca, is the most important place of pilgrimage in Bolivia. A row of stalls protected by white sunshades surrounded the cathedral gates. They were selling model houses, cars and televisions. A buy-and-bless sale. Buy a model Land Cruiser, get it blessed and God would soon give you a real four-wheel-drive. But I didn't need a model. I had brought the real thing – my bike. Instead, I chose two garlands of red flowers, one each for the front and back of my bike, a bottle of cheap champagne and some firecrackers from the adjoining stall.

'Nomine padre, nomine madre,' said the priest as he dipped a bunch of plastic flowers into a red plastic bucket and flicked the holy water over my bike's handlebars and seat, then over my head. His prayers and incantations lasted for two minutes, which seemed very good value. All the important bits of my bike received attention: the wheels, engine and top box. He would bless anything if the price was right. I gave him ten bolivianos ($1) and he turned away and started on the grey Mitsubishi 4 × 4 behind me.

The packet of thunder flashes had seemed rather small, so I bought another and lit them both at once. They were a lot louder than I expected. Duly fortified, I shook the champagne to build up some pressure and handed my camera to a German tourist to record the momentous event. A small crowd had gathered to watch. The plastic cork exploded over the spectators' heads and as the foam emerged

I shook the bottle, Formula 1 style, and emptied it over my bike. I retrieved my camera and thanked the tourist.

The champagne dried into a sticky mess. I washed it all off back at my *hostal*, La Cúpula, and then checked the photos. He hadn't taken a single shot.

Later that day, as I sat on the grass and gazed out over Lake Titicaca in an almost trancelike state, I couldn't stop smiling. Something significant had changed and I was suddenly seeing my bike in a different way. I'd been on the road for a year now and it was starting to dawn on me that this wasn't just a 22,000-mile journey from New York to Tierra del Fuego then on to Cape Town and back to London. It was also a way of connecting with my father, and my motorbike was the link.

A motorbike is a like a Spitfire. It is freedom, excitement and a scalpel: precision, poise and purpose. Stopped by nothing, you slice through the traffic, past the caged egos and peacocks in tin boxes, wasting space and going nowhere. With another burst of acceleration you fly through the gap and into the distance. Out of the city, the road crests a rise through red maples and dips down into a series of S-bends where a long line of cars, queued behind the slowest like sheep, crawls towards the first corner. With surprise, momentum and nothing coming the other way, you overtake them all in one go, strafing them and painting graceful arcs, perfect parabolas and the smoothest lines through the bends. Art on a bike. Using the brakes means your speed was too high, you failed to anticipate: an error of judgement. You don't get many chances to get it wrong in a Spitfire.

I felt bonded to my bike. I relied on it completely, to keep me safe and not let me down. It had no soul of course and was simply a mechanical tool, a mode of transport. But the blessing had made me feel strangely unsettled. The priest had 'christened' my bike and now, even though I am an atheist and not at all sentimental, I felt I had to give my bike a name. I decided to call him Fred.

Fred is what my father used to call me. He died suddenly when I was sixteen. I never really knew him nor will I ever know how similar we are. But my journey was bringing his memory alive, and Fred was the key.

I am a long-distance rider. This is my job. This is what I do. Every day I wake up somewhere new, get on my bike and go. The former loneliness of the long-distance rider has gone. I am no longer alone, because my bike and I are one. I am happy now.

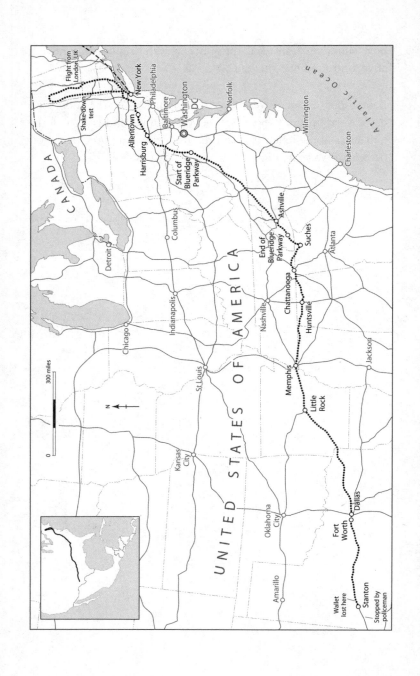

1

A GIANT TARMAC
QUESTION MARK

With only two weeks to get to the Mexican motorcycle rally from New York, I jumped on to my bike. I'd have to take the shortest route through Texas, rather than explore the deserts of Baja California, but at least I'd have time to take the slow roads.

Instead of getting more and more excited as my trip approached, I had constantly seesawed between 'I will go' and 'I won't go', like pulling petals off a daisy. Gnawed by self-doubt and indecision, I'd worked my way through my list of things to do, having completely underestimated how much time it would take to get a new bike ready. As the rally loomed ever closer there was no time for a shakedown test, I'd have to do it on the road.

Finally on my way, I took a deep breath, relaxed my shoulders and hoped that I hadn't forgotten anything. It felt strange to be on the road again, but I knew that would pass.

Relieved to get off interstate 81, about 300 miles from New York, and on to smaller roads, I was looking forward to the November fall colours, winding roads and views from the Blue Ridge Parkway. The single-storey Fox Diner reminded me of 'Happy Days' and I expected to see several finned Cadillacs and Buicks parked outside, not a Jeep, a Honda and an old white Mercedes. Inside, the chrome fittings and Formica tables kept the Happy Days theme going, but a burger and fries weren't the way to keep slim. I left feeling bloated and pulled into the nearby 7-Eleven knowing there would be few, if any, petrol stations in Shenandoah National Park.

'It just gets better and better the further south you go,' said Darlene as she handed me my change. Her blonde hair and startling blue eyes made me want to stay longer. 'Why sit on an interstate when you can have beautiful scenery and beautiful views all day? It's the best road in the world.'

President Roosevelt built the Blue Ridge Parkway during the 1930s Depression, to create jobs for unemployed engineers and construction workers. It connects the 105-mile Skyline Drive in Shenandoah National Park, Virginia, to the Great Smoky Mountains National Park 470 miles further south. Designed by Stanley Abbot, an architect rather than an engineer, it follows the crest of the Blue Ridge Mountains like a forest roller coaster, in a continuous series of swoops and swerves.

Climbing through low hills and fields, the Skyline Drive emerged on to the ridge, where westward views over the fields and farms below appeared through gaps cut in the forest. The sun was low when I pulled into the Dickey Ridge Visitor Center. I stopped beside a fellow biker. André was still quaking from a scary encounter with a bear a quarter of an hour earlier.

'I was so lucky. It ran across the road in front of me as I was going round a bend. I lost time getting the bike upright and more moving a finger on to the brake lever. I was so close I saw the hairs on the back of his head as I went past.'

He was so spooked I offered him a drink but he was in a rush to get home in time for work the next morning.

As André headed off I began to wish I hadn't left my cooking equipment in New York in a last-minute 'travel light' moment. He'd recommended Mathews Arm campground 15 miles away, but an hour had slipped past and it was now dark. Day one and my first golden rule was already in tatters: don't ride at night. The forest marched beside me as the sharp shadows from my headlights flickered through the trees.

The 'generator-free zone' at the campground was on the crest of a hill away from the other campers and RVs. Tiny lights shone in the valley below; the distant cry of a blue jay and the sweet smell of fallen leaves drifted past on a gentle breeze. Cocooned in my tent, dreaming of the days to come, I wondered if two weeks was enough to make the Horizons rally in Mexico. Suddenly some twigs cracked close by and I was alert in an instant. André's bear? Too scared to move I kept reassuring myself that it was only Bambi and eventually fell asleep.

The next morning, bursts of orange and ochre interleaved with glorious greens as the ribbon of asphalt sashayed from side to side, dancing through the autumn splendour. Gaps in the trees revealed hills rolling into the distance like standing waves and a giant tarmac question mark on the crest ahead. I frequently stopped to soak up the colours, breathe in the dying leaves and gaze at the views. A blaze of orange pumpkins filled a trailer beside a post-and-rail fence. A large American flag flew above, taut in the wind. A hundred yards further on two trestle tables sagged under the weight of yet more pumpkins. The two on the top grimaced at me through their hollow eyes. A hand-painted sign leant against a trestle leg: $1. Ten days to Halloween.

Something was bothering me, and it wasn't a fear of Halloween ghosts. I'd felt a similar unease at the beginning of a previous trip, when I'd taken nearly a week to get into the rhythm of the road, but this was deeper. This was about money. I had chosen to fund this trip with my savings and with a so-called Open-Plan Mortgage, which allowed me to borrow up to the entire value of my flat. The prospect of blowing not only my savings but perhaps my flat as well was making me very anxious. Should I – could I – enjoy the present at the expense of the future? A dilemma that was to become something of a recurring theme.

Darlene had been right. The road cut straight through forest with a wide grassy clearing on both sides. Hogging the centre line for the smoothest ride, my speed crept up on the long straight as it arrowed towards the yellow birches, red maples and orange sassafras in the distance. Sunday morning is a great time to ride. The Shenandoah National Park was deserted. I accelerated a bit more and my nerves tingled. My suspension soaked up the bumps, flowing over them like soft cushions. The road curved left ahead, and a few hundred yards before the bend a kaleidoscope of autumnal colours shimmered in the sun. I couldn't see around the corner but felt it tighten. I checked the bend again and looked up at the trees. A white truck was reflected in the leaves.

I snapped the throttle shut and moved to the edge of the road. I couldn't brake because I was leaning into the bend and there was nowhere to go. Suddenly a huge white truck appeared in the centre of the road and whooshed straight past me. I shuddered, shocked at my luck. It should never have been there. National parks prohibit commercial vehicles. I slowed down, relieved I had reacted so quickly and shivered as Obi-Wan's words came to me: 'Use the Force'. How could leaves be a mirror? They aren't silvered. It made no sense. The more I thought about it the odder it seemed. What was the logical explanation? Had the leaves been at the right angle to act as a mirror? Do things happen for a reason?

Three days into my journey, my anxieties were fading as I rolled through the curves, the warm late-October weather enveloping me like a blanket. Riding through a tunnel of golden leaves, dew sparkled in the morning sun and misty hills exploded from openings through the trees. Like a slow symphony, the haze gradually lifted to reveal the autumnal forests stretching to the horizon. The sense of space and adventure sated my soul.

The reflection of the white truck in the autumn leaves still turned over in my mind. Had I imagined it? Was it my sixth sense, the little voice of my intuition? After all, dogs and other animals possess a vestigial sixth sense and we are all related through common ancestors.

I had learnt to listen to my little voice and intuition while I was an in-patient at the Priory, a private mental-health hospital. I'd admitted myself to the Woking branch one summer's afternoon feeling dizzy and scared. For a month the earth had been moving continuously under my feet, as if I was walking on a rolling deck. I couldn't relax, couldn't sleep and for the first time in my life was having terrifying panic attacks. I thought I was dying. I lay on my bed at home and cried for hours at a time. I needed professional help.

I was burnt out from my job as an IT consultant, mentally and physically exhausted from an intense two years of high stress, long hours and almost no time off. Obsessed with paying off my mortgage, I ignored what my body was telling me, dismissed the obvious signs and soldiered on. Eventually I became so wired I couldn't sleep, running on adrenaline until my brain shut me down.

Just like a computer, I needed to reboot. I'd locked up and needed to restart. The wires in my head were so taut they short-circuited, filling my head with irrational thoughts. A breakdown is just what it says. I lost my self-confidence, identity and personality. Familiar feelings and emotions were stripped away by the failure of my system to cope. Behaviours and layers built up over the years evaporated and left me raw and vulnerable like a child.

A close friend later said that my breakdown could turn out to be the best thing that happened to me, and she was right. I discovered I had suppressed anger for years and was startled when I felt the raw emotion again. Perhaps I had suppressed mourning my father's death too. My craving for cash and the rat race had polluted my priorities. I had completely confused what I wanted with what I needed. I was lucky. Though I hit the depths of despair, all it took was time. Time to relax, recover, and realign the wires.

I emerged a changed person, far more relaxed, free and alive. I saw everything clearly, no longer distorting my desires in the shallow pursuit of meaningless possessions. I appreciated my good luck and health like never before and listened to the little voice I had ignored for so long.

The little voice had told me to go on a big ride and worry about the money later. Had it also told me to get the hell out of the middle of the road because a hulking great truck was about to mow me down?

André had recommended the bikers' Two Wheels Only camp in Suches, Georgia, and the closer I got the more motorcycles appeared on the road. The climbs are so steep through the Chattahoochee National Forest that many of the hills have two lanes up and one down. Just as I passed an old Suzuki two-stroke belching blue smoke, five sports bikes zapped past me and made me jump. The cars kept right, hugging the kerb to keep out of the way. The line of bikes followed their leader, falling from side to side with every corner, like synchronised windscreen wipers.

It was impossible to miss Two Wheels Only on Highway 60: rows of motorbikes were parked outside a rust-coloured house with white shutters and a tin roof. Inside, a small stuffed brown bear lay on top of a wooden chest. Four rough-cut timber poles supported the bare beams, and a brown cardboard Harley hung from the ceiling. Trophy animals filled every nook and cranny. The Roadkill Café Menu on the wall caught my eye: 'You Kill It, We Grill It: Chunk of a Skunk $1.95, Flat Cat $2.95. For the adventurous there's Guess that Mess, or if you're in a rush, Bag 'n Gag, our daily take-out special: Anything Dead in Bread.' Chunk of a Skunk sounded interesting, but they didn't say which end you'd get. 'When in Rome' flashed into my mind but in the end I gave Smidgeon of Pigeon and Narrow Sparrow a miss and opted for the safety of a cheeseburger.

I pitched my tent beside one of the wooden tables that dotted the forested campsite. Twenty yards away was a far grander set up. The garlic-and-herb smell coming from the frying pan made it rude not to say hi.

Ara Gureghian was a personal chef to rich Floridians and he travelled in style. His bike, a big BMW, even had a fridge. A fold-out trestle table stood under the awning. A little juice shone on the white chopping board on which he'd just prepared 'a simple linguini and tomato sauce', beside which was an open roll of professional cook's knives. His meal looked mouthwatering. Maybe I should follow him.

Ara took his time talking and thought a lot about what he was going to say. There was a big melancholic air about him, as though he carried a heavy weight on his shoulders, and I soon found out why. His son Lance had recently passed away from cancer; he was 26 and Ara's only child.

Ara had been on the road ever since, with his dog Spirit in the sidecar. Spirit had his own black helmet and goggles. 'Writing is my therapy,' he told me, 'replacing my pink and blue pills after my son passed away. I just write for myself.'

Perhaps writing could be my therapy too.

Two Wheels Only seemed like the obvious place to devote some time to my bike. Since I'd spent so long getting it ready I hadn't even had a chance to run it in. I'd bought a brand new silver KTM 640 Adventure for this, my third long-distance bike trip and, as an invet-erate tinkerer, had made over sixty modifications to it. One of the changes was adding a Scotts steering damper to prevent 'tank slap-pers' (uncontrollable lock-to-lock shaking of the handlebars). The £300 Scotts damper is bright gold and can be stolen in seconds; so I painted it matt black with emulsion. One thing led to another and soon I was covering all the shiny bits I could find. By the time I finished, the whole bike was matt black.

I had to do the first service and check for nuts and bolts loosened by the single-cylinder vibrations. It is extraordinary how different identical machines can be when they're made from the same parts but with slightly different tolerances. To minimise the vibrations, ex-KTM factory mechanic Martin Marsh, or 'Swampy' to his friends, had stripped, balanced and rebuilt the engine, making it as smooth as possible. It also made it more powerful.

That evening I met Sue Galpin in the Roadkill bar. A blue-eyed blonde with a wicked glint in her eye, she's a racer and ambassador for BMW motorcycles, having ridden over 500,000 miles on BMWs, and also teaches people how to ride safely. She was in Suches for the upcoming True Grits Fun Run, an annual 70-mile race for 50 cc bikes which was due to be held the following week, at the end of October. She'd won the race twice before – 'the boys don't like to be beaten' – and said she'd be happy to show me the route.

We went for a ride round Blood Mountain, which is said to have got its name after a battle between the Creek and Cherokee Indians. As we climbed out of the valley through the trees, there were continuous double yellow lines and corners so tight that '15 mph' signs warned of hairpin bends. A momentary crest and then a plunge down the other side to the stream below. There were constant corners through a myriad of twists and turns, a mad ride through a forest where beeches dripped copper leaves like confetti. Exhilarating and exhausting at the same time. A pillion would soon be seasick despite the smoothest roads I've ever been on. If the crash barriers were higher it would make a perfect marble run – for giant marbles. The longest straight was only a few hundred feet and often there was none at all. The road was never flat, even for an instant, constantly changing elevation, up one valley then down the other side through a tunnel of green, orange and brown. Sue was fast. Fast and fearless. Totally committed round blind corners ridden on faith and reflexes. Too fast for me. It was hard to keep up with her even though she was going slowly and too polite to call me slow.

Time was slipping by. Checking my map on the wooden table under the trees I traced a route west through Chattanooga, Nashville and Memphis, places that felt familiar from songs and films even though I'd never seen them. I'd have to hit the interstate so made a beeline cross-country on Highway 72 through Florence to catch the I40 at Memphis. It was beginning to feel a long way to Mexico. I needed to keep my eye on the calendar.

I crossed the Tennessee River at Florence in the warm afternoon sunshine. It didn't feel like I was in the richest nation on earth. The box-girder bridges on Highway 72 looked like they'd been built from a Third World Meccano set. The steel girders didn't look strong enough, especially the horizontal ones with such big slots punched through them that less than half the steel remained. The faded green paint had long been overtaken by rust but they still took the weight of the huge trucks. Maybe UK bridges were just massively over-engineered.

By the fourth day out of Two Wheels Only I'd found my rhythm. My day always started slowly while I let the engine warm up and myself settle down. I kept below 60 mph for the first fifteen minutes, before accelerating to cruising speed. It was another dry day, but the heavy clouds cast a gloom over my mood. All the cars seemed to be grey. I was free to think, free to wander. I was making good miles to the Horizons biking rally in Creel and wondered who else would be there. Then my heart skipped a beat and my hopes of making Mexico evaporated in an instant. The throttle wouldn't open any more. It was against the stop and I was losing power, only doing 66 mph and slowing down. Ring failure? Valve trouble? Had I not checked them properly in Suches? It took me a few moments to realise I'd been going up a long, gentle slope into a strong headwind in top gear. I changed down and accelerated away.

I turned on to the I20 and resigned myself to motorway monotony. It was dull and overcast and the dry grasses, flat light and drab buildings merged into one shade of concrete. The buildings were boxes: simple, effective, and cheap. Nothing looked like it was made to last. Everything was constructed to maximise profits and minimise costs, and the roads felt the same: two lanes of poorly made and maintained tarmac, built down to a price not up to a standard. The cheapest road to a cheaper country. Even the telegraph poles looked drunk and disorderly, each one at a different angle, the horizontal bars leaning this way and that and never at the same height.

Two hours later the wriggles set in. After three, I was starting to dance on my seat, continually moving my bottom to avoid the ache. I'd never have lasted so long without my piece of sheepskin. Without it two hours was agony. I wanted to keep going and go faster so I had to concentrate more. I have always felt alive at speed, even as a child. I remembered sitting on the front armrests of my father's car, aged nine, on the way to Cornwall to pick up my eldest sister. The dead-straight dual carriageway descended a long hill, went under a bridge and climbed up the other side. I was bouncing up and down urging my father to go faster. 'We're doing 125 mph and it won't go any faster,' he said. I was disappointed as the speedometer went up to 140 mph. Now, thirty years later, I wondered what my father would have thought of my trip, whether he might have wanted to come too.

Those warm and cold fronts on weather maps really do exist. You feel the caress of a warm front or the chill of a cold one as you ride through the invisible lines. I wondered how cold it would be at 8,000 feet in Creel, Mexico. It was downhill all the way into the afternoon and concentration was easier. I was cruising, wondering how far I'd get before dark and looking forward to the first beer. I played with my best gadget, a Touratech IMO ('Intelligent Motorbike Computer') digital speedometer with ten screens of data. The two I used the most were the one that showed the miles done on the current tank and the mpg on the last tank, and the one that counted down the miles to my destination and calculated the expected time of arrival. It said there were 243 miles to Presidio on the border and my ETA was 18.30. As it wouldn't get dark until 7.30 p.m. I could be in Mexico that night. But that was rule number one again. Don't ride at night.

I looked up from the digital speedometer and saw a car going slowly 100 yards in front of me. It looked like it had a roof rack, but I soon realised it was a row of lights. My stomach lurched. I slowly edged past the patrol car, while the driver was on his radio, hoping he might lose interest. Just as I thought I'd escaped all the lights went on.

'Good afternoon,' I said in my best British accent.

'Hi, how are you?'

Texans are so polite.

'Good, thanks. What's the problem?'

He looked confused. 'Your licence plate doesn't exist.'

'I'm from England and it's a British bike.'

'Show me your registration papers and driver's licence.'

I opened my top box and showed him my V5, the bike's registration document.

'Show me your driver's licence.'

I reached into my chest pocket, but it was already open and empty. My heart sank.

'Oh, fuck, fuck, fuck. My wallet must have fallen out. It had everything inside: my passport, credit and ATM cards, UK and international driving licences, and about $150 in cash.'

I jumped up and down with frustration and anger, and thinking that a bit of hamming it up might get me off a speeding ticket, I jumped up and down a bit more. I could see the judges holding up the 'artistic interpretation' and 'star quality' marks over his shoulder. All nines. I'd left the zip undone before but it had never actually fallen out. (Low scores for the intelligence test then.)

'The strong crosswind must have sucked it out of my pocket. It must be lying somewhere on the I20.'

It wasn't a total disaster as I had a second passport but he didn't need to know that. What worried me was whether I could get into Mexico without a driver's licence, and how to get a new ATM card.

'When was the last time you stopped?'

I flicked through a few screens on my IMO bike computer, carefully bypassing the one that showed my maximum speed in very large numbers and exactly when I did it – about half an hour earlier.

'Exactly 133 miles ago when I filled up with gas.'

'You could go back and look for it, but it would be like looking for a needle in a haystack,' the patrolman said, then wished me luck and drove away.

More like a complete waste of time, I thought. At least I hadn't got a ticket.

It was 4 p.m. and there were still 200 miles to the border. But I could ride back, spend the night near the petrol station, potter down the hard shoulder looking for my wallet and still get to

Presidio the next day. It would be a long day but at least I would have tried.

A few hours later, feeling really tired, I pulled into Town and Country service station in Roscoe. As I stopped I put my left foot down in to a pool of oil and it slipped from under me. Another superb display of advanced riding skills was rapidly approaching. With consummate grace and skill I hopped off as best I could – and then watched my bike crash to the ground.

'Er, can someone help me pick it up please?'

The three men standing around a nearby 4 × 4 gawped but didn't move. Perhaps they were waiting for an encore. Then a big man in a red checked shirt came over and we heaved it upright. I thanked him profusely. Lonnie had broad shoulders and rough hands. He was a cotton farmer, 'just one of the small guys', with a mere thousand acres rather than the ten thousand the big boys farmed.

His parting words caught me by surprise. 'Don't worry, you'll find your wallet.'

How could he know? Logically he was right. It lay somewhere on that 133-mile stretch of interstate highway, lonely, hoping to be found, and yearning to go shopping. That's what wallets do. All I had to do was look in the right direction at the right time.

I woke at 6 a.m. feeling strangely optimistic. Hopefully the strong northerly crosswind would have blown it on to the hard shoulder. I rode down the hard shoulder at 30 mph, but it was too fast to scan the amazing variety of roadside detritus so I slowed to 20 mph. t-shirts, shoes, tapes, even huge pieces of wood, littered the sun-bleached grass. The service road made it easy to double back but every time it was something else: paper, cloth and once a pair of knickers.

After an hour and a half it was beginning to look futile. At the rate I was going it would take six hours to reach the lay-by where the patrolman had stopped me and another three hours to Presidio, longer in the dark. After two and a half hours I'd half given up and was going much faster past the tall grass, zooming over bridges and embankments without a second glance. Three hours in and I'd done only 70 miles. And then I found it near a bridge just beyond Odessa.

Unbelievable. I'd found it after 75 miles. Lonnie Orman had been right. How could he have known? Was he in touch with the other side? Everything was still inside my wallet although the zip was now buggered because it had been run over. You'd think drivers might take a bit more care with other people's property.

At the next petrol station, Phillips in Stanton, warm macadamia-nut cookies and a cold Coke felt like Christmas. 'You sure are lucky,' said the women behind the counter. 'Nothing exciting ever happens around here, although we did find a handgun in the trash once. Now we have a story to tell. We could become part of an "Interesting gas station tour of Texas".'

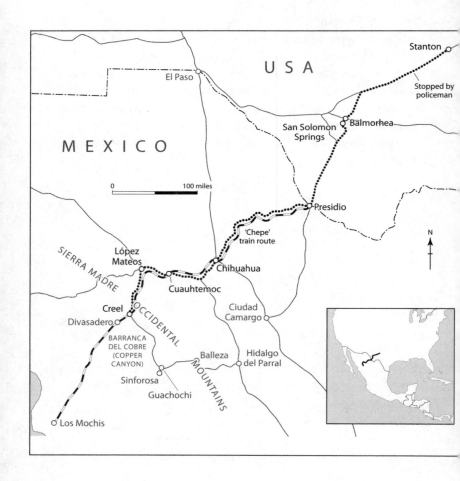

2

CASEY JONES

A herd of ugly black donkeys dotted the dry, dusty and treeless plain. Their movement was so slow I only noticed it when I stopped. Perhaps they were anxious not to miss a single drop of oil. I turned south at Pecos, Texas. It was a joy to be off the motorway at last after a week of droning across the southern interstates, through miles of mind-numbingly dull dried grass and fields. A low hill shimmered through the haze, promising curves to come. Maybe there were mountains beyond. I wanted to reach out and touch them.

At last bright green fields blossomed on either side of the road. In Balmorhea, 100 miles from the Mexican border, a small channel flowed with crystal clear water. Balmorhea is an oasis, fed by the San Solomon Springs, an artesian well which was once an important spring for the itinerant Mescalero Apache who watered their horses here. The Apache ranged over the southern part of what is now New Mexico and into Mexico, fighting the Spanish (who arrived in Mexico in the early 1500s), then the Mexicans, honing their famous guerrilla tactics during these wars before perfecting them against the US Government. It was said that an Apache could run 50 miles without stopping and travel more swiftly than a troop of soldiers. By the mid-nineteenth century, however, Mexican farmers had settled around Balmorhea. They dug the first irrigation channels to water their crops and changed the name to San Solomon.

Once out of the lush Balmorhea valley, the thin, treeless scrub returned; patches of bare earth and tufts of coarse grass were my only companions. I smiled at the first real corners all week, taking exaggerated turns through the bends and leaning over as far as possible. I whooped. It felt like my birthday so I went back and rode them again. I yearned for the border, eager to get away from the big distances and into Mexico. Every time I crested one hill another appeared, and then another. They started to come faster and faster until giant interlocking fingers of rock forced the road to loop back and forth. I used the full width of the empty road, aiming for that perfect line in my Spitfire, clipping each apex while keeping an eye out for Huns in the sun. Perfect biking country. I grinned through the sweepers, wondering how to celebrate my last night in the US. Rocky outcrops guarded the top of each spur. This was Indian country. Thin stunted bushes appeared on the skyline. Small puffs of cloud in the sky looked suspicious. Smoke signals?

Presidio's main street sliced through town to the border, giving little reason to stop. You only came here on the way to somewhere else. The streets were clean, laid out with sterile grid orderliness, but there were many vacant lots. Something was missing. 'City Hall' said a sign above a small white bungalow on a street corner, rather optimistic in a town of 5,000 people.

Outside the Riata Inn Motel a tall man with black hair and a black enduro jacket and jeans was removing his panniers from his motorbike. Like me, Gerardo Ibarra was on his way to the Horizons rally in Creel; his brother, Juan, was the rally organiser. The brothers were both born in Mexico but Gerardo now lived with his family in Indiana, where he worked as an engineer. He had the slightly hollow cheeks of the very fit, which figured, given that he'd once been in the Mexican National International Six Days Enduro Team. I doubt even God could make a national ISDE team. I could only dream of having his skills. With that in mind I decided not to join him on the ride to Creel the following day, preferring to travel at my own pace.

As I paid my bill the next morning the lady receptionist warned me: 'Mexico's a Third World country. You be careful.'

'Have you been there?'

'Nope, and I ain't going either.'

After an easy US border crossing I rode over the Rio Grande into Mexico. The Mexican Customs officials were super friendly, and in half an hour I was zipping through Ojinaga with a 90-day visa and a 90-day temporary import permit.

Ojinaga looked and smelt different. A blue rust bucket belched past in a cloud of blue smoke that rasped my throat. The car had no badges at all. There were fewer vacant lots here. Bright red and blue shops lined both sides of the road. A pale stone building with crenel-lated walls belonged to the Alamo but white houses with red roof tiles gave the place a European flavour. It felt like home, except for the tangle of telephone wires hanging overhead like black spaghetti. The pavements were crowded with people, many just chatting beside the road. Cars were not king here.

I rode the elation of being in a new country, passing through a lunar landscape devoid of farms or fields. I shouted, happy to be in Mexico and riding curvy roads again, until I reached Chihuahua, the state capital. There weren't many tiny dogs about (or normal-sized ones for that matter). The traffic on Highway 16 crawled through the industrial part of the city, past cement works and chemical factories, through a fog of evil smells where tall chimneys belched grey soup into the sky. I slowed to cross the railway tracks laid into the road. There were no barriers but the rails were shiny with use. Heavy traffic and heavy lorries carrying Uncle Sam's dirty deeds. I would pick up the railway line again, 100 miles southwest, in Copper Canyon, a railway buff's dream.

The Mexican Government must be run by a secret cadre of car mechanics: there were hundreds of topes (speed humps) and they were often hard to spot. Just like the state's eponymous little dogs: annoying, small and vicious. But speed was good: the faster I went the smoother they became. I would stand up just before the bump

21

and hardly slowed at all as my suspension sucked them up into barely a ripple.

If only life's little ripples could be dealt with so easily. After checking out of the Priory I'd decided to fulfil a dream and ride my motorbike from London to Cape Town. But since I'd already given up twice before (once heading south from London and once north from Cape Town), I decided to start my third attempt from New York.

An advert for a Horizons Unlimited biking rally in Mexico three months away caught my eye. I could fly to New York then head south by joining the dots on my must-see list: the hibernating butterflies in the Mexican Sierra Madre Mountains, the Galápagos Islands, the Inca ruins of Machu Picchu, a ride across the Salared Uyuni, the world's highest salt lake, a stop in Ushuaia, the world's southernmost city, then a wander among the giant stone statues of Easter Island. Leaving South America from Buenos Aires, I'd fly to Cape Town and ride back to London through East Africa. I would be away for a year.

But, right now, at the very beginning of my odyssey, I was wondering what I was doing on yet another trip, especially so soon after my last one. A chartered accountant then IT consultant by profession, aged 39 and still single, I should be working and trying to settle down and raise a family before it was too late. Too stubborn to be sensible and save, I'd run away from restlessness and responsibility. I had decided it was better to go alone than not at all, better to reach for a dream and fail than always live with regret. I didn't want to get to my death bed with my list of must-sees still intact. But why doesn't a decision stay made? Why did the dilemma keep resurfacing?

I turned south towards Creel at López Mateos, beside green cornfields. The air was cooler. Long straights undulated over the contours as scattered pine trees morphed into small copses, then it was as if someone flicked a switch and I started winding through forested hills. My spirits rose on the winds as I leant into the corners, flicking from left to right, flying along each arc, aiming for the vanishing point, until the view exploded again. My speed increased with the rhythm of the road when suddenly a donkey's backside appeared around a corner. I stood the bike upright and braked hard. The burro didn't move, his head was hanging down, staring at the ground in front of him. There were no fences.

The Sierra Madre Occidental Mountains start near the Arizona and Texas border and extend 700 miles southeast through the heart of Mexico. Creel, a logging town, is 200 miles from the border. Twisting and turning, I climbed through pine forests, and the closer to Creel the steeper the road became. The scent of wood smoke filled the clear, clean air. As I rode into town past wooden shops with raised verandas, I expected to see people carrying skis. There were bright colours, but they were the pink and yellow floral skirts of the local Tarahumara Indian women.

A whistle blast called me to the other side of town. A shortcut through unmade backstreets and I caught a glimpse between two houses that required a double take: a long line of RVs floating above the ground. Another blast shattered the silence. A blue loco, spouting a plume of black smoke against the blue sky, was noisily shunting a long line of motorhomes on flat-bed cars into a siding. They were on their way to Los Mochis on the Pacific coast, a journey of only 225 miles that would take twelve hours. Like everyone else, the RVers had come to Creel to see Barrancas del Cobre, Copper Canyon, which is deeper and prettier than the Grand Canyon. My other reason for coming was the awesome railway itself. But first I had a Horizons Unlimited motorbike rally to attend.

Grant Johnson, the rally organiser, smiled warmly, welcoming me to the Hotel Villa Mexicana. Bearded and wiry, the former road-racing and motocross champion has been a motorcycle traveller since 1987, when he and his wife Susan quit their jobs and headed for Panama. They run the best website for motorcycle overlanders, HorizonsUnlimited.com, both an amazing source of information and a network of worldwide contacts known as Horizons Unlimited Communities. The annual Horizons rally is organised via the site as a chance for bikers from across the globe to chat and swap stories. This was their first Mexican meeting and there were forty of us in all, among them Daniel Toader, also on a KTM 640 Adventure; Marc, a Belgian economics professor who lived in Thailand and whom I'd get to know when we met again in Valle de Bravo 1,100 miles south; Leah and Dom, an Aussie-Irish couple on their way to Buenos Aires on Kawasaki KLR650s, whom I'd also meet up with further south; and Leroy, a retired crop duster from Texas, who knew Mexico well and looked much younger than 79.

Grant gave a presentation on packing. I wondered how exciting that could be, but was surprised to learn that only Daniel and I put all our kit into colour-coded stuff-sacks. It saves so much time since you know which pannier it'll be in and what colour to look for. Other bikers presented slides from their own trips and shared 'top tips', like 'hide some cash on your bike,' and 'don't keep your top-up engine oil inside your luggage'. The latter was a bit late for me.

Juan Ibarra, the brother of enduro rider Gerardo whom I'd met at the US border, was in charge of all the local arrangements. A poet, author and veteran motorcyclist, he had organised for the Tarahumara to perform a traditional dance. The Tarahumara are the local Indians, the second largest tribe in North America. Originally from the fertile lower plains, in the sixteenth century they retreated into Barranca del Cobre to escape the Spanish and then the Mexicans, both of whom forced them to work in their mines. Now they are under pressure from the drug gangs who grow marijuana in the remote and road-less canyons. They make a living from farming and selling arts and crafts to tourists, like their exquisite baskets made from pine needles and sisal grass.

There were seven dancers, four women and three men, all of them short and heavyset, with black hair and Asian features. The women wore their traditional dress of fluffy-layered red, blue and white skirts, which flew out when they spun round, and tall headdresses hung with streamers that dropped below their waists. They danced with the men and sang to a guitar and drums like large tambourines.

As an encore they gave a demonstration of rarájipari, their national running game, a sort of hybrid of cross-country running and football. The group split into two teams, each with a wooden ball about the size of a baseball. Starting at one end of the hall, a man from each team pushed the ball on to the top of his toes using his other foot, and at the shout slung the ball down the room. Everyone rushed after the two men, shouting and yelling. Another man flicked one of the balls back again. One of the women used a forked stick to throw the other ball towards the post. A mass rush and the balls whizzed back to the start. After five laps the winning team danced a celebratory jig.

Juan filled us in. 'The Tarahumara love to run,' he told us, 'and call themselves the *Rarámuri*, the running people. They agree the course and number of laps before they start, but usually it is many miles through canyons and up and down huge hills along paths we can't even see. Think of starting at the rim of the Grand Canyon with the finish on the banks of the Colorado thousands of feet below. The games often last for one or two days non-stop, with runners refuelling with pinole [ground corn] and water. They also use their endurance to chase deer until they either trap them or wear them down from exhaustion.'

The next morning I walked to the station through the chilly morning air to book a ride on the famous 'Chepe' ('Chihuahua al Pacifico') train through Barrancas del Cobre, one of the ten greatest railway journeys in the world. Thin ice lay cracked like broken glass beside the road. I was glad I wasn't camping. Outside the station a Tarahumara woman in bright yellow scarf, red blouse and turquoise skirt sat surrounded by a sea of equally colourful Tupperware bowls. She was weaving a small basket. The colours were so strong, I longed to take a photo, but resisted, mindful of Juan's advice that some Tarahumara believe that you steal their soul when you take their picture.

With peaks exceeding 10,000 feet, the rugged and inaccessible Sierra Madre Occidental mountains hindered Spanish exploration, economic development and transport so much that it took sixty-four years to complete the railway. Started in 1898 and designed to compete with the Panama Canal, the railway begins in Los Mochis on Mexico's Pacific coast and rises to 8,000 feet at Creel before descending to Chihuahua and continuing east to enter the US at Presidio. The land is so mountainous that en route it crosses thirty-seven bridges and passes through eighty-six tunnels. The most spectacular sections are the twists and turns through Barrancas del Cobre: in one valley the train makes a loop through a tunnel and emerges above itself.

There are only two trains in each direction every day, a fast luxury one for tourists and a slow one for the locals. The local train stops at every station and can be hailed like a taxi. In the 1990s one village decided to rob the tourist train at a brief, unscheduled stop. While the tourists were handing over their cash, one of the bandits spotted a camera being pointed at him. He gestured that the tourist should hand over his camera. The man refused. A more agitated demand met with a similar but unwise refusal. The bandit shot him dead. Another reason not to take photos uninvited. Ever since, every train has had an armed guard.

Two huge red Ferromex locomotives pulled the train. A cow catcher almost touched the rails. The door of the cab was way above my head. I got the driver's attention and pointed at myself then the cab, using my most fluent gesticulations. The driver smiled and nodded to the rear of the train. Disappointed, assuming he wanted me to sit with all the other tourists, I looked up enquiringly again. He pointed a bit lower. At the ladder! I climbed into the cab and offered the ten dollars I'd been waving in my hand.

'Non!' He waved it away.

Jesus ('Hay-zoo') was also standing in the cab, hitching a lift to a nearby village, just past Divisadero. My Spanish was non-existent, so we communicated through drawings and mimes. I still have the piece of paper. The climbs are so steep each train needs two locomotives. Each loco weighs 300 tons and houses a 200-litre, 3,000-horsepower diesel engine to pull the train over the mountains. Suddenly the driver opened the throttle and the quiet rumble grew to a deafening din. The train was alive. We had to hold on to stay upright, and shout to hear each other. You felt the huge weight of the train as it lurched up the track. This was a real man's job, with two enormous throbbing engines and just two controls: a throttle and a brake. I pointed to myself and then the driver, but Jesus shook his head.

'No permiso.'

I mimed a 'Casey Jones' whistle blast with another enquiring glance. Another shake of his head.

The engine's constant movement was raw and primeval. I was inside the animal, not a passenger. The power of the engines flooded through me as we pounded our way up the track. Jesus signed that he was getting off soon, opened the left-hand door and beckoned me to follow, pointing at my camera. The train rocked so much, I held the guard-rail tightly, my camera flapping about my chest, as we worked our way round the deck, to the very front of the loco. Jesus leant forward against the steel rail, pointed to the spot in the middle of the train beside him, and raised his arms above his head. I copied him and leant against a chain drooping between the posts.

At that moment we rounded a bend and entered a tunnel. The noise was immense. The temperature plummeted, there was a strong stench of diesel and a dot of light ahead. I put my fingers in my ears, but Jesus made me raise my hands again as the driver increased the revs into a monumental wall of sound. The light approached and we crashed into the blinding sunshine, emerging suspended over a narrow gorge, with a pure void below. We floated and rocked through space, to the symphony of the thundering loco. The thin concrete sleepers did not look strong enough. I stared at the thin worm of a stream, hundreds of feet below. Another tunnel loomed in the face of an orange cliff. We grinned at each other, and raised our arms again.

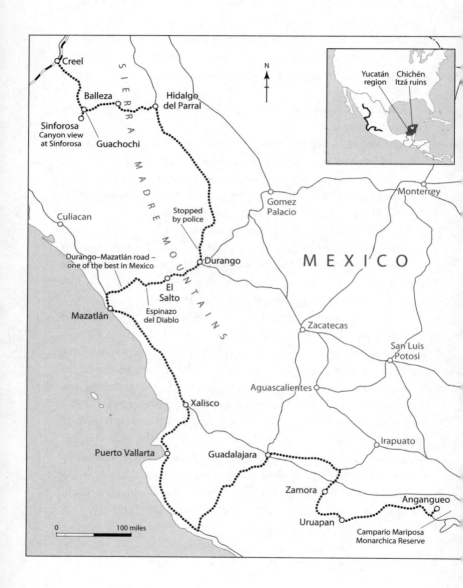

3

FLYING WITH THE MONARCHS

The small white shack stood in a field near Guachochi, its hand-painted 'Trucha' sign leaning against the rusty gatepost. It seemed an unlikely place to find the best trout in Mexico, but Leroy, the septuagenarian crop duster from the Horizons rally in Creel, had been unequivocal in his recommendation. Inside, there were four small tables and a mix of red and blue plastic chairs, but no sign of a kitchen. The señorita smiled at me and pointed to a table with a red top.

'Buenos días. La carta por favor.'

She shook her head. No menu.

'Entonces, trucha y un Coca por favor.'

She disappeared out the back and various thrashing and bashing noises ensued. I wondered how big the trout were around here. After twenty minutes my stomach was making as much noise as she was. Finally she returned with two huge steamed trout, their tails flopping over the edge of the plate, a mound of hand-cut chips and a bowl of peppers, tomatoes, onions and avocado. The trout was moist and melted in my mouth. I crunched the peppers, eating slowly to make it last longer. It was the best meal I had in the whole of Mexico.

Leroy had been bang on about the trout, so I had high hopes for his other top tip: the canyon viewpoint at Sinforosa, only ten miles from the restaurant, was 'the best of all of them' he'd said.

I'd seen a sign to it just before the restaurant, but never saw another one. How could I miss a canyon over 6,000 feet deep with a GPS? Quite easily it seemed. After a couple of abortive attempts I finally stopped to ask a man in oil-splattered white shirt and black hat. His face was heavily lined and his smile revealed two missing teeth. He pointed back the way I'd come from, then lost me in a blaze of Spanish. Finally noticing my bewildered look, he raised a hand. 'Momento!' Turning on his heels, he pointed to his car, then me, and drove off. I followed him through several turns until we emerged on a larger track which ended in a car park. He honked, waved and drove off. I didn't have a chance to thank him.

A small path sloped gently down through tall pine trees. The cool air and scent of fresh pine were a welcome relief after the dust following his car. A glimpse of white through the trees and then I stood on the edge of a vast wound in the side of the earth. The scale was hard to take in. Orange cliffs plummeted vertically beneath my feet, but so many trees and bushes clung to the slopes at crazy angles that the canyon was green. The ridges were so sheer, as if a giant axe had cleaved the earth asunder, the Rio Verde a tiny thread at the bottom of the canyon, more than a mile below.

Pulling in to the Pemex petrol station in Balleza a few hours later, I thought I heard an ominous noise from the engine. I stopped and revved the motor, listening intently, but it was 'Just My Imagination (Running Away With Me)'. The song played on a continuous loop in my mind. Normally it was my imagination, rather than an imminent catastrophic failure. The torment of the long-distance rider: too much time to think, too much time to listen. Hadn't catastrophising been my favourite thinking error in the Priory?

Every action, every turn of the bars and change of gear had a feel, a familiarity that became ingrained, so a sudden change was obvious. But things wore out slowly, too slowly to notice. It only became apparent when it was obvious. In my job as an IT consultant there were no problems, only opportunities: an opportunity to learn something new. But with my bike it was different; I identified the worst outcome and worked out how to stop it happening.

This time, my paranoia was justified. There were spots of oil on the ground and the once-clean sprocket was glistening black. I wiped it clean, but it was covered again half an hour later. If it suddenly got worse, it could pump the sump dry and the engine would seize. Weeks stuck waiting for parts. I had to get to an internet café to find out what parts I needed.

Every Mexican town has a heart, the Plaza de Armas, a central square where people congregate to see or be seen, or just sit on the shady benches. Normally the main road goes straight to the centre of town but Hidalgo del Parral was different. I followed the 'Centro' signs, but they disappeared at a fork. I guessed left, but it felt wrong. I was lost. I approached five cyclists in white t-shirts and black trousers, chatting on the other side of the street. Policías, policemen, on shiny white mountain bikes. Eventually I got them to understand that I was looking for Hotel Acosta and one of them beckoned me to follow him. We rode through a maze of tangled streets clogged with parked cars and crowded with people on their evening amble, over a bridge spanning a dried-up river and across a square with a red-roofed rotunda, like a bandstand. It was so much easier with one's own police outrider.

Once checked in, I called the UK from the first internet shop I found. It was run by Jesus, who spoke English and charged me an absurdly cheap rate to use his phone. His kindness embarrassed me, but he waved aside my protestations. The call didn't take long.

'There's very little risk,' said Brian from Motorite. 'Just keep an eye on the oil level and if it gets worse replace the sprocket seal and 'O' ring.'

I ordered the parts and arranged to pick them up at the nearest KTM dealer, in Puerto Vallarta, 'an international resort with excellent golf courses' according to my guidebook. Puerto Vallarta was 750 miles away and I had five days until the parts arrived.

Later that evening as I entered my hotel foyer the concierge approached me.

'You want a lady?'

I looked nonplussed.

'I have a lady for you,' he said, pointing towards the front of the hotel, still smiling broadly. 'Very nice lady. She's ready now.'

I'm sure she was, but it was only 7 p.m. I tried to say I didn't really want one right now, and headed for the stairs. At that moment, the lady herself emerged from the shadows. A very attractive woman, smiling broadly, with a fantastic figure, walked towards me across the foyer. It was Jessica, Jesus's wife. They'd been looking for me, wondering whether I could join them for dinner.

The restaurant was surely one of the best in town, with coats of arms lining the walls and a full complement of linen napkins and wine glasses. Jesus ordered a seemingly endless parade of dishes – the smokiest refried beans, tacos, corn and wheat tortillas, enchiladas in a peanut and almond sauce, steak with peppers sizzling on a skillet, sautéed chicken breast. Suspecting, correctly, that they wouldn't let me pay, I thought of ways to thank them. During dinner I told them about strange English foods like Marmite, Bovril, Horlicks and horse-radish sauce and the next day I asked my mother to send them a jar of each from home. Two weeks later Jesus emailed his thanks, diplomatically reporting that 'the flavour was something very different for me. I have never tasted anything with that strong flavour before.'

I was sad to leave Parral. By 11 a.m. the sun had burnt the haze away, leaving a cloudless sky. The road meandered through low treeless hills covered in brown grass and dotted with small green bushes. It was rarely straight for long so there was a single yellow line down the middle. This made it fun to ride, especially when combined with the national sport of motorbike baiting. Almost every time I came up behind a car, there was a telltale puff of smoke as the driver floored it. Usually they gave up at 60 mph, because the cars were too old to go any faster. But one black pickup with four big lights on the roof went off like a chilli tortilla, blasting down the short straights in a deep-throated roar, braking heavily and tiptoeing around every corner, then accelerating away again. This went on for half an hour, until I overtook him on a bend and he vanished from my mirrors. Mexican *machismo* in action.

The traffic increased as I approached Durango, a city of half a million people and the heart of the Mexican steel industry. To the north is the Cerro del Mercado, a hill of nearly pure iron ore and one of the world's largest deposits. I overtook a truck and the roof of the approaching car suddenly sparkled with red and blue flashing lights. I pulled over. Would this be my first request for a bribe? As I got off my bike, it leant over too much on the slight slope and I fell off. While I was lifting it up it suddenly became much lighter. The policeman was helping me. We were both laughing. Perhaps he'd let me off? I'd drop my bike every time if it worked.

'You were going too fast.'

Unfortunately, his English was perfect.

I tried to look apologetic.

'There are no signs to tell me what the limit is.'

He led me to his car and pointed to a display on the dashboard.

'Look at your speed.'

'117' leapt at me in big red numbers.

'The limit is 100.'

A second patrol car pulled in. The driver emerged slowly and deliberately. He had wrap-around reflective shades, black hair greased and groomed to perfection, an immaculate uniform and polished black boots. He checked himself out in his wing mirror before having a rapid conversation with my accuser. I assumed they were planning a two-pronged attack to fleece me. I recalled advice from veteran Harley-Davidson travellers Peter and Kay Forwood, who had ridden through 193 countries but never paid a fine outside their home country of Australia. They'd stressed how important it was to delay the officer as long as possible, to deny any wrongdoing, even if it was obvious you'd broken the law, and to never bring up or enter into a discussion on the subject of a bribe or payment of money. Taking the moral high-ground was the thing.

I steeled myself ready for the fight.

'Mexicans are crazy drivers. Go slowly,' he warned and walked away.

I was spending too much money, hitting the ATM every three days. I wasn't even out of Mexico and I was worried already. I checked into Hotel Ana Isabel, Durango, parked my bike in the courtyard and resolved to sleep in cheaper hotels from then on. After all, when you're asleep there's no difference between sleeping rough and a five-star hotel. You could be anywhere. The real cost is the rate per hour when you're awake. However, my desire to save money wasn't strong enough to make me camp. It takes much longer to find a campsite, pitch a tent and cook than it does to find a hotel and a restaurant, so I could get further, faster by staying in hotels. It was a constant dilemma: should I travel slowly, see and spend more, or go faster and see less? Money worries kept me moving. Besides, there was so much to see and so much to do, I couldn't do everything. The places would always be there, so I could see them on another trip. Right now I wanted to get to the Yucatán and visit the Mayan-Toltec ruins at Chichén Itzá, the extraordinary stepped pyramids that conjure up despotic rulers, sacrifices and Tintin. But my immediate target was Puerto Vallarta on the Pacific coast to pick up the KTM parts.

Leaving Durango the next morning, I headed for Mazatlán, on the advice of Juan, who'd said it was one of the most fantastic roads in Mexico. Mazatlán is a large town only 200 miles from Durango, and I imagined reaching the Pacific Coast in the early afternoon, finding a small fishing village nearby and sinking a cold beer while the sun set over the sea.

The road narrowed as it climbed away from Durango and up into the Sierra Madre. A crest revealed El Salto below, where thousands of tin roofs filled the valley; some flashed in the sun but most were dull and rusty, tightly packed, a sprawling shanty town to harvest the timber. There were no terracotta tiles here. Out of town the character of the road changed into a meandering monster, constantly twisting, turning and climbing into an ever-thickening web of forest. Juan had been right. What other roads had he recommended?

Cool air flowed over my cheeks. Motorcycling is the purest form of motorised travel. It is immediate. You taste the land and the weather, feel the cold air as you ascend, ride into a cold front or into a pool of still air in the bottom of a valley, and smell the cornfields before you see them.

I sewed a thread through the fabric of forest, back and forth around corners so tight they had 6 mph warning signs. I was fluent on a bike in a way I could never achieve with words. I rode the line I'd seen in my mind, flowing around the tin boxes, sitting or crawling along.

I could never have enjoyed a ride like that on my first attempt at London to Cape Town, three years earlier. I'd bought a new KTM 640 Adventure, the perfect bike for an African trip, but it vibrated so much I couldn't hold my teeth together. 'Oh don't worry about that,' Austen the salesman had assured me, 'they all smooth out after a few thousand miles.' Austen was an owner of Bracken's, the London KTM dealer, and had done London to Cape Town three times on a motorbike. Fired by his enthusiasm and tales of exciting adventures, I read voraciously and was soon hooked. The 'lost' city of Petra, Jane Goodall's chimpanzees at Gombe, Tanzania, Dianne Fossey's gorillas in the mist in Rwanda, the Serengeti migration, Mount Kilimanjaro, and the world's first inhabitants, the San in the Kalahari Desert – I had to see these things for myself. Unfortunately, the engine never did smooth out, even after 5,000 miles in three months, so I sold the KTM quickly, at a huge loss, and bought a Honda XR650L for the trip instead.

Even with the smoother bike, my dream of riding from London to Cape Town didn't last long. A strange feeling of disorientation and discomfort crept over me in Turkey, exacerbated by camping for two nights at the Syrian border post while waiting for my lapsed visa to be renewed. A few days later I stopped at the turning into the desert to Palmyra and spent ages trying to decide whether I really wanted to ride 100 miles into the desert to see another ancient city or just head south to Damascus. The road arrowed east, the asphalt shimmered in the heat haze, blurring into the pale blue sky. I leant into a crosswind and after half an hour my glasses suddenly started to vibrate up and down so fast I couldn't see at all. I panicked, turned tail and headed for Damascus. On the dual carriageway south, headlights came straight towards me and I freaked out again. Workmen were driving a lorry the wrong way up the fast lane, dropping off new streetlight poles as they went. No one took any notice at all. Failing to recognise culture shock, I fled through Damascus and on to the familiarity of a McDonald's in Beirut. I flew to Milan three days later. The dream had only lasted eleven weeks.

But now, snaking up the mountain to Mazatlán on my third attempt at a big bike trip, I was flying. The constant corners and helter-skelter of twists and turns became hypnotic, until a double left-hander caught me by surprise, as did the first truck on my side of the road. It couldn't take the hairpin any other way. Caught in an endless tunnel of trees and blind corners, I burst out on to the ridge of the Espinazo del Diablo (Devil's Backbone). A knife-edge of rock about 100 yards long, hanging between two peaks like a suspension bridge. A small café tucked under an overhanging rock urged me to savour the views, but I was having too much fun to stop. A glimpse through the tips of the pine trees took my breath away. I was riding on the edge of the world. The ground dropped away vertically beneath me, while successive jagged peaks seesawed across the horizon to the clouds gathering over the sea 50 miles away. That tiny strip of rock was the drawbridge out of the Sierra Madre Mountains. Throwing my Spitfire into a dive, I headed for the sea. We descended into the soft soup of tropical heat surrounding the Pacific Ocean. It was like wearing a steam blanket. I could taste the extra oxygen, after the thin mountain air. As we came in to land, I knew my trip was finally starting. The ocean was a milestone, a notch in my belt. I kicked off my boots on the beach and the warm sand oozed between my toes.

The coastal road from Mazatlán meandered south through tropical palms and on to Puerto Vallarta, a day's ride away, where my new gearbox seals and 'O' rings were waiting for me. Then it was inland to Angangueo, 310 miles east. The sun cast giant shadows over the patchwork of pale brown and yellow fields as it hovered above the mountains. After climbing for an hour my fingers felt the altitude at

8,000 feet. Then blinding sunshine made me screw up my eyes as I crested the last hill. Angangueo stretched along the narrow valley below. Terracotta roofs glowed red, pink and mauve in the soft sun, pierced by the church spire.

'Si, si,' said the manager at the first hotel, when I asked if he had secure parking. I never left my bike on the street at night. It was always locked away, out of sight. But despite the manager's encouragement, my bike was too wide to fit through the front door, so I looked for another. The next one up the hill had wide double doors opening on to a small flower-filled courtyard. I didn't even try to negotiate, as I liked the landlord and the place.

It took me barely a minute to get my kit out of my panniers for the night. I had at least learnt something from my first Cape Town attempt three years earlier. On that trip I'd left London with so much stuff it used to take me ten minutes to unpack. My Honda XR650L screamed 'Novice!' from the amount of gear I carried: aluminium panniers on each side, a top box behind me, a tank bag, a backpack for water, and another, larger backpack strapped to the rack above my headlight. I had everything I could ever need and more. By the time I got to Italy, I sent three loads of stuff home.

The one thing I regretted not bringing on this trip was a coffee filter. The next morning I longed for a cup of real coffee with my *huevos rancheros*. The national dish of Central and South America is a hearty plate of eggs, corn tortillas, refried beans and salsa, the main variation being in the colour and palatability of the refried beans – from a light crimson to black, and from aromatic to smoked train soot. Today's were strong and smoky. My courtyard hostal only offered chicory coffee, which I loathe. I had ground coffee in a pannier along with my cooking gear (which I'd had sent to me in Texas in a last-minute brainwave), but no filter. Salivating at the thought, I boiled some water on my petrol stove outside my room. The stove roared like a jet engine, but there was no one else to hear it. To avoid getting a mouthful of coffee grounds I used a corner of my newly washed t-shirt as a filter. It smelt wonderful, even if there was a strong aftertaste of detergent.

The Campario Mariposa Monarchica Reserve, one of the terminuses of the longest insect migration in the world, was only six miles from Angangueo. Every year about one hundred million monarch butterflies arrive here from North America, flying 3,000 miles to escape the freezing winters of southeast Canada and northeast USA. The journey is so extraordinary scientists only discovered the route in 1975. (There are two other routes: from the west of the Rockies to southern California and Baja, and from Florida towards Yucatán, but exactly where the latter route ends is still not known). They average 13 mph, using currents to glide rather than energy to fly, and take about two months to get to Mexico, arriving in late October. They never get very high over the ground, ranging between 30 and 150 feet.

The hibernating areas are at about 10,000 feet on steep, southwest-facing slopes. When I reached the Reserve's entrance, I wondered if I'd come to the right place, since there were no butterflies and very few people to be seen. It was 17 November and the butterflies had not yet starting arriving so the Reserve would not open for another three days. No wonder I was the only tourist in town. Returning a few days later, I followed the path up through the aromatic oyamel fir forest. Soon flashes of orange against the greens and browns of the trees revealed the first solitary monarchs. Many rested on the ground. The numbers were increasing by the minute, in the air, on the ground and in the trees. There were 14 to 15 million butterflies to the hectare. On warm days they wake to drink and millions take to the air at a time. When they cross local roads, the police slow traffic to a crawl to protect them. Hundreds danced up and down in front of my eyes. A hundred yards away some of the trees look as though they were diseased and dying. The middle sections were completely brown with thousands of hibernating monarch butterflies, their wings closed to conserve heat and energy. They choose the middle branches to protect them from the weather. Heavy snow can kill thousands, creating an orange and white carpet. I sat by a small stream and watched them drink as they uncoiled their proboscs into the water, equivalent in scale to an elephant with a thirty-foot trunk.

There were so many beside the stream, the edge of the water blinked orange and white as they flexed their wings. They flew the same aerial dance-way to the stream and back to the trees, using air currents I cannot detect.

The monarch is North America's largest butterfly, with a wing-span of four inches. The orange colour of the wings tells predators that monarchs are toxic; they contain a drug similar to Digitalis and if eaten will cause the predator to either vomit or die. There are four or five generations of monarchs born each year, but only one of these migrates. Their lifespan depends on what time of the year they are born, with the migrators living the longest, at up to seven months. No single butterfly makes the complete round-trip because they don't live long enough. They navigate by using an internal compass and clock that make adjustments for the change in the sun's angle every day. It is astonishing that such a tiny insect can make such complex calculations. Is it hardwired into its DNA, or does it have to think where to go? What is a thought? Everything is made up of atoms. Atoms combine into molecules, and molecules into proteins like RNA and DNA, the building blocks of life. At what point in the chain does thought arise? I am a large collection of atoms and everything that I think, feel or do is the result of chemical reactions between my molecules. Who does the thinking: the atom, the molecule or me?

I was sitting on a log in the forest enveloped by a mist of monarch butterflies. They filled the air and the trees above me, the bushes beside me, and carpeted the ground as if the forest had shed every leaf in one go. The floor was a moving mass of black, white and orange. Some landed so softly on me that I didn't even realise they were there. They landed on my clothes, my hair and occasionally on my face. I thought I had been bitten when tiny claws dug into my skin. It was a forest of flut-tering wings, like the constant whisper of cotton-wool waves breaking on soft sand. I closed my eyes. The sound of millions of wings, the flashes of orange and the smell of the firs mingled in my mind.

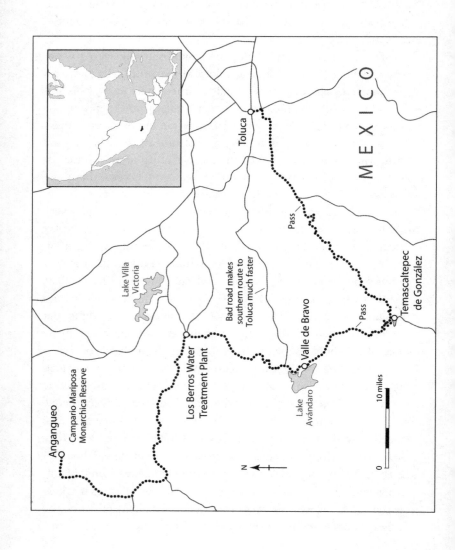

Angangueo

Campario Mariposa
Monarchica Reserve

Lake Villa
Victoria

Los Berros Water
Treatment Plant

Bad road makes
southern route to
Toluca much faster

Toluca

Pass

Valle de Bravo

Lake
Avándaro

Pass

Temascaltepec
de González

MEXICO

N

0   10 miles

4

HAPPY VALLE

I fell in love in Valle de Bravo. As soon as Rosa tore up the hill on her scooter, her long black hair flowing behind her, I knew I was in trouble.

Valle sits on the edge of a large lake surrounded by pine-forested mountains. It's a small, attractive town 90 miles west of Mexico City, a popular weekend retreat for wealthy second-homers. A myriad of tree-lined roads threaded over the hills, hiding the largest houses from sight. Among the old Toyotas and battered pickups, Mercedes and BMWs with blacked-out windows cruised around, wanting to be admired but too scared to show themselves. At the top of the rise into town, sand-wiched between two houses, was a very expensive grocers, the Fortnum & Mason of Valle, full of imported delicacies at eye-watering prices. I couldn't stop myself from pulling in for a fix of plain chocolate digestive biscuits, then continued into town, weaving my way through the narrow cobbled streets lined with whitewashed buildings and terracotta roofs.

Juan Ibarra from the motorcycle rally had invited me to stay. The warmth of his invitation dampened any doubts I had about staying with someone I didn't know. He was 'the community' for HorizonsUnlimited.com in Valle. An HU community is simply local motorcyclists volunteering to help visiting bikers find spare parts, a dentist, or just a place to pitch their tents; there are communities in many countries around the world. Juan was the perfect host and many bikers have camped in his garden. Dom and Leah, the Aussie-Irish couple from the rally, were already there.

I called Juan when I reached Valle and immediately recognised Leah's voice at the end of the line.

'Buenas tardes, Juan por favor.'

Total silence.

'Er, Juan's not here,' said Leah after a slight pause.

'Hi Leah, it's Jerome. How are you?'

'You bastard. Where are you?'

'I'm in the town square. Where are you?'

'I've no idea, I'll hand you over to Rosa, I'm sure she'll be able to help.'

'Hello,' said a friendly voice at the end of the line. 'What can you see?'

'A big, twin-towered church, several bright-red Coca Cola umbrellas in the square and lots of orange flowers in the tops of the trees.'

There was a giggle from the other end.

'Everywhere in Mexico has Coca Cola! Go to the gas station, there's only one in town and I'll meet you there.'

Easy for her to say. The tangle of small streets was made worse by a confusing one-way system so I soon lost my sense of direction. It was a public holiday and the streets were crowded. It took me five minutes to find the gas station near the lake. Someone beeped and I turned round to see an attractive Mexican woman in jeans and a white t-shirt sitting on a scooter behind me, her long black hair tumbling over her shoulders. She smiled and waved.

'Follow me,' and she zoomed off up the hill, overtaking cars on both sides of the road, wherever there was space.

Juan's house was built into a steep hill at the top of a narrow wooded valley. The hill fell steeply away, revealing Valle's lake in the distance, where every night the setting sun flooded the valley with soft orange light. Living in someone else's house felt strange after the anonymity of a *hostal* and the familiarity of my tent. I set up

42

my camping mattress beside a weights machine in his gym. Even though Juan was just about to set off on his third biking trip to South America, he was very hospitable. 'You are welcome to stay as long as you wish,' he said. 'You see I have an open house.' As well as Dom and Leah from the rally, Marc, the Belgian professor, was also staying. He was an old friend of Juan's and seemed to spend most of his life riding a dirt bike in different parts of the world.

Juan is interested in the paranormal and that evening he told us about an unusual dinner party he'd recently hosted for six of his friends.

'They were the local coven,' he began, 'and I wanted to test whether any of them really were witches. I picked up an object from one room and put it down in another. When I returned I asked each person in turn what item I took from where and which room I put it in. There was no way they could see what I'd done as I'd shut the door on the way out. I walked into my bedroom, picked up a mug and put it down in my office. One by one I went round the table asking them what I had moved. One lady got the bedroom but nothing else, another the mug but both rooms wrong. The last one got it spot on: "You went into your bedroom," she said, "picked up a blue mug and put it down on the table in the study." I repeated the exercise several times and she got it right every time.'

The witch was Rosa.

The night before Juan set off on his South American trip he gave me a bronze monkey head. It was the size of a cherry and had gold earrings and a bell inside its head. He told me it was a good-luck charm from Guerrero in southwestern Mexico, made by indigenous peoples. Monkeys represent joy of life, friendship, jest and communication. 'It will bring you good luck,' he said. I still take it with me every time I travel.

Marc left the same day as Juan and Don and Leah left a day later. I said I'd be moving on too but Juan invited me to stay as long as I wished. He preferred a lodger to an empty house. And of course there was Rosa.

Realising that I'd have to learn Spanish to travel through South America, I wondered if I could do so in Valle instead of in Antigua, Guatemala as I'd originally planned. Rosa introduced me to Hanny Pechir of Interanglo and I booked an hour's lesson a day for a month.

My Spanish improved slowly but Rosa's English grew in leaps and bounds. We were on exactly the same wavelength and often knew what each other was thinking, being able to complete each other's sentences. It was scary but exhilarating at the same time. Bright, strong-willed and the youngest of five children, Rosa had run away from home at fifteen. Now 21, she worked for a local estate agent but always had cash problems; most of her income came from commission, which she only received when the property was paid for. Her big passion was Carindapaz, the family ranch one hour's drive from Valle. Her father had started a business there supplying flowers, pork and shiitake mushrooms to Mexico City, but he'd died intestate and now everything was a mess. None of her siblings wanted to keep the farm, but Rosa was determined to make it work, not least because it kept her father's memory alive.

I worried about the twenty-two-year age gap between us but she said she wasn't worried at all.

'The problem is only inside your head.'

While working on my Spanish I needed something to get me out of Juan's house when Rosa was working, so I decided to buy a bicycle. Rather than ride my motorbike into town I could cycle to my Spanish lessons and save petrol, see more of the mountains and get fit. Valle, a town of just 5,000, had five bicycle shops. There were dealers in several international brands and in the end I settled for a Santa Cruz Blur. At $3,700 it was a huge chunk out of my budget, even at 40 per cent less than the UK price. Eduardo, the cycle shop owner, clinched it when he agreed to buy it back for $3,000 one month later. I'd be renting a top-of-the-range bike for a fraction of what it would have cost me back home.

Over the next few weeks I discovered trails through the pine forests and around the lake. I soaked up the pine scent, kept in the shade to stay cool, and discovered La Torre, the tall iron tower high above Valle where the parapentists soared into the sky. I relished the purity of cycling, especially after all those weeks on a motorbike. No noise, just the quiet whir of the chain and soft crunch of the tyres. No petrol, only muscles. I felt inside nature. Birds called and twigs snapped beneath my wheels. I could smell flowers before I could see them.

As part of my Mexican fitness training Rosa decided I should eat a real Mexican omelette. I was excluded from the kitchen while she cooked. With a flourish she laid it in front of me. Folded in half, it looked and smelt like an omelette, dotted with what seemed to be squares of potato, red and green peppers, and inch-long brown beans. It tasted good and spicy until I bit into a bean. It crunched and had a soft centre and a nutty taste. Bits stuck in my teeth. I tried another and it too crunched as it went down.

'They are grasshoppers!' Rosa laughed, then showed me the bowl full of mahogany grasshoppers like straight baby langoustines with two long legs.

My stomach turned.

'You are very lucky. This is the grasshopper season.'

Mexicans like eating insects. There are some four hundred on their list and the practice dates back to pre-Columbian times. It's likely that people from all the major civilisations – Olmecs, Zapotecs, Toltecs, Aztecs and Mayans – ate them. They are a food source that needs no tending, only foraging skills; a supplement in good times and an emergency supply should the main crops fail. Mine were chapulines, but maguey worms and escamoles (ant pupae) are also popular. People from Africa, Asia, South America and Australasia all continue to eat insects, the only races that do not are Europeans and North Americans.

Actually, we Europeans and North Americans do eat insects, we just don't know it. Insects are so numerous and pervasive it's impossible to remove every trace from every item of food we eat. In its inimitably accessible style the US Food and Drug Administration allows the following extras: Chocolate: 60 Insect Fragments per 100 grams;

Ground Pepper: 475 Insect Fragments per 50 grams; and Wheat Flour: 75 Insect Fragments per 50 grams.

There is also a growing interest in entomophagy (the eating of insects) because the nutritional value of insects is so high. Per kilo they contain more protein than corn and more energy, protein and vitamins than chicken. Being cold-blooded creatures, they are far more efficient at converting themselves into food than cattle, pigs or sheep because no energy is wasted maintaining a high body temperature. They also breed much faster, don't emit huge quantities of greenhouse gasses and need far less water. This is significant for space travel, as NASA is unlikely to take cows into space, but it's also significant for a planet that's suffering from population pressures and a growing problem with water and global warming.

Mexico City, just 100 miles from Valle, will surely be a major beneficiary if entomophagy helps tackle some of these issues. It already has a chronic drink problem. With a population of 20 million it is the third largest metropolitan city in the world and needs ever larger quantities of water. Ironically, in its earlier incarnation as the capital of the Aztec city-state of Tenochtitlán, the city used to be an island in the middle of Lake Texcoco. When Hernán Cortés, who conquered Mexico by defeating the Aztec empire, captured it in 1521, its population of 200,000 was sustained by a system of fertile *chinampa* (floating islands). However, as the city grew it expanded beyond the lake, which was eventually drained altogether. Being in a basin, boreholes have since been the main source of the water supply, but the ever increasing extraction rates have had unfortunate side effects: the land keeps sinking. Between the late 1940s and 1950s it sank by nearly ten feet. In the 1970s two lakes were created to sate the city's thirst, one of which is the lake at Valle de Bravo. The water is pumped over two 10,000-foot passes between Valle and Toluca, and Toluca and Mexico City. The latter is 2,000 feet higher than Valle. It takes 6 per cent of Mexico City's annual electricity supply just to keep the pumps going.

I loved living in happy Valle. An hour's Spanish lesson in the morning, a cycle ride every afternoon and seeing Rosa in the evening filled my days. I extended my visa in Toluca, dutifully making two freezing trips over the now snowy passes to submit the required sixty-four pages of documentation that would allow me to stay another blissful ninety days. Christmas, then New Year passed. My Spanish wasn't improving that quickly, despite my coaching, but I couldn't stay here forever. I asked Rosa to come south with me but for weeks she was strangely silent on the matter.

Then one day in February, Rosa asked me to meet her by the pier in Valle. I knew it wasn't going to be good news.

In my room later that night, I stewed on how I'd got her, us, so wrong. She loved me, she'd said, but she loved the ranch more. Perhaps I'd mistaken a holiday romance for something more serious.

5

WHAT DO YOU WANT
FROM THIS CEREMONY?

Gorgeous, blonde BMW 650 biker Catalina had invited me to join her and her wealthy friends in Acapulco. Her father was a lawyer with a holiday home in Valle but every alternate weekend Catalina and her friends Ale and Guillermo went to Acapulco to hit 'the best disco in Mexico'. I wasn't so keen on the disco but I did want to see Acapulco's *clavadistas*, the crazy cliff-divers. Catalina assured me the trip wouldn't break the bank and I didn't need any more persuading. It could be just what I needed to distract me from Rosa.

We agreed to meet in Acapulco 300 miles away a week later and in a rare bit of planning I researched places to see on the way there.

First stop was Taxco, the best place to buy silver in Mexico. Silver has been an important local industry ever since the Indians paid tithes to the Aztec empire, and they were still mining it when the Spanish arrived in 1521. The following year Hernán Cortés overthrew the Aztec empire and started large-scale mining. Taxco became Spain's primary source of silver in the New World and today Mexico is the world's largest silver producer. Taxco is built on a narrow ledge halfway up a steep valley. A brown statue of Santo Cristo (Christ) with outstretched arms looked over the town. The cobbled streets entwined like creepers around the hillside, either following the contours or taking the direct route straight up and down. Some were too steep to walk without a handrail. The roads were so narrow that there was a one-way system through the town, but no one seemed to heed it so it was a bit like driving in Italy.

Every other shop sold silver, from tiny kiosks with only a few rings and chains to large shops with rows of different sized tureens, cutlery services and cups sparkling under the spotlights. It didn't look too far up to Santo Cristo but the narrow lanes were very confusing. I walked up every staircase between the houses as a shortcut. The last one came out on a single-lane dirt track above the town. An old blue VW beetle slowed down beside me.

'Dónde es Santo Cristo por favor?' I asked, pointing the way I was walking.

'Si.'

The driver smiled and beckoned me into his car. He looked kind. His black eyes smiled too, beneath thick black hair and a neatly trimmed moustache. His hands were rough and calloused. His name was Neto and he was, naturally, a silversmith. He agreed to show me his work after I'd seen the Santo Cristo.

A jagged line of forested hills receded into the distance in the early evening mist and the twin towers of the Santa Prisca cathedral poked through the terracotta tiles that carpeted the slopes like Lego. The hillside was too uneven for a park or big square so the pink sandstone Santo Cristo statue simply gazed out over the town, hundreds of feet below us.

Neto's house looked like a child's painting: a white two-storeyed square with four black windows and a door. He yelled to his wife to bring the key to the tiny windowless workshop next door and she hurried down, shooting me a shy smile. Neto's speciality was bracelets made from rolls of 3 mm silver wire produced in Taxco. The town was one big production line, with five hundred people employed at its silver mine and many more doing the smelting and the silversmithing. He wound the wire around a drill, cut the spiral into loops and soldered them into chains, hand-twisting the links into ovals then hammering out bevelled edges. Two blows and it was done. Neto and his two partners took two days to make a hundred bracelets from scratch, just enough to support all three families.

Wandering down the hill in the midday sun through the tangle of tiny streets I criss-crossed my way towards the cathedral and emerged on to a cobbled street. A couple of one-way signs listed drunkenly on their poles and drivers seemed to be following suit. A white VW Beetle drove the wrong way down the street, but no one took any notice. A blink-and-you-miss-it café, Borda's, caught my eye. I dodged the enormous hole in the middle of the street, big enough to swallow a car but with no signs to warn hapless motorists, and climbed the stairs to Borda's narrow balcony. The tiny table for two made the perfect place for people-watching and gave me an excellent view of street maintenance, Taxco style. I wondered idly what Health and Safety would have to say about the man changing the bulb on the streetlight opposite. He was sitting astride the upside-down bucket of a JCB excavator, a good 30 feet above street level, his legs dangling over the sides. Reaching towards the lamp, he undid the relevant bolt, pulled a new bulb from his pocket, wiped it clean on his shirt and swapped it with the old one. He smiled with satisfaction as it lit up.

He was in no hurry and nor was Borda's elderly Señora it seemed. My request for *huevos rancheros* had apparently caused her some concern. Perhaps asking for a breakfast meal at lunch in Mexico was even more of a faux pas than having a cappuccino in the afternoon in Italy. Or maybe it was my accent again.

Lentamente. Mexican food complements their towns. There is a timelessness, a sense of permanence and lack of urgency in the daily rhythm of most Mexican towns. Filled with five-hundred-year-old buildings and invariably centred around a Plaza de Armas, they haven't been swamped by shopping malls, supermarkets and cheap prefabricated offices. They are still low-rise and residential. Every evening the Plaza de Armas comes alive as families, friends and lovers meet and mingle or just drive around slowly in their cars.

Back on the road, it was all about speed. Riding fast and overtaking everything in sight on the road to Acapulco gave me my first fix for

51

months – that intoxicating rush of immense joy and contentment at being alive. The KTM Adventure is a hard bike to beat on so many counts: it is the tool of choice for the Paris–Dakar race, with many wins under its belt, it has fantastic suspension and a long range. The KTM 640 Adventure I bought for my first trip in 2000 had vibrated so much I'd had to replace it with a Honda XR650L. From fast and furious to safe and secure. True, the XR engine was blissfully smooth in comparison, but it was so much slower, it felt like a fat slug. After three months riding it from London to Beirut and back, I was really pissed off with it. It was slow, heavy and didn't handle well at speed. I ended up with two speeds: off and full throttle, revving the bollocks off it to make it go as fast as possible. For my second trip I'd eventually found a smoother engined KTM Adventure, and now here I was on my third KTM, the best and smoothest yet, barrelling towards Acapulco.

It got hotter and more humid as the autopista descended to the sea, and felt strange to have summer weather in February. The three-lane traffic slowed to a crawl in front of the ten toll booths stretched across the entrance to the tunnel into Acapulco. The deep note from my exhaust reverberated off the walls like a Ducati.

Catalina and her friends Ale and Guillermo were waiting for me at the Fairmont Princess, a huge, glisteningly white five-star hotel on the beach. Acapulco is built around a deep semi-circular bay and is one of the best natural harbours in the world. Full of concrete tower blocks, big flashy hotels and neon signs, the city is the Las Vegas of Mexico and was far too big and brash for me. I chickened out of going to the disco, opting for a moonlight walk along the beach instead. For me the *clavadistas* of Quebrada were a much more interesting prospect.

Quebrada was much harder to find than I expected for the cliffs were folded into steep wooded hills at the western end of the bay. The road lurched drunkenly from side to side before emerging at the top of the narrow rocky cove used by the cliff divers, the *clava-distas*. In 1934, the *clavadistas* started doing elegant swan dives here to impress the girls. It's a 110-foot drop into the sea below and the rocks are peppered with shrines commemorating those that didn't make it. There are two dangers: the cliff slopes out at the bottom so the divers must leap a considerable distance to clear the rocks below, and the water is so shallow that the diver must time his or her leap so that they hit the water when the wave is 'in'. If it is 'out' it's not deep enough and they'll hit the rocks at the bottom.

As I watched from the tiered seats built into the cliffs specifically for enjoying the *clavadistas* spectacle, six athletic divers started climbing the cliff, one of them a young girl. The girl was the first to stop, at about 30 feet. She turned and waved to the crowd, launched herself horizontally into space, arching her back and plummeting vertically into the sea, then emerged to a burst of applause. The next three divers stopped halfway up the cliff. They were young, fit and famous. One by one they lapped up the applause before leaping into the air. Each surfaced to more claps and cheers. The last two *clavadistas* dived from the very top. The first waved to the crowd, flexed every muscle with his arms outstretched like an Olympic gymnast, then leapt forward, arching his back in a perfect curve before slowly somersaulting into the water. It must have hurt from that height. The second did a double somersault. When I looked at my photos afterwards I noticed that they hit the water with their fists clenched.

I escaped from Acapulco to Pie de la Cuesta, a tiny village six miles north. Eleven miles of white sand disappeared into the distance. I sat in the shade of a palm tree with a cold beer in my hand and gazed out over the water. A fisherman walked past playing a conch shell. It was a Sunday.

I watched as a fishing boat loaded with people approached the shore. Ten men jumped off and swam to the beach, the last one carrying a rope. The boat turned and two men paid out a net; then the boat made a slow U-turn and dropped the rest of the crew 200 yards up the beach. The two shore crews started hauling on the rope, tug-of-war style, inching closer together with every pull. A shout went up when one team had pulled the net to the shore and the water started to boil with jumpy, panicking fish. The waves became a problem, carrying the net swiftly up the beach and then back into the sea again. Passers-by joined in to help and gradually the water drained out. Three men stood at the bottom of the net and scooped escaping fish into their buckets. At last a big cheer and the net stayed clear of the water, a writhing mass of silver bodies slithering and flapping in the sun.

We rode back to Valle in the Sunday evening maelstrom, exchanging the sea warmth for mountain pines, slicing through the traffic that laboured through the hills. The next day Ale invited us all for dinner and a *temazcal*, the Aztec sauna. Her house was high up in El Pedregal, an exclusive residential estate off the Toluca road, 400 yards above Valle. I rode past the lone gateman and followed the road as it wound past vacant lots waiting to be developed. The house had fabulous views over forest and farmland towards Valle. The only blemish was the line of pylons marching up the middle of the valley.

I'd heard a lot about *temazcals* and was excited to have been asked to one. *Temazcal* is the Nahuatl word (the language of the Aztecs) for a herbal sauna used in the healing and easing of medical problems. The conquistadors, Cortez's compatriots, believed them to be a pagan ritual and hotbed of orgies because both sexes entered the domed *temazcal* tents, or *inipis*, naked. The Spanish banned the practice and destroyed the *inipis* they found. Anyone who disobeyed was given a hundred lashes and left in the market place with their hands tied for two hours. All that did was drive the practice underground. Four centuries later, many Mexicans still follow the ancient customs.

Ale said we should wear swimming things, though going naked was more authentic, and that we shouldn't talk when we were inside the *inipi*. At dusk we each took a towel and walked through her garden towards some low trees. A domed shape appeared in a hollow. A small stream broke the still air and sweet wood smoke drifted past. The temperature was falling fast.

Ale introduced us to the shaman, Miguel Ehekamitl, from the El Camino Rojo sect. He looked about forty and had a weather-worn face with deep lines round his eyes. Ale explained that Miguel would lead the purification ceremony. He had chosen the best place to build the *inipi*. As a representation of the womb of Mother Earth, the *inipi* had to be away from the house and in the right position. Water was important, as were the right materials. It looked like a large upturned beige umbrella and was made from the trees around the spring. The distance to the trees used in the *inipi* was important for spiritual energy. Inside, the water and the fire would purify us. The single opening through which we entered pointed south; this was 'the pathway of the dead', which begins with birth and ends in death.

'What do you want from this ceremony?' Miguel asked, via Ale. He needed to use the right prayers and herbs.

One by one we made our requests. We were all there for different reasons. Guillermo wanted to get his flying licence; I asked for a safe trip.

The shaman smiled and bade us enter the *inipi*.

'You can take your clothes off now.'

Ale slipped off her shawl and crawled into the *inipi* through the low door. I followed her on all fours, circled clockwise and stopped near the entrance, facing the hearth in the centre. It was too low to stand up. The last person lowered the heavy cloth flap and sealed the five of us inside. It was black and I couldn't see a thing. Legs and arms intertwined as we moved around the edge. Someone giggled. Silence. My eyes adjusted to see silhouettes. I tried not to shiver.

The flap was raised from the outside and something thudded on to the ground. Miguel placed it on to the hearth. Another then another. The air warmed. They were hot rocks. The temperature climbed. Miguel chanted some prayers to the gods and sprinkled herbs on the rocks. A soft scent filled the air. The heat was very pleasant and I felt my shoulders drop as I started to relax. A murmured prayer and a loud sizzle. It got much hotter. Water fizzed off the rocks. Sweaty silence in the darkness.

Someone farted on my right. Guillermo.

The steam rose to the top of the *inipi* and worked its way down. The different levels of temperature represent the different 'skies' within the *temazcal*. The highest and hottest spot represents the celestial world, and the lowest and coldest the Earth. The healing properties come from the shaman moving the cosmic forces between the 'skies'. A wave of heat flowed around my head then sank over my shoulders and caressed my chest. The first flush was delicious, but it kept getting hotter. More water fizzed until the only sound was my breathing. I thought of Rosa and wondered if I'd had a lucky escape. The steam got ever lower. I was being poached. I lowered myself on to the ground to try and keep beneath the heat. It was intense. Miguel added more water. The silence and calm was peaceful but so hot, too hot for me. I was the first to leave and the first to sleep.

Lost in Rosa I had forgotten about Ushuaia at the southern tip of South America. It was time to think about moving on. I'd been in Valle for nearly three months and itched to be on the road again. Ushuaia is so far south the warm-weather window is very brief: December to February. It was now late February so I had nine months to get there before it warmed up again.

I spread out all my stuff on Juan's floor and reorganised it into piles. What could I leave behind? I opened my first aid kit. It contained six syringes. I hadn't even known they were there, let alone how to use them. Would leaving unnecessary kit be like jettisoning beliefs that served no purpose? By travelling light on the road would I be travelling light in my mind?

I spent the rest of the morning going over my bike. The rear tyre needed changing after only 6,000 miles: the heavy load and high speed on the interstates must have accelerated the wear. I adjusted the chain, checked the oil, water and tyre pressures and finished by scanning my whole bike inch by inch. All was well except for the steering-head bearings, which clicked when I turned the handlebars through the straight-ahead position. Maybe I'd been taking the *topes*, the sleeping policemen, too fast. The bearings could be easily replaced the next day in Moto Altavista, the KTM dealer in Mexico City, only two hours away.

Mexico City's reputation is of muggings, murders and appalling air pollution. I stuck to the main roads to try to avoid getting lost, but the rush hour was mayhem. Luckily, I had only one turning to get right: on to Boulevard Adolfo Lopez Mateos, one of the main north–south motorways. Amazingly I was not shot or robbed at the first traffic lights. Good fortune doesn't make the news or sell newspapers. The lanes were wide and with no panniers I rode the white lines, through three lanes of stationary traffic. I'd rather do 100 mph in completely the wrong direction than 1 mph the right way but many cars moved to one side to let me through.

The workshop manager introduced me to Patrick, the chief mechanic. He was huge and spoke perfect English; his father was from Cork in Ireland and his mother was Mexican. We chatted as he worked on my bike. It was nice to speak English after three months of pidgin Spanish in Valle. He seemed a gentle giant and told me that he'd travelled all over the world as a ships' engineer but had lived in Mexico City on and off for years. Now he had itchy feet. Something made me ask if he had any children.

'I have seven,' he replied. 'All with different mothers. All are in different countries.'

Patrick noticed some wires chaffing around the headstock that would soon short out if left alone. We had just put the fairing back on at the end of the job when the manager said something to Patrick. Their exchange rapidly escalated into a shouting match. Patrick loomed over the manager and I thought he was going to hit him, but he slammed down his fist on to the steel workbench instead, his face red with anger. He gave me a quick glance, like a lost soul, silently put his tools into his tool chest and carried it away.

Everyone in the five other work bays stopped and stared. The manager signalled to the nearest orange-overalled mechanic to follow Patrick out.

'I am sorry. He has worked here before but no more.'

'What did he do?'

The manager shrugged and walked away.

Now that my motorbike was fixed, there was only one thing to sort out before I left Valle for good. I wanted to take my bicycle with me. All I had to do was figure out a way of carrying it on my motorbike while still keeping both panniers. I visited the steel fabricators on the main road to see what they could do. After an hour of considering the various options, Alberto, the owner, and I came up with a design that would carry my bicycle sticking up into the sky on a custom-made frame behind the back wheel. Three U-shaped sections held both wheels behind my bicycle. Everything was complete by 7.30 p.m. One person working all day cost $45.

My worry was how my bike's handling would be affected by having the weight so far behind the rear axle. There was only one way to find out.

I went for a test ride the next day fully loaded. The serpentine hill out of Valle was a great test track. It's a continuous series of tight turns with double white lines. A slow truck creates huge tailbacks for cars but it's great fun on a motorbike. A strafing run. See a gap in the traffic, accelerate hard, and slot back without using the brakes, only the throttle.

I liked the eccentricity of taking a bike on a bike, but found myself being surprisingly practical. I worried about it getting nicked and having difficult border crossings. Customs officials could have a field day. My carnet stopped me selling my motorbike for a profit but I had no such document for my bicycle. (Customs stamp and remove 'entry' and 'exit' sections from your carnet. The matched sections prove the vehicle has left the country so no duty is due). Then another problem dawned on me. I dropped my motorbike a lot because the seat was so high. Many times I'd put my foot down only to discover it was wafting in thin air because of the camber. One fall could wreck my bicycle. Even more sensibly, how often would I actually use it?

The test ride was a disaster. The ride was awful. The front wheel wandered over the road, making pinpoint positioning impossible and it wheelied under acceleration – not ideal when overtaking on narrow roads. Putting the bicycle frame across the seat behind me improved the weight distribution but made my bike far too wide. It was scary, so reluctantly I left it behind. At least I tried. I took the bicycle back to Eduardo to get the agreed buyback price.

'I can't pay you now,' he said. 'I don't have the money. I pay you when I sell it.'

I needed the money: It would last me two months on the road. But I couldn't hang around waiting for a buyer. I'd just have to trust him and keep phoning up to check on the sale. I loaded up my bike ready to get up and go the next morning. Something made me check my wallet: passport, cash and cards. My heart sank – my ATM card was missing.

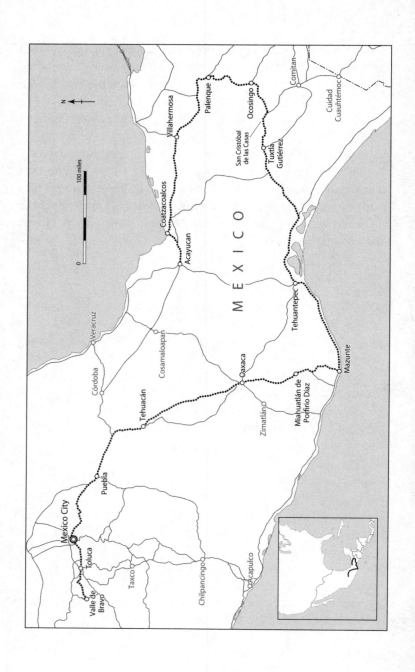

6

ONE MISSED CALL

Getting a new ATM card from England could take weeks, but I had only used it a few days earlier at Bancomer in Valle's town centre. I still had the receipt and cash. Maybe I'd left it in the machine? Very likely as my short-term memory is not good – a trait inherited from my mother so not my fault at all. That was why I also kept my bike's keys on a bright yellow plastic cord. Annoyed with myself and dreading the calls home I raced down to the bank. After a 'Buenos días' and several smiles I gave the receipt to the cashier. He disappeared into the back office. A few minutes later he returned stony faced and sat down. He looked up, then showed me a small grey card and beamed from ear to ear. The person who'd used the ATM machine after me had handed it in! No Mexican I have since told the story to can believe that it actually happened.

Everyone jaywalks in Mexico. It is automatically the driver's fault if you hit a pedestrian. People constantly crossed the road without looking. What if someone ran out in front of me? I always rode slowly in towns, constantly scanning for jaywalkers. I intended never to ride at night because it was too dangerous. With no warning signs you expect the unexpected: unlit streets, vehicles driving without any lights at all or broken-down ones left unlit on blind corners, animals crossing or sleeping on the warm road, potholes or parts of the road washed away altogether. You had to be able to stop in the distance you could see was clear.

Darwin's theories work: risk reduces speed. Health and safety is unnecessary. Thousands of form fillers and do-gooders protecting people from their own stupidity. The UK has the most road signs of any country I've ever visited and is so obsessed it's often impossible to read them all even at 30 mph. Try it.

Everyone has a level of risk they are comfortable with. You don't need speed signs to tell you how fast is safe. Many countries have few speed signs – if any at all. (In Zambia the signs were removed as fast as they were put up to make pots and pans, until the authorities drilled the aluminium sheets with hundreds of holes.) Information constantly pours in from scanning your surroundings.

Today I was already past Tehuacán, 250 miles from Valle, and it was a lovely dry day with a cloudless sky. I felt great. I rode near the middle of the road to get the best possible view ahead. Two fingers rested on the front brake lever. My speed depended on perceived danger, how I felt, what I saw, heard and smelt. A wandering car: maybe the driver is drunk or on a mobile phone. Overtake him soon. A dog. Maybe he'll run across the road. Raw diesel fumes. Diesel is like ice on the road. Trust my intuition and thread my Spitfire through the sky, leaving invisible contrails and the tin boxes behind.

My shoulders relaxed as once again I was flying into the unknown. I'd had the same feeling when I rode through the Karoo only two days out of Cape Town, South Africa on my second trans-Africa attempt. I suddenly realised that it was the start of many more trips to come. It was a deep comfort, just knowing it was meant to be, so I began to think of where to go next. I loved Africa and wished I had been born there, but how could I be so sure when I had never even been to South America? I listed the places I wanted to visit in my mind. However, the constant stress of always being on my guard got to me after eight months. Instead of my jaw dropping at an extraordinary sight and reaching for my camera, I just thought 'Oh, yeah, another amazing sight,' and rode on. I finally gave up in Marsabit, Kenya after nearly being shot by the *shifta*, the bandits who rob vehicles on the Moyale road into Ethiopia. Back in London, the novelty of hot baths, toast and TV wore off after three months and I felt cooped up, hemmed in and yearning to be on the road again. And here I was.

I reached Oaxaca, a colonial city of wide tree-lined avenues, on my first night out of Valle. My second, in Mazunte on the Pacific coast, was my first under canvas in Mexico. The Alta Mira Hotel sat on the top of the cliff above the mile-long crescent sandy beach. I perspired unloading my bike and pitching my tent. The warm, humid air was a welcome change to the chilly evenings in Valle. I had come to visit the Turtle Museum. Mazunte used to thrive on the illegal trade in turtles and turtle eggs – some Mexicans believe turtle eggs are more effective than Viagra – but it is now home to the Centro Mexicano de la Tortuga, the Turtle Museum. Wandering down the narrow palm-lined road, past the one closed shop with a rusty red 'Coke' sign, I was annoyed to find a large chain and padlock around the museum gates. But the side gate was open so I walked through and started my own self-guided tour, slipping a five-dollar bill to security guard Enrique so he didn't feel the need to alert his boss, snoozing in a nearby room. It was hardly worth the bother: most of the inhabitants were stuffed and in a sorry state, with bits of fluff coming out of their ears. I imagined them crawling up the beach in the moonlight to lay their eggs.

The wind rustled the palm fronds as I lay in my tent that night. Only three days away from Valle and I felt unsettled and unsure. Was this how I'd felt at the start of my trip four months earlier, when I left New York? Was it traveller's stress, fallout from the continual daily stream of decisions: 'Where am I going? Can I get there before dark? What can I see and do on the way? Or should I just do as many miles as I can? Who do I trust?' I was always on my guard. Being careful what I ate and drank – no tap water, salads, or unpeeled fruit. Trying not to get ripped off.

Being constantly on the move, never in one place for very long, takes its toll, but it seemed too soon for that. Turned out it was my old bugbear: money. That was what I was worried about. I was spending too much. Happier that I'd at least identified the problem even if I wasn't about to resolve it, I let my thoughts turn to Palenque, my first Mayan ruins, a mere 500 miles away. I'd be there soon.

Two days later signs for Palenque hotels and restaurants were becoming ever more frequent. Jungle encroached on the road and it was so hot and humid that I opened the vents under my arms and across my back. It was like riding in a green soup. The road hugged the contours, sweeping in and out of tiny valleys; bananas grew in every garden and huge leaf-laden branches hung over the tarmac. Round one corner half the road was missing, a gaping wound gouged by heavy rains. There were no warning signs so it would be lethal at night. I kept close to the side, ready to stop at any time.

The ancient Mayan site of Palenque sits on the edge of a ledge in the foothills of the Tumbalá mountains and is surrounded by jungle. The path to its famous ruins meandered through a forest of stunted rhododendron-like trees. Gnarled roots twisted into the damp earth like a mangrove swamp. My cotton t-shirt made me sweat. Dark green mosses hung from the branches like long beards. Streams played their tunes as the water hid from the trees only to emerge, laughing, further down the slope. The muddy path squelched underfoot and suddenly burst out on to grassy fields where two massive stone pyramids pierced the sky.

I climbed the wet, uneven steps up a grassy hill to the unrestored Temple XIV, whose two upper windows looked like giant keyholes. Two spindly trees grew out of the roof. A four-tiered watchtower like a giant wedding cake rose from the Great Palace but it had been over-restored, its perfect white limestone colour-contrasting with the black decay and dying stonework. Raucous birds called from the trees as if urging the forest to cover the stones in its ever-growing embrace.

The eight-tiered 75-foot-high pyramid known as the Temple of Inscriptions looked just as it did in *Tintin and the Picaros*. I expected to see a Mayan running out with Snowy in pursuit. Inside were three huge stone panels covered in glyphs, in such good condition that they have enabled historians to decipher the Mayan writing system. In 1948

Dr Alberto Ruz Lhuillier, a Mexican archaeologist, discovered near one of the inscribed panels a stairwell that descended 80 feet and emerged into a chamber. He described his findings in his Exploration Notes of 1952, which are translated at pakalahau.wordpress.com.

> Out of the dim shadows emerged a fairy tale, a fantastic, ethereal sight from another world. It seemed a huge magic grotto carved out of ice, the walls sparkling and glistening like snow crystals. Delicate festoons of stalactites hung like tassels of a curtain, and the stalagmites on the floor looked like drippings from a great candle. The impression, in fact, was that of an abandoned chapel. Across the walls marched stucco figures in low relief. Then my eyes sought the floor. This was almost entirely filled with a great carved stone slab, in perfect condition.

The chamber was 30 feet long, 13 feet wide, and with a vaulted roof 23 feet high. After a while he realised the walls went below the floor and that the 'great carved stone slab' held a secret. Finally, in the summer of 1952, Ruz Lhuillier discovered a second chamber beneath the slab. Inside was the sarcophagus of the Palenque king Pakal the Great, the first tomb discovered in a pyramid in Central America, which had lain undisturbed for over a thousand years. The inscriptions told that Pakal the Great was born on 26 March AD 603, acceded to the throne when he was thirteen, and ruled until his death sixty-seven years later. The three stone tablets built into the walls of the temple were king lists, documenting his regal line through the ages and using Mayan mythology to justify his inheritance and prove his legitimacy. They paved the way for his son, Chan-Bahlum II, who extended the king list all the way back to the divinities who created the cosmos, and constructed a trio of temples known as the Group of the Cross – the Temple of the Cross, the Temple of the Foliated Cross and, my favourite, the Temple of the Sun. Through these temples father and son created the Golden Age of the Maya.

Different people have different reasons for visiting Palenque. One of the wackier commentators on Mayan culture is the Swiss author Erich von Däniken. He saw proof of extraterrestrial beings having visited the Mayans in a carving that shows an upright god wearing a huge headdress, carrying two staffs and with wavy lines coming from his feet. Von Däniken talks about it in his book *Chariots of the Gods?*: 'Could primitive imagination have produced anything so remarkably similar to a modern astronaut in his rocket? Those strange markings at the foot of the drawing can only be an indication of the flames and gases coming from the propulsion unit.' He caught the mood of the times. Published in 1968, the book, subtitled '*Was God an Astronaut?*' has sold over 20 million copies and has never been out of print.

I had no spaceship, only my earthbound motorbike to carry me onwards. I woke in a strange mood. I felt tired but had slept perfectly well. Yucatán was my next destination, with its Mayan city of Chichén Itzá and the meteor crater, Chicxulub, which reputedly killed off the dinosaurs (and 70 per cent of the earth's living species) 65 million years ago. From there I'd loop down through Belize and into Guatemala to visit the Mayan city of Tikal. I rode slowly because I couldn't concentrate very well. The further north I went the more unsettled I became. My photo count had plummeted over the last few days.

Did I really want to travel 1,000 miles to see two more ruins? I had so overdone ruins on my first African attempt through Italy and Greece that when I'd reached the huge amphitheatre at Pamukkale, Turkey I simply mumbled 'nice view' at the vista across the plain, took a distant photo, and left. I did the whole site in fifteen minutes.

I stopped to look at my map. If I forgot about Yucatán and doubled back to San Cristóbal de las Casas I could take the 190 directly into Guatemala. A brochure had shown tantalising views of Lake Atitlán and Antigua Guatemala. Impulsively I abandoned Yucatán and Tikal and headed straight for Guatemala.

A heavy black cloud still pulled me down. I wanted to cry. I stopped on a rutted lay-by cut into the side of the hill. Normally a decision made the anxiety disappear in an instant. I was scared. This was all wrong. I stopped again but I was losing it. I stared at my map, hoping for inspiration. I couldn't make up my mind at all. The tears wouldn't come.

Suddenly I realised it was the money. I didn't want to spend all my savings and use my mortgage to pay for my trip. I'd already spent half my savings and I wasn't even out of Mexico. And an email from the taxman the day before said he was taking half the rest. I only had enough for a couple of months at the most, nowhere near enough to reach the Galápagos Islands, let alone Ushuaia at the bottom of South America. Why had I bought that bicycle? I sat on the ground as my dream collapsed around me. I'd convinced myself I could spend my savings and the balance available on my mortgage loan and get another job when I got home, but now, as the moment arrived, I crumbled. The thought of spending everything I had and then borrowing even more was too much. If I flew home and got a job I could return with more cash. In an instant I decided to fly home from Mexico City and started planning my next trip.

I turned round again and picked up Ruta 186 to Mexico City. Arriving in a daze at Acayucan, almost halfway to Mexico City, I just wanted to bathe in luxury and dry white wine. I checked into the Kinakú, the smartest hotel I could find, curled up on my bed and cried. Tears of failure, loss and loneliness. I had so wanted to visit the places of my dreams – the Galápagos Islands, Easter Island, and Machu Picchu, Peru. But it made sense to go home, earn more money and come back again.

I woke the next morning, thought of Rosa and glanced at my mobile phone. We hadn't spoken since I'd left Valle de Bravo.

'1 missed call.'

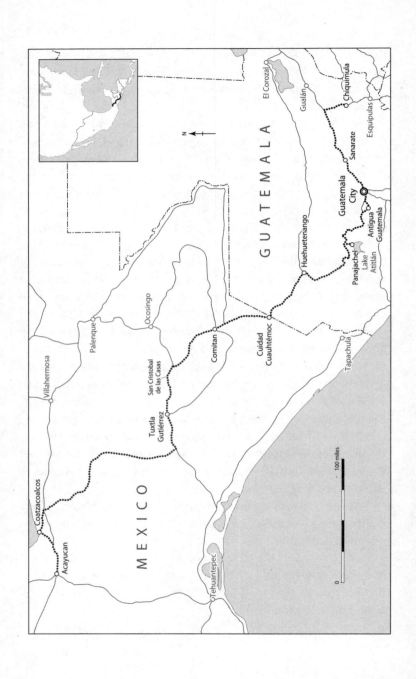

7

FRIDA'S RESTAURANT

'What is wrong? I think you are upset,' said Rosa.

'How could you tell from 400 miles away?'

'It is just a feeling. I can usually do it with people I care about.'

How could she know? Was she really a witch?

'I'm giving up. I don't want to use my mortgage to fund my trip and have decided to go home, get another job and come back again next year.'

'What is wrong with your bike?'

'Nothing, it's fine.'

'Are you OK?'

'Yes.'

'But if you and your bike are fine, why go back now? You told me you can get another job when you get home.'

She had the annoying habit of always being right. It did seem foolish to give up now when I was so close to South America. My 'don't spend what you haven't got' upbringing was holding me back.

I had to break out and leave it behind.

The previous night I'd been consumed by regret. Regret at not having the courage to do the things I wanted to do. I'd thought of Bert Munro, 'the World's Fastest Indian', who, at the age of sixty-eight, had set a 183 mph land speed record on an Indian motorcycle at Bonneville salt flats. 'When you're dead, you're dead,' he'd said. I

69

didn't want to lie on my deathbed thinking of all the places I'd meant to see but hadn't. With Rosa's words ringing in my ears, I resolved to try and let the future take care of itself. Tears washed my doubts away. From now on I would live for the moment and enjoy every day that I wasn't stuck in an office. My world turned in an instant. The buzz came back. A renewed zeal and sense of freedom flowed through me as I conjured up thoughts of the Galápagos Islands, the first big thing on my must-see list. I could be there in a few weeks.

In an hour I was on the autopista headed for Comitán de Domínguez and the Guatemalan border. The expensive autopistas were almost traffic-free and made for easy riding – a chance to watch the hills, fields and valleys go by, and a chance to think.

Two days later I rode into Ciudad Cuauhtémoc, two miles from the frontier. With only 2,000 souls it is the smallest 'city' I've ever seen. The narrow road wound up a small valley between hills carpeted with dried grass and small trees. Wooden sheds with tin roofs, breeze-blocked buildings smaller than a garage and a large flea market warned of the approaching border. Two men rode past on three-wheeled bicycles loaded with cooler boxes and big drinks containers. A brown dog lay asleep in the gutter.

The formalities on both sides of the border were straightforward: passport stamps and a thirty-day visa for me and a temporary import permit for my bike. It all took little more than an hour. The Guatemalan border guard raised the black-and-yellow barrier and I was in. Plastic bags, bits of cardboard and empty cans lay in the road. The cars were older and more battered.

Three red tuk tuks waited for a fare as another buzzed past me, leaving a trail of two-stroke exhaust. Had I been beamed into Thailand? They were the real thing, the same as those on the streets of Bangkok, made by Bajaj of India. Another example of globalisation.

Making a mental note to always try and use small border crossings like this in the future, I rode the euphoric new-country high down the valley, through a blaze of pink and orange blossom and past strange trees bearing fruit like green apples. The Panamericana Highway wove through low green hills towards Huehuetenango and Lake Atitlán 110 miles away.

After half an hour I began to feel the effects of the previous night's celebratory chicken. The road switched back and forth up a valley, offering no cover for a swift pit stop. Eventually I turned off on to a deserted track and stopped behind the only bush. No cars or buses in sight. I took my loo roll from my top box (handily placed for such emergencies) and squatted on the ground beside my bike. The crunch of tyres made me look up. A flat-bed truck had pulled in at a gate ten yards away. The driver stopped the engine, opened the gate, drove his truck through, closed the gate and drove away, ignoring me completely. Then an ancient yellow bus crawled past. Smiling children waved frantically through the window, all white shirts and black hair. Their laughter rippled over the sound of the engine as I squatted with my trousers round my ankles, trying hard to keep my balance. The driver honked twice and saluted. I waved back with the loo roll in my hand and nearly fell over.

Aldous Huxley called Lake Atitlán 'the most beautiful lake in the world' and the view from the little shoreside town of Panajachel didn't disappoint. In the clear morning light, two huge forested volcanoes rose up behind the lake in perfect cones. A collar of cloud obscured the peaks beneath whipped cream. The wakes of two fishermen in wooden skiffs like small wardrobes rippled across the smooth water. Tourists almost outnumbered Guatemalans and the main street down to the lake was one long avenue of white-roofed tents, restaurants and corrugated-iron shacks. Mayan women in red and blue shirts and long cylindrical skirts sold groceries, vegetables and brightly coloured textiles; ageing gringo hippies flogged tourist tat and a couple offered me hash. I booked into the faded Hotel Atitlán just out of town to get away from the noise and the hippies and chose a musty room that looked out over the garden.

Later that evening I wandered past the now empty stalls until I heard the sweet sounds of 'Blowing in the Wind' drifting down the street through an upstairs window. The guitarist had a good voice. Climbing the *hostal*'s creaking staircase beside a mural of a Mayan god covered in snakes, I reached a green door with a badly painted number '1' on it. I listened to make sure I had the right room then hammered on the door.

'Por favor, Señor Conte, stop that dreadful noise!'

Silence. An annoyed man with a fringe over his eyes opened it to see who was complaining.

'Sergio! Cómo estás?'

His face quickly changed to a big smile.

'Jerome! Muy bien, y tu?'

We had an Italian hug. I'd first met Sergio on the Ilala ferry in Lake Malawi three years earlier on his Cape Town to Dar es Salaam trip and he hadn't changed at all. His long brown hair still flopped around his face and he was as tanned as ever. Sergio's family had a sign-making business on the island of Ischia, off Naples, Italy, and because it was seasonal he was able to spend three months backpacking every winter. A week earlier he'd emailed to say he'd be hanging out at Lake Atitlán for a while before heading south. He always travelled with his guitar, playing and singing his way round the world. And now he was annoyed with me because he'd been serenading a girl in a yoga class across the street.

'She came out for a break,' he grinned, 'and I was really getting somewhere until you hit my door.'

We spent the evening together and agreed to try and meet again in Bogotá, Colombia if our itineraries coincided. Leaving Sergio I wandered back to the Hotel Atitlán and went to sleep. I woke in the middle of the night feeling a strange vibration, but was too sleepy to be scared.

Antigua Guatemala is only 40 miles from Lake Atitlán and lies in a natural bowl surrounded by three volcanoes. Everything was green: the valleys, hills and cones. Founded in 1543, after the two previous capitals had been abandoned, it was the seat of the Spanish colonial government when Guatemala included what is now the state of Chiapas in Mexico, Belize,

Honduras, Nicaragua and Costa Rica. The seat was moved to Guatemala City after the earthquakes of 1773 but the grid of wide streets and imposing colonial buildings still exuded a faded majesty and air of authority, like a low-rise and rundown tropical Whitehall. White paint peeled and stained the plaster of the ancient colonial buildings. Everything felt decrepit but genuine and not over-restored. Cobbled streets kept vehicle speeds very slow and added to the rustic, dilapidated charm.

Antigua is also known for its Spanish language schools. My original plan had been to learn Spanish here, but meeting Rosa in Valle de Bravo had changed all that. Thoughts of Rosa reminded me to call Eduardo and check on the sale of my bicycle. An injection of $3,000 would ease my money worries considerably. 'No I don't sell it yet,' Eduardo told me. 'It is in my shop so everyone can see it. It is an expensive bike so there are not so many people who can buy it, but the price is good. You must wait.'

Parque Central is Antigua's Plaza de Armas, a square of trees, tidy flower beds and the cool spray of a fountain. The magnificent Palacio de los Capitanes Antigua runs the length of one its sides in a double colonnade of twenty-seven arches. Built around 1543, for more than two hundred years it served both as the seat of the Spanish colonial government and the home of the Captain General. These days it houses government offices. The northern side of the square had a coffee bar squeezed in between a tourist t-shirt shop and the post office. I ordered a latte, grabbed a Guatemalan car magazine, sat at a table outside and started reading about the busiest roundabout in Central America (in Guatemala City). I was glad of the distraction when two young English women sat at the next table. Karen had started her trip in Panama and was on her way down to Costa Rica, while Jane was just joining her for a month, her first backpacking trip. She clearly wasn't enamoured. 'How can a girl take so little stuff?' she groaned. 'It's ridiculous!' They were good company, and Karen in particular had a fantastic sense of humour and radiated energy. We arranged to meet at Frida's restaurant that night.

Frida's is named in honour of Frida Kahlo, the famous Mexican artist and beauty, one-time wife of the painter Diego Rivera and known for her many tempestuous affairs with women (including the African-American singer Josephine Baker) as well as men. The walls were covered in posters and mural reproductions of her work and the front wall had a strange Daliesque picture of her in the nude encircled with barbed wire. Other murals showed a beautiful woman with a gaping hole exposing her heart. As the waitress led us to a table, Jane asked her about the barbed wire. She told us Frida Kahlo had been severely injured in a traffic accident when she was only eighteen and that from then on she suffered continuous pain, which she expressed through her art. She added that the artist had had 'many lovers, men and women', and that she died in 1954, at the age of forty-seven.

Jane kept the waitress talking for ages, but it was only later that Karen confided in me that they had actually been sussing each other out to see if things might go further. Jane and Karen were both bisexual and Jane had slipped the waitress their hotel name and room number during the conversation. She didn't take up the invitation.

Over a mixed nacho starter so generous it could have sustained a family of five – a huge wooden bowl of tortilla chips served with green and red peppers, onion, tomatoes, lettuce, guacamole, hidden chilli, beef, chicken and chorizo – I asked Karen if she might want to ride south with me.

'I'd like to,' she said, 'but I have a hammock I bought in Belize, a blanket from Panajachel and my backpack. There isn't even enough room for my backpack on your bike!'

Taking a bicycle would have been easy in comparison. Later that week we laid her stuff out on the floor: not only did the hammock have long poles, but Karen also had a drum, several blankets and shawls, as well as her forty-litre backpack. Even if Jane took half of it home it would still be unmanageable. Thwarted by too much kit, we arranged to meet ten days later on the sandy beaches of Puerto Viejo in Costa Rica.

Ten days for 700 miles as the crow flies, but by road it meant leaving Guatemala, and crossing Honduras, Nicaragua and almost all of Costa

Rica. First I had to tackle Guatemala City, 20 miles away. As with the horror that was Mexico City, I decided to do it on a Sunday morning. At 10 a.m. Guatemala City was deserted, but soon after entering the city limits I wondered if I was coming down with something. My eyes started to itch and run. My throat rasped when I swallowed. I pressed on, keen to get out of the polluted hell as soon as possible. If I could get to Chiquimula, an hour's ride from the border, by 3 p.m., I could cross into Honduras that day. Tales of nightmare border crossings in Central America danced through my head. Were corrupt Customs officers circling even as I rode?

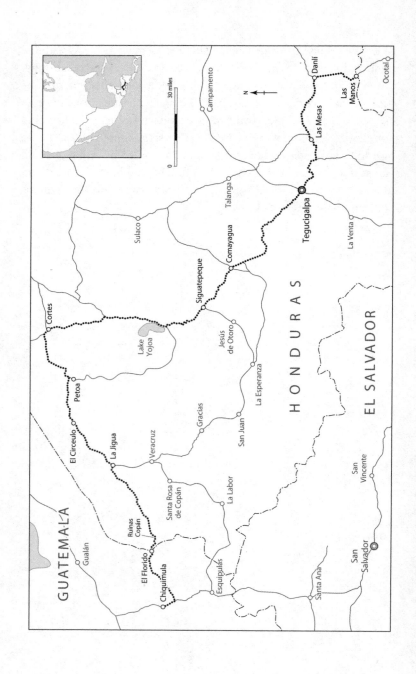

8

AN ANGEL

I'd read about horrendous border crossings where agents swam like sharks looking for easy prey. Hardened pros would surround you when you arrived, calling and heckling. They relied on your fear of the unknown, saying it was 'muy complicado' and would take a gringo hours. You had to select one to make the others go away. The most unscrupulous ones avoided any mention of money so they could go for the kill at the end.

Getting out of Guatemala proved reassuringly easy and luckily no agents appeared on the Honduran side of the border. But after ten minutes queuing at Honduran Migración the official said I needed five copies of my documents before I could even start. There was only one place to get photocopies and the small office hidden down a dusty side street was closed. The afternoon disappeared in front of me as I sat down to wait. A siesta could last for hours. I made a mental note to cross borders in the mornings. My tummy rumbled. There was a packet of biscuits on my bike. I was just about to get up when a short, middle-aged lady with black hair opened the door. An old Xerox photocopier stood on a desk surrounded by empty cardboard boxes and old toner cartridges. A television sat on the other desk displaying its guts to the world. Two dollars for five photocopies. I shuttled back and forth between offices, collecting stamps in a language I didn't understand, but eventually it was done, and with not a shark in sight.

I punched the air as I left El Florido an hour later, exhilarated at getting into a new country. The border approach roads are often new. I drove slowly down the clean tarmac but resisted the urge to accelerate before I'd settled in. Do brake lights work in Honduras? What animals wander across the roads here? A cow was OK but goats were bad news. Unpredictable and fast, they can suddenly stop, do a 180 and dart back across the road. It always took me a couple of days to get used to riding in a new country.

I'd chosen this crossing because it was close to Ruinas Copán, a Mayan city of twenty thousand people in its early-ninth-century heyday. I was intrigued by a photo of Copán's ball court, which seemed strikingly similar to a tennis court. The path sloped down through a fogged mass of gnarled trunks and roots. Streams ducked and dived between the trees until the shadow of giant steps was suddenly projected on to the branches ahead of me. *Tintin* country again. Giant faces and gods with many arms. Another ruin claimed by the jungle. The path split and I stumbled between overgrown stones the size of tables without having any idea what I was looking at. I never found the ball court, where 'tiered rows of benches lined the two longest sides', or any big open area. I was glad I hadn't gone miles out of my way to get there.

Bananas are big in Honduras. Plants grew by the roadside, along the edges of fields and in huge plantations. As I wound through the shallow valley, huge banana leaves flopped down like giant tongues. All bananas are infertile. They are seedless cousins of a wild herb and cannot reproduce sexually. They propagate by sending off shoots from the main plant, so each sibling is a clone. The lack of genetic diversity makes plantations very vulnerable to pests and disease so commercial growers use weekly applications of pesticides to protect their crops. One third of the production cost of bananas is spent on pesticides, the highest of any fruit in the world. As it takes eighteen months to create a new variety by cloning grafts, growers prefer to research new pesticides instead of new varieties.

Honduras is the original banana republic. It declared itself independent from Spain in 1838 but alternated between unrest, rebellion, civil war and changes of government. In the second half of the nineteenth century US companies started buying land for bananas. Shipped to the southern states, the bananas massively undercut other fruit like apples yet still generated high profits. The share of bananas in Honduran exports grew very quickly: from 11 per cent in 1892 to 80 per cent in 1929. The American companies soon dominated Honduran politics and rival banana companies fought through rival political parties for favours and influence. The two main protagonists were the United Fruit Company (now Chiquita) and the Standard Fruit Company (now Dole). In 1912 the US President William Taft sent marines to protect American banana investments threatened by an uprising. In 1975 the US Securities and Exchange Commission published a plan by another major player, United Brands, to bribe Oswaldo Arellano, the Honduran President with $2.5 million if he reduced export taxes. But the greatest price is paid by the locals who work on the plantations for small wages to put cheap bananas on foreign tables thousands of miles away. Today just five companies control 90 per cent of internationally shipped bananas and two of them – Dole and Chiquita – control over 50 per cent.

As I rode south through rolling hills, banana leaves partly obscured a sign for a hotel that had seen better days. White paint had peeled away in slabs from the mildewed walls and a drainpipe lay dismembered on the ground beneath two broken windows. Half an hour later I regretted not stopping. My map showed several towns along my route south, but none had a hotel. Finally a billboard for 'Lago Hotel' and then the hotel itself. Unprepossessing, but it over-looked Lake Yojoa and would do.

With relief I unloaded my stuff into the cabin nearest the lake and checked out the shower. It was damp and musty. There was only one tap. The water stayed cold but there was a shower-head heater. The wire came out of a hole in the ceiling straight into the shower head. Even lukewarm water would be good after the heat. Perhaps

I should stand on a rubber mat? As I snapped the switch, a buzz of electricity fizzed through my fingers. I decided against using the bedside light and retreated to the restaurant for a Victoria beer. The veranda looked over reed beds to the lake, which glowed orange. A fisherman emerged from the reeds and rowed slowly through the reflecting hills, his wake rippling the mirror behind him. A warm and gentle breeze cooled my face. The tilapia from the lake was sweet and the hand-cut chips fat and hot. As I flicked through my guidebook, planning the next day's route, I came across a special section on the Copán ruins that I hadn't noticed before: it was the third largest site in Central America, had a museum on the Mayan civilisation and an immense plaza famous for its stelae and altars. In my hurry I'd completely missed the main ruins.

An English voice interrupted my reading. Tom and his Uruguayan girlfriend, Maria, were on their way south to visit her family with Jif, a four-month-old Labrador cross. He bounced all over the place with puppy playfulness and paws far too big for his legs. His lead was a surfer's ankle strap. We talked about South America and Tom agreed that Central America paled in comparison. 'All the big stuff is in the big bit', he said. Maria and I swapped books. In exchange for *Memoirs of a Geisha* she gave me two tiny books of poetry, each slightly larger than a packet of cigarettes and written by Manuel, a friend of hers from Montevideo.

As I was checking out of the hotel the next morning I noticed several books behind the counter. One, a *Reader's Digest*, was in English. Manuela, the receptionist, spoke perfect English and the books were hers. She had lived in the States for twenty years, but on a family visit back home to Honduras her handbag had been stolen, along with her USA residency Green Card. That was seven years ago. Despite her many requests, the US Authorities never issued a replacement so she was stuck in Honduras. She no longer wanted to live in the US but said she would have liked to return to tie up loose ends.

'Last year twenty US RVs stopped by on their way south,' she told me. 'When they found out I loved to read they got a collection of books together for me. That's how I got the *Digest*.'

She was eyeing my *Uncommon Grounds: A History of Coffee* by Mark Prendergast but I wanted to finish it. The gravel crunched harshly under my feet as I walked across the drive. I could buy another one. I was not a prisoner in my own country. She read to escape. I retraced my steps to her office.

'I thought you might like this.'

Her eyes lit up with pleasure as I offered her the book.

Back in my room, I looked at the three new books that were lying on the bed with the rest of my stuff and felt greedy. How would I feel if I was starved of books?

'Manuela, would you swap *Lost Discoveries* by Dick Teresi and *Under the Volcano* by Malcolm Lowry for a litre of water?'

'Is that all you want?'

I took the litre of water.

'You are an angel. These mean more to me than you can possibly imagine.'

Honduras is a small country. It was only 150 miles to the Nicaraguan border at Las Manos. A crowd of hustling 'helpers' surrounded me within seconds of my arrival, but this was a minor border crossing and I hadn't expected any at all. I felt intimidated, and fought the urge to choose one so the rest went away. There's only ever Customs and Immigration so how hard could it be?

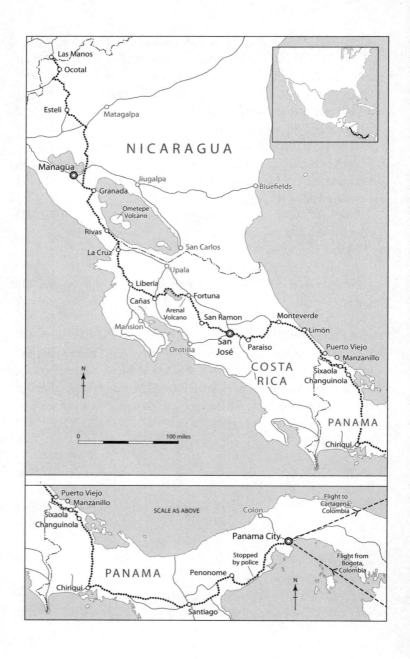

9

COSTA RICA'S PR TRAIL

Three men and four boys crowded round me at Las Manos before I'd even got off my bike. I pointed to the most honest looking and he beamed back. The others melted away. We agreed a price and he smiled again. I'd overpaid. I followed him to the first of many offices to collect a form I didn't understand and took it to a window in the adjoining building. A hand took the form, my passport and five dollars, then stamped the form twice. Lots of offices, forms and stamps and twenty-five dollars later we're done. I handed over $5 and my guide looked very happy. Too happy. I'd massively overpaid.

Nicaragua is even smaller than Honduras and I was through another easy border into Costa Rica by mid-afternoon.

It was extraordinary how everything changed after crossing an imaginary line. Costa Rica was like a garden, the leaves and grass were greener, as though fed by underground springs. Trees with bright orange flowers peppered the hillsides and glistening black tarmac flowed under my wheels. I'd crossed three borders in three days, racing from Guatemala to Costa Rica via Honduras and Nicaragua, seeing nothing of the last two countries as my cash concerns propelled me south towards the Galápagos Islands. But I would linger a while with Karen in Costa Rica.

Costa Rica has the highest per capita income and is the most democratic of all the Central American countries. It has had a stable government and no army since 1949. Quite an achievement when it's surrounded by revolution, resistance and rebellion. Small family farms and coffee seemed to be key to the country's success.

In AD 850 in Ethiopia, a goatherd called Kaldi noticed his goats becoming hyperactive and disobedient one day while eating the red berries of a tree he'd never seen before. Since they recovered the next day he tried the berries himself and soared. He (or his goats) had discovered coffee. It would be another eight hundred years before the craze for coffee drinking reached Europe and a further couple of centuries before the berries became an important commercial crop in Central and South America. The berries are picked by hand so need a pool of cheap labour. Other countries in the region had large Indian populations that the Spanish could easily exploit. In Guatemala the huge *latifundia* estates used Indian slave labour to pick the coffee, but Costa Rica's Indians had all but been exterminated by Spanish settlers and their diseases, so, instead, small family farms were the norm. However Costa Rica had its own form of apartheid. In the late 1930s Panama disease decimated the banana crops around Limón on the Caribbean coast, forcing many people of African descent to move west to the Pacific coast plantations. A law was subsequently passed in 1935 prohibiting Pacific coast plantations from employing 'coloured' people. Another important factor inhibiting *latifundias* was that coffee was grown on virgin land near San José, rather than on land already occupied by Indians who were forcibly removed and used as pickers, as occurred in El Salvador and Nicaragua. These days, 80 per cent of Costa Rica's population is of Spanish descent, more than any other country in Central America, making it the most homogenous society.

Still on my new-country high I passed a red Land Rover going the other way. It had two headlights on the roof and a British number plate. Michael and Sandy were one year into their three-year round-the-world trip in a custom-made six-wheeled Land Rover called Nyathi (buffalo in Swahili). With a single cab and windowless panels to the rear it looked like a monster sandwich truck. They'd come from Ushuaia in Tierra del Fuego and were on their way to New York.

'Tea and cakes?' asked Sandy. She opened the side panel behind Michael's door, slid out a tray and removed three china mugs and an electric kettle, filled the kettle from a purified water tap under a flap outside then plugged the kettle into a socket between the seats. An inverter that ran off the batteries powered the kettle and their computer as well.

A small table and two folding chairs appeared. It reminded me of an Abercrombie and Kent brochure for Africa. The vast Serengeti plains stretched out in all directions, bisected by a black line as thousands of wildebeest munched their way to the Grumeti River. A table covered in white linen and full silver service stood in the foreground. The ladies wore long dresses and the gentlemen dinner jackets. I felt slightly underdressed in my dirty jeans and faded t-shirt.

The cab looked like the cockpit of a small aircraft with a long row of switches above the sun visor. On Sandy's side a flat computer screen folded neatly into the roof and the full-sized keyboard slid under the glove box. She typed while Michael drove, updating their website with campsite GPS co-ordinates, daily miles done, weather conditions and what they had for lunch. The day before they'd had cereal, baguette, avocado, cheese and pizza. It had taken them about three years to build Nyathi, to a design that had been refined over a previous round-the-world trip. The extra axle was for carrying spares – a spare axle, drive shafts and a differential among them. Nyathi weighed over three tons and did only 15 mpg on diesel.

An occasional jacaranda tree covered in purple flowers added to the rush of colour. An hour later, crossing a plain of ricefields, I stopped, stunned at the brightest greens I had ever seen. A flock of white birds with yellow beaks sat on the edge of the paddies beside the road. I wanted to hold the vibrant colours in my hands.

Half an hour later I saw a cyclist up ahead. I slowed so we could chat without having to stop. Jodie was riding to Ushuaia and hoped to be there in nine months. She'd left Colorado six months earlier and would have cycled the whole length of the Americas on her own.

She'd obtained a place at the Royal College of Music in London to study the clarinet but had decided to go for a bicycle ride instead. We agreed to meet up in Liberia 25 miles away.

That evening over energy omelettes Jodie told me how she tried to do 60 miles every day. 'But sometimes it's just not possible,' she said. 'You can't avoid the hills but the wind is the real killer, especially if it's gusty. I shout and yell at it to "fuck off". It doesn't, but it makes me feel a lot better.'

I felt guilty. All I did was just sit there. If I encountered a hill or a headwind I simply twisted my wrist. If it got really steep I changed gear. It was all over in seconds. Jodie carried forty kilos of kit. Forty kilos to grind to the top of every hill. I got there quicker but I missed out on the silence, the sounds of a village afternoon and the natural high from being so fit. She talked and exchanged greetings with locals as she cycled past. The traffic was scary of course. Twice the vacuum from passing trucks had pulled her into the middle of the road and almost into oncoming cars; once she'd been blown right off. All she had was a helmet. No gloves, knee or shoulder protection. I envied her mental and physical strength and her extraordinary determination, drive and patience.

The Costa Rican countryside was incredibly lush, with amazing flowers and the most vibrant greens, but the towns were something else. Liberia reminded me of Croydon, England. Its buildings had neither character nor antiquity. Everything was formless and func-tional, slab-sided 1960s-style concrete; angles and straight lines with not a curve in sight. The cathedral was the ugliest I'd ever seen, its belfry a cross between a chimney and a rocket.

I came to see the whole of Costa Rica as a tropical Croydon and found the Costa Ricans arrogant and used to an easy dollar. Give me Guatemala any day. Jodie felt the same. We agreed to meet again four days later in Monteverde near the Caribbean coast.

With bicycles much on my mind, I called Eduardo the Valle bike-shop owner again. He still hadn't sold my Santa Cruz.

Inspired by spectacular photos of orange lava exploding into the air like a giant firework, red rivers flowing down the slopes and an eerie nocturnal glow, I headed to Arenal, an active volcano just 75 miles from Liberia. I pulled in at La Fortuna, a one-street town near the volcano, and scuttled into the first *hostal* I found. For two days I waited for the majestic Arenal volcano to reveal itself, exploding fireworks and all, but the only thing I saw was two brown lines disappearing into the low cloud. The publicity photos could have been from anywhere. That night I woke with a wobble. What was going on? I was alone but something moved. My bed. Surprisingly alert in the middle of the night I realised what was going on – a small earthquake. Not many of those in Surrey. By the time I left La Fortuna I was beginning to think that the Arenal 'volcano' was a Costa Rican public relations coup. No tourist I spoke to there had seen the volcano or even believed it existed either. The clever Costa Ricans had discovered how gullible tourists were. I suspect the photos were taken in another country and photoshopped.

Next stop on the Costa Rica PR trail was Monteverde, 125 miles southeast. Some 10 per cent of Costa Rica's land mass is preserved as national park, the greatest proportion of any country, and the Monteverde Cloud Forest Reserve is one of the jewels in their crown. It's 4,500 feet above sea level and is home to 400 species of birds, over 2,500 plants (including 420 orchids) and tens of thousands of insects. Jodie arrived and we set off to explore some of its trails. The dark and damp forest floor was cool. Trees dripped with orchids, vines, and mosses. We walked on a suspended bridge high in the canopy but saw little to get the blood running.

We hoped to see hummingbirds but had to settle for the aviaries of the Hummingbird Garden, where over a hundred are kept in captivity. Their iridescent greens and blues flashed in the light as they darted from flower to flower. They are extraordinary fliers because they can rotate their wings in any direction so can generate lift on both the down stroke (as all other birds do) and the up stroke. They are the only birds that can fly backwards, and left and right like a helicopter. To hover, the hummingbird flaps its wings 70 times per second. We humans see this as a blur, because our 'flicker fusion rate' is about 20 frames per second (which is why we see films shot at 36 fps as moving rather than as a sequence of still images). A monarch butterfly, on the other hand, can see every beat of a hummingbird's wings.

The name 'Cloud Forest' evokes a lovely, fluffy, dry image, but it rained steadily for the two days Jodie and I were there. The PR department hadn't mentioned the soggy reality. Maybe they'd photoshopped the vibrant greens too. Another Costa Rican marketing triumph.

I waved goodbye to Jodie, agreeing to try and meet again in Cuenca, Ecuador.

Puerto Viejo, the small, laid-back hippy town of bars, beaches, cheap eats and palm trees, was an easy couple of hours' ride south down the Caribbean coast from Monteverde. There was no tarmac, just dusty tracks. Signs for 'Cabinas' and 'Surf Rental' dotted the tiny main street, urging surfers to try out the Salsa Brava, the biggest wave in Costa Rica. Many of the buildings were little more than driftwood shacks with palm-frond roofs. Someone told me that an English woman had stopped by earlier that morning, asking about a man on a motorbike, and soon enough I found Karen, deeply tanned and smiling as ever, browsing a shop whose t-shirts and sarongs were displayed like national flags. Since leaving Antigua ten days earlier, she'd slow-bussed her way south and now had just three days left before her flight home from Panama City.

It was hard to decide what to do. Once the cool morning breezes evaporated in the humidity and fierce midday heat, it was too hot to move. I'm indecisive but Karen's from another planet. An expert faffer, she can spend hours deciding what to do and then do nothing but gaze out to sea. We spent most of the morning deciding where to have lunch.

After a few hours Puerto Viejo felt crowded so we cruised to Manzanillo, the easternmost point in Costa Rica, where the road ended. Nine miles further south, the River Sixaola formed the natural boundary into Panama.

The smell of garlic and the sounds of reggae music drew us to Maxi's Bar, a wooden beachfront house with a rust-coloured corrugated iron roof. We sat on the upstairs veranda and watched the waves break through the palm trees. The food was so deliciously spicy, with a distinct Caribbean flavour – red snapper for me, chicken with rice, beans and fried plantains for Karen – that we returned for more the following day. Many locals are descendants of Jamaican workers who arrived in the nineteenth century to work on the Atlantic Railway and the banana plantations. They were obliged to live on the Caribbean coast rather than the Pacific coast because Costa Rica had, until 1949, an apartheid law that banned Pacific coast banana plantations from employing 'coloured' people.

Three days passed in slow motion. We could have stayed for months. But, sadly, Panama City called.

Ruta 36 sliced through low-lying banana plantations to the border at Sixaola, 20 miles south of Puerto Viejo, where an old single-track railway bridge spanned the river. The latticed steel girders arched over the water and into Panama.

I waited for a white truck that had just set off from the other end and completely filled the road. The driver honked as he passed me. The 'road' was two pairs of railway sleepers laid end to end on each side of the rusty rails, with a six-inch drop-off the edge. To allow space for the train's wheels there was a three- or four-inch gap between the rails and the sleepers – a perfect fit for my front tyre. Chicken wire fenced me in. The river flashed below me but I daren't look down, worried my tyre might get caught as I rode the wooden tightrope into Panama.

Panama had even more bananas than Honduras. Plantations lined both sides of the road through Changuinola, stretching across the hot and humid plains to the Caribbean Sea. I needed speed to cool me down. After Almirante the road turned south to join the Pan-American Highway along the Pacific coast. There were few cars, perhaps because it was a Sunday. The road twisted and climbed through deforested hills as I came up behind a lumbering truck in the middle of the road. I could pass in a flash if I could see ahead. The faster the overtake, the safer it would be. I accelerated but just as I passed the end of the trailer it suddenly moved towards me. I swerved on to the edge of the tarmac, avoiding the heavily rutted verge, blasted my horn and accelerated hard. I squeaked past with my heart racing. He'd swerved to avoid a pothole. I hooted before I overtook the next one, to make sure I'd been seen. He was also in the middle of the road. I hooted again. No reaction. I started to overtake and he swerved towards me. I accelerated away. I needed a louder horn. Was bike-baiting a national sport in Panama?

As I crested a rise, the sudden view took my breath away. There was no horizon. The clouds merged into the distant haze. Three islands of forested ridges floated on the mist below. The forest nearby was so bright it looked wet. A new road surface, smooth and fast, meandered down to the Pacific coast. The flip-flop sequence of successive hairpin corners kick-started my adrenaline but it was hard not to be mesmerised by the view. A quick glance and I nearly missed a corner.

There were still 230 miles to Panama City and my IMO bike computer said it would be nearly dark when I arrived so I went faster. Treeless hills and gullies hinted at clearcut logging. Panama had noticeably fewer forests than Costa Rica. As I rejoined the Panamericana going east at Chiriqui the country began to show a strong American flavour. Hoardings advertised Western Union, Sony and Hewlett Packard. A kink in the middle of an extended straight invited me to overtake a long line of cars – right in front of a patrolman leaning against the side of his car. His hand shot up and he ran to the side of the road, waving madly. He switched effortlessly into English and I couldn't even pretend not to understand.

'You have committed a grave offence. That is a $50 fine.'

'It is my first day in Panama.'

I was pathetic, but no amount of apologising or pleading cut any ice.

'You ride over the line. You must pay.'

Other drivers honked and waved as they went past. Perhaps stopping gringos is another national sport. He tasted victory in my rush to move on.

'$30 and you go now.'

I didn't want to arrive in a new city in the dark, which would mean having to stop under streetlights to read the map and possibly riding into a dodgy area by mistake. So I gave him $10. It got me away but he'd still stop the next tourist. Annoyed with myself, I vowed not to pay again.

Two hours later I rode into what I hoped was the centre of Panama City. The streets were clogged with yellow taxis and evening rush-hour traffic. One-way systems and tall buildings that cut off my GPS signal conspired to send me round in nightmarish circles. Tired after my long ride, I approached the nearest taxi and asked him to lead me to Hotel Costa Inn. It was the best $2 I'd spent in ages.

Exploring the streets on foot next morning, Panama City felt brusque and business-minded, like America. People were friendly, well dressed and clean. Skyscrapers dominated the city centre and loomed over the Pacific – the Miami of Central America. Everywhere I looked there were McDonald's, huge shopping malls and advertising hoardings screaming from the rooftops. Gleaming Mercedes and BMWs mingled with the taxis.

Karen and I had our parting dinner at the Miramar, Panama City's most panoramic restaurant. The sun set across the bay from the eleventh-floor balcony as tropical warmth soothed our skin. The next morning we said our sad goodbyes. I was listless and lonely as soon as she'd gone.

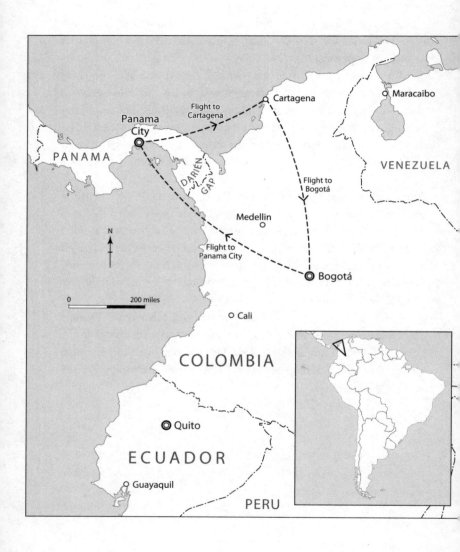

10

THE KNOCK

There is no road into South America. The Darién Gap is 75 miles of mountains on the Panamanian side and marsh and myriad rivers and tributaries on the Colombian side, where building a road is impossible. Besides, many Colombian groups – guerrillas, drug gangs, paramilitaries and smugglers – make it far too dangerous to attempt. It is the only gap in nearly 30,000 miles of Pan-American Highway from Alaska to Chile.

Darién is a region of the easternmost Isthmus of Panama. Most people fly over or sail around it. But there are always those who have to do it the hard way. As far as I am aware only four motorcycles and their riders have made it across the countless rivers and documented their journey with photos and testimonies from the authorities: Ed Culberson, Helge Peterson, Braga Antonio and Loren and Patricia Upton. In his book *Obsessions Die Hard: Motorcycling the Pan American Highway's Jungle Gap*, Ed Culberson states: 'Nothing I had experienced in Africa or Southeast Asia compared to the utter desolation and forbidding nature of this jungle.' In 1980 on the proposed Highway route, engineers failed to find solid ground before reaching the limit of their drilling rigs. With an annual rainfall between 70 and 170 inches (the average for southern England is 30 inches), the whole region is a floating mudbath.

For me and my bike, the easiest option would be to fly over the Darién Gap, but where should I fly to? Was Columbia safe? Or should I fly straight to Ecuador? I received lots of advice from people who weren't Colombian. The worst people to ask are usually the neighbours. They often think the next country, city, town or village is full of strange, scary people who eat foreigners. It was the same story here. 'Several entire states were not under government control'. 'The main roads are heavily patrolled by the army'. But Ecuador was only two days' ride from Bogotá. How dangerous could it be? I'd heard one story of an American hiker who'd been kidnapped by guerrillas but was such a pain they let him go. I wasn't going on a jungle trek and wouldn't hang around. I needed local knowledge and contacts. I had contacted the Horizons Unlimited Community in Bogotá a few weeks earlier but hadn't received a reply. Then an email from Sergio (my Italian, guitar-playing friend whom I'd last met in Antigua, Guatemala) introduced an alternative possibility.

'Cartagena is a beautiful city,' he wrote, 'and the Colombian women are the most beautiful in the world. I will be there in a week.'

I decided to leave my bike temporarily in the shipping office in Panama City and fly myself first to Cartagena and then Bogotá. That would give me a feel for Columbia and I could then decide where to have my bike flown to. If I didn't feel safe in Bogotá I'd ask the Panama office to fly it direct to Quito.

Next day at Girag, the shipping office, Dalys organised everything and told me what to do.

'Disconnect the battery,' she instructed. 'Tape the wires. No gas.'

I drained most of the fuel, leaving what I hoped would be enough to get to the nearest petrol station at the other end. This was so different to the strong and sturdy custom-made box I had fabricated at Heathrow at the start of my trip. In Panama City, the agent simply rolled my bike onto a wooden pallet and strapped it down.

I walked off the plane in Cartagena into a wall of damp cotton wool. Waves of heat rolled over the tarmac and it was exciting to be in a new country but a part of me was missing. It felt strange to be without my bike. The Customs agent asked me to open my bag. His eyes lit up when he saw my two Nikon SLR cameras, one with a telephoto and the other a wide-angle zoom lens. (When I see a shot I know imme-diately which lens I want and take it without getting off my bike.)

'Where is the invoice?'

I gave it to him and he walked away. He returned a minute later.

'You must pay duty of US$1,000.'

'I am not paying anything,' I retorted. 'I am a tourist. Every tourist has a camera and pays nothing. Why did you not stop *him*?' I pointed to a man walking past with a camera hung round his neck.

He ignored me.

'You must pay $1,000.'

'I pay nothing. Either you let me pass or I fly back to Panama.'

He went away again and returned a few minutes later.

'Go.'

Sergio was right. The Colombian women were beautiful, dark and sensuous. It was too hot to traipse from hotel to hotel trying to save $10. Hostal San Diego was right in the centre of the oldest part of town, a jumble of Spanish colonial architecture just five minutes' walk from the sea. The brick streets were only wide enough for a horse and cart and their two-storey houses created a rainbow of pastel shades like a new box of artist's crayons. Pink and red heliconia flowers cascaded from wooden balconies. The branches of a fig tree in a big clay pot reached round a window. Terracotta tiles covered every roof and the streets were clean. A child in a yellow t-shirt slept curled up on the narrow pavement.

That night, knocking sounds woke me from a deep sleep. It took me a while to realise it was my door. No one knew I was here. I hoped whoever it was would go away. Then came a woman's gentle voice. I wrapped a towel around my waist and opened the door. Without my glasses on I could only make out a tumble of long brown hair and a shapely silhouette.

'Oh, I am sorry. I wanted 105 not 104.'

She seemed a bit embarrassed, made a few signs and then started knocking on the opposite door, 105.

I went back to bed. It was 6 a.m. She kept on knocking on 105 but nothing happened. I was starting to get annoyed. It was a Sunday morning and all I wanted to do was dream. She knocked on my door again. I ignored it. More knocks. I tied a towel around my waist, put on my glasses and opened the door. She walked straight in. She was very pretty and smelled nice.

'Sorry. Can I use your phone to call 105?'

'Yes, go ahead.'

Something went wrong and she handed me the phone. I didn't want to talk to the receptionist, couldn't understand what she was saying anyway, and handed it back to her. Dominga replaced the handset, tried again, sighed and put the phone down again. She sat next to me. Close to me. She was very attractive, with warm dark-brown eyes and an inviting cleavage.

'What is the problem?'

'I left something in the room.' She paused. 'Would you like to do something?'

'Yes,' I thought, 'go back to sleep.' She was looking at me in a different way. 'Do what?'

'Sex.'

Well, I suppose that made it fairly clear. I was still very sleepy but waking fast.

'How much?'

'One hundred dollars.'

'Wow, that is a lot of money.'

She laughed and laid back on the bed.

'Eighty dollars.'

Later that morning I had the urge to indulge in a proper Sunday, a day of newspapers, cold beer and lounging by the pool, but my *hostal* had none of those. I needed to blag my way into a proper hotel for the day, one with lots of stars and a selection of English newspapers. A quick flick through my guidebook revealed the Santa Clara to be just what I was looking for. Two men in immaculate white uniforms stood outside its high wrought-iron gates. Two more stood inside. They looked like orderlies waiting for the ambulance to arrive. All jumped to attention as I approached. I nodded and strode confidently through the lobby into a colonnaded courtyard filled with trees, fragrant flowers and a fountain. An invitingly cool mist enveloped me. A dark archway led to a large swimming pool fringed by tall palms and overlooking the sparkling bay. A waiter took my order for coffee and led me to the buffet breakfast. Eight tables were loaded with temptation: freshly squeezed mango, passion-fruit and papaya juices, six different types of fresh fruit, seven different hot foods as well as an omelette chef standing by, and a bread table covered in chocolate, almond and plain croissants, and countless other cakes and pastries, even miniature pork pies. I resisted asking how much it was and no one asked for my room number.

There was still no word from Sergio so I flew to Bogotá. At 8,000 feet, it was refreshingly cool after the heat of the Caribbean. Small crowds and big, wide streets made it feel relaxed but the buildings had an air of decay. The Museo del Oro, with its horde of pre-Hispanic gold and the four largest emeralds in the world, was just about the only sight. Its vast array of ornaments and artefacts were once used by shamans to appease and honour their gods, and there were amulets, rings and extraordinarily fine filigree-like earrings as well. All the treasures had been hidden from the Spanish conquistadors, who melted down everything they found before shipping it back to Spain.

I wandered the streets trying to decide whether I felt safe enough to ride from Bogotá to Quito. On the way to lunch the next day a man in jeans shot out his hand and said, in English, 'Give me money, gringo'. It happened twice more in an hour. The beggars were more aggressive, demanding money as their right. Everyone else I met was friendlier than they had been in Central America. An email from Bogotá's Horizon Community brought brief relief. I'd asked if it was safe to ride from Bogotá to the Ecuadorian border.

'Start riding at 6 a.m. and stop at midday,' the email instructed. 'Do not ride in the afternoon. The guerrillas are not good at getting up early. Find a hotel and leave the bike out of sight. With brown hair and blue eyes you cannot be South American!'

The next day I was accosted and followed twice while walking around the city centre. I didn't like the atmosphere. It was tense and unsettling.

I phoned Dalys at Girag, the shipping office in Panama City, and asked her to send my bike to Quito.

'We cannot fly it to Quito. You only pay to Bogotá and it costs more to Quito. You have to sign the papers.'

No matter what I offered – to pay by credit card, fax the documents, use couriers – she wasn't having any of it. She insisted that I fly back to Panama City, pay over the counter and sign the documents in her presence. So that's what I did.

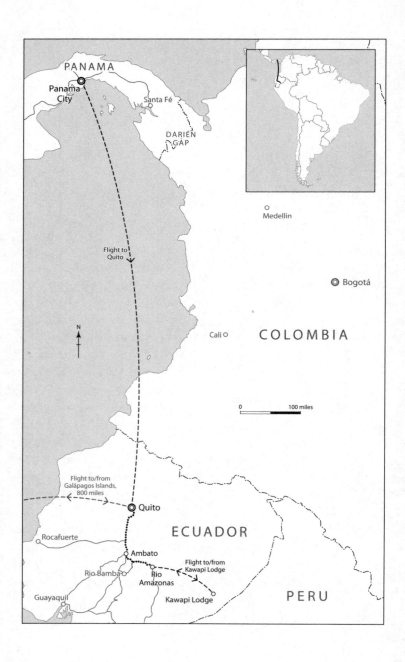

11

THE KEYS TO THE TOYSHOP

Ricardo Rocco is a great bear of a man, a six-foot-three version of the Armenian-French singer Charles Aznavour. I expected him to burst into song at any moment. A former Ecuadorian rally champion, he is Horizons' Quito 'Community' and quite a legend. Four years earlier he had set off on an 'Around the World for Peace' expedition, spreading a message that was pro-peace and against drug abuse. After an exhausting trip around South America he was in Colombia and almost home when he got kidnapped at a roadblock by the Ejército de Liberación Nacional (ELN, the National Liberation Army), who looked for wealthy people to ransom. They took him and several other hostages deep into the mountains. The ringleader started going through Ricardo's luggage and found the folder of his expedition press cuttings detailing his peace campaigns and anti-drug stance. After two hours alone in a barn he was taken to see the commander in a nearby town. Ricardo thought that was it. But the commander congratulated him on his charity work and let him go!

I met Ricardo at his home in Quito and was touched by his generous offer of hospitality. But as he'd had a motorbike stolen from his locked garage only the week before I decided to remain in my hotel as insurance. Ricardo told me how whenever he arrives in a new town the first thing he does is visit the local brothel 'to get a flavour of the place', but I wasn't about to follow his example. I was quite happy with my hotel. It was in Mariscal Sucre, Quito's tourist hub, where the streets were lined with cafes, a bewildering variety of restaurants – Chinese, Italian, seafood, Latin and grills – backpacker hostels and small hotels, travel agencies, tourist shops and internet cafés. It was a relief to be cool again too: at 9,200 feet above sea level, the days were crisp and the nights clear.

A childish joy defused the tension from Bogotá. I felt I had just been given the keys to the toyshop for the weekend. With excitement I spent a week trawling through the travel agents' brochures. There were so many things to do and I wanted to do them all: jungle treks and meeting native tribes in the Amazon, hiking and mountain biking in the Andes, visiting active volcanoes and of course cruising the Galápagos Islands.

If only I hadn't bought that ludicrous bicycle in Mexico, I'd have had more money to indulge my dreams now. A fool and his money are soon parted. Chasing Eduardo, the bike-shop owner, was becoming an increasingly painful thorn in my side. When I phoned him from Quito he claimed he hadn't yet sold it, but Rosa thought he was lying. Who to believe? In the meantime, I would have to call the Woolwich and arrange another two grand on my mortgage.

It was hard to know which of the many Galápagos tours to choose, but in the end I took the advice of a British girl who'd bought the cheapest trip available and regretted it. 'It was meant to be the highlight of my trip, but it was awful,' she told me. 'I went on the cheapest boat to save money but it was a big mistake. My cabin was tiny, smelt of diesel and was next to the engine. The food was awful, God knows what it was supposed to be. I was sick from that and the sea. The guide was surly and no one spoke any English. We even ran out of water and had to borrow some from another boat. I wish I'd gone on a better boat.' With all that in mind, I negotiated a 40 per cent discount off the last cabin on the *Beluga*, a steel-hulled motor yacht, which was to sail the following week.

Dan Walsh, a journalist from *Bike* magazine, had arrived in Quito and suggested meeting for a beer in the Turtle's Head. He was riding south on a BMW 650, funding his trip by submitting monthly features to the magazine – the perfect way to travel. The Turtle's Head was run by Albert, a Scottish former dispatch rider, who produced his own microbrews. Dan introduced me to four other Brits on bikes – Brian Coles (Colesy), Trys and Richard and Jane – and regaled us with tales of Colombia, which he'd loved. He'd ridden from Bogotá with a big government number on his jacket so that the army didn't mistake him for a member of FARC (Communist Freedom Fighters) and shoot him on sight. I wished I hadn't been so wet.

The Turtle's Head became our local. Colesy was on an Americas trip, worked in computing and could talk forever. Trys was an artist who'd been badgered into the trip by Dan even though he'd never ridden a motorcycle before; Albert commissioned him to paint a larger-than-life portrait of him on a regal chair with his two dogs at his side. And Richard and Jane were on their honeymoon; having finally tied the knot after fourteen years together, they were celebrating by riding their BMW GS1000 from Calgary, Canada to Buenos Aires, Argentina. All of us were heading south.

In between sessions at the pub I worked on my bike. I'd met Armando, who owned an identical KTM Adventure as well as a fleet of thirty taxis, and he'd kindly invited me to use his workshop where he serviced and repaired his taxis. His mechanics even washed my bike before I started servicing it. Through the whole of Central America I'd thought my bike was making a funny noise. I'd put it down to my paranoia as I only heard it at slow speeds and couldn't work out where it was coming from. Eventually I realised it was the chain, but did nothing about it. At Armando's I took the chain and found that four of the rollers were very thin and one had split in two. Armando generously gave me his spare so that I didn't have to wait until I got to the nearest KTM dealer, 240 miles away in Cuenca. He refused to accept anything for it so I took him and his girlfriend out to lunch. Where would they like to go?

'McDonald's,' said his girlfriend. 'It has just opened.'

Before my Galápagos cruise there was just time to squeeze in a visit to the Amazon. I booked a room at the Kapawi Ecolodge, deep in the rainforest near the Capahuari River, a tributary of the Amazon and close to the Peruvian border.

It is run by the Achuar, a self-sufficient nation of 6,000 spread out across 3,000 square miles. The only way in is to fly by Cessna. Low cloud and rain made me nervous as we flew over the vast expanse of virgin rainforest, broken only by sinuous rivers and a few tiny villages. Almost every village had one white building amongst the brown huts.

'They are churches built by missionaries,' the pilot informed me. 'Some of the oil companies use them to "soften up" the natives. Ecuador is the third largest oil exporter in South America.'

A thin brown line appeared below. It didn't look long enough but we skimmed the trees and only used half of it. I mopped my brow after a short walk through the forest to a waiting canoe. The noisy outboard pushed us upriver against the fast-flowing current and provided a cooling breeze. The Achuar lived in isolation here until the early 1970s when the missionaries and oil companies arrived. They intend to keep their lands free of roads, logging and oil, wanting to avoid what's happened to other tribal lands in the north, where towns have sprung up in the middle of the forest, kept alive by the new roads. Many indigenous people in the Amazon have been ignored, displaced, or killed by disease. There are stories of appalling pollution, and in a decades-long case against Texaco (which merged with Chevron in 2001), the Ecuadorian court fined Chevron almost $10 billion. Chevron has appealed. A few years before I arrived a plane landed at a remote airstrip in Achuar land and the occupants emerged with gifts for the community. They were oil company executives. The community held them captive for a few weeks before releasing them.

The lodge was made from forest materials. Raised boardwalks connected eighteen thatched wooden huts on stilts set round a lagoon. All the guests were English-speaking. As well as a wealthy British couple and their daughter, who'd just chartered a boat to sail around the Galápagos Islands, there was an irritatingly opinionated American mother-and-daughter combo, a pair of dour Irish doctors, and two Canadian conservationists who were having an uphill battle persuading Ecuadorians that they weren't from the US. Scottish couple Dale and Lynne had been married for a week and were on their honeymoon; they quickly escaped the first night's dinner and sat close together on the balcony with their legs entwined. I'd meet them again on the Galápagos cruise. The final couple were Ozzies Pam and Jane. Pam had terminal cancer and not long to live. She had come to try the local hallucinogenic drug, natem (ayahuasca), a vine, which she'd found terrifying. 'I felt like I had lost my mind,' she told us. 'Without Jane beside me I don't know what would have happened. I was out of control.'

Antonio, our guide, was half Achuar and half Ecuadorian. On our first full day he and a naturalist led us on a hike. The forest was so dense it was impossible to walk in a straight line for more than a few paces. Our eyes soon adjusted to the darkness. The smell of damp decay mingled with bird calls. There was something new to see with every step. Huge hollow fig trees, a black butterfly with a bright orange band on its wings, and huge seed pods like coconuts. A black frog the size of a walnut. Another large tree with hundreds of finger-like branches that fanned out at the base like a spaghetti rocket. We stopped to stare at the ground. Bright green dots slid across a rotting black log: leaf-cutter ants were carrying bits of leaf high above their heads on their way back to the nest.

That afternoon Antonio briefed us before we visited the chief of the local Achuar community. 'The chief will ask each person to introduce themselves, where you come from, how old you are and why you have come to his house. I will translate. Wait until the chief asks you a question before you speak. You will be offered a slightly narcotic drink but you have to have a lot before anything happens.

It is rude to refuse completely. Do not wander off and take photos, especially of the women's houses, and do not take photos during our session with the chief. At the end of the meeting the women will display their handicrafts for us to look at and buy if you wish. The prices are fixed so there is no haggling.'

After a short canoe ride we scrambled up the bank and followed a path to three huts. The chief's house had open sides, a dirt floor and a roof thatched with leaves. We sat on small three-legged stools. Two chickens pecked at the dirt beside me. As Antonio and the chief talked, they often spoke at the same time, each confirming what the other had just said. The chief's wife poured some grey liquid into several bowls. Whitish lumps floated to the surface. It smelt like warm wallpaper paste and tasted like it too. She made it by chewing leaves in her mouth for several minutes. Only one of us finished their bowl. Neither of the Irish doctors even picked theirs up.

'Please introduce yourself to the chief,' said Antonio.

The chief then introduced himself and added that now we knew each other we could proceed. Antonio fielded our questions but warned us not to ask about the oil companies as it made him angry. We learnt that the chief had lived in the village all his life and had no thoughts of moving. 'Everything I need is here,' he said. He and his people believed in many different spirits, who helped them live in harmony with the forest and the animals, and they communicated with them by using hallucinogenic plants. He couldn't understand why we Westerners were always rushing everywhere. What was wrong with tomorrow?

As the meeting closed I looked across at Morgan, one of the Irish doctors. His camera was half out of his bag and as the lens peeped over the side he pushed the button. I couldn't believe what I was seeing when we had been specifically asked not to take any pictures. Later that night I asked him if my eyes had deceived me or whether he had taken a photo during the meeting?

'Sure,' Morgan said. 'He didn't notice.'

'That is not the point,' I replied. 'We were specifically asked not to take photos, so why did you do it?'

'There are many places where you're not supposed to do things, like use mobile phones in aeroplanes, but everybody does it.'

'But you were a guest in his house and were expressly asked not to take pictures.' I was really angry but he couldn't see it at all.

'It's just about money. They are all the same.'

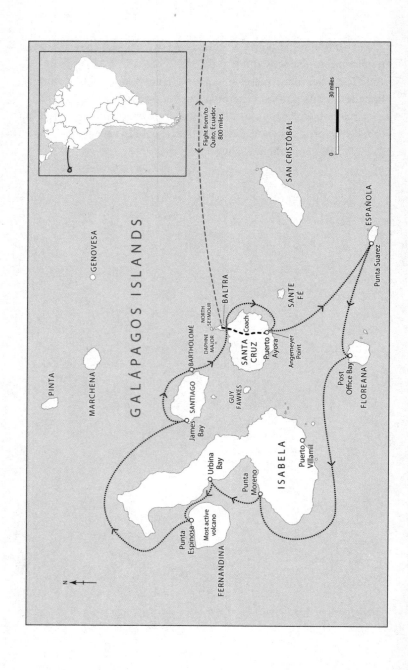

12

RED POUCHES AND BLUE FEET IN THE GALÁPAGOS

Darwin put the Galápagos Islands on the map. Ironically, the twenty-two-year-old had only agreed to join the trip on the *Beagle* as naturalist (and the captain's companion) to avoid entering the Church. The *Beagle*'s mission was to complete the South American surveys begun on its previous voyage and obtain a complete circle of measurement of longitude using twenty-two chronometers. Refitted for the journey with an extra mizzen mast and two inches of fir on the hull, the ninety-foot, ten-gun bark left Portsmouth on 27 December 1831. Darwin's cabin, the chart room, was 9 feet by 11 feet with a 5-foot ceiling, a 4-foot chart table and the mizzenmast coming through the floor. It was to be his home, on and off, for almost five years.

The ship arrived on the island of San Cristóbal on 18 September 1835 and Darwin no doubt spoke these immortal words as he stepped ashore: 'The *Beagle* has landed.' He certainly wasn't looking for the origin of species, which theory only dawned on him much later. Indeed, there is a general misconception that Darwin devised his theory of evolution all by himself, but this is not true. Darwin was exceptionally well connected and well informed. One important influence was Sir Charles Lyell. Darwin took the first volume of Lyell's *Principles of Geology* with him on the *Beagle*, which argued that geological features are the result of tiny changes over immensely long periods of time. On his return to England Darwin became friends with Lyell, who may have recommended a book about the Canary Islands by a German geologist, Leopold von Buch. Darwin was particularly taken by von Buch's belief that, in isolation, species change to the point of becoming different species. This was exactly what Darwin came to believe had happened on the remote and isolated Galápagos Islands.

The archipelago of fourteen large volcanic islands and about forty smaller ones straddles the equator 700 miles off the coast of Ecuador. Only five are inhabited – Baltra, Floreana, Isabela, San Cristóbal and Santa Cruz – as there is so little water. When Darwin arrived, in 1835, the islands were uninhabited. Today the population tops 20,000 and is growing rapidly. The main centres are Puerto Ayora on Santa Cruz and Puerto Villamil on Isabela. Most of the islanders make their living from tourism or fishing.

On the flight to Baltra island I sat next to two salesmen from Mumbai who were in South America to sell drugs to the Ecuadorian government. We discussed evolution and how all life rapidly becomes resistant to new drugs.

'Evolution works in our favour,' said one of the salesmen, 'because drug-resistance always generates new sales. For malaria, for example, the secret is to never get bitten in the first place. It's called preventative medicine.'

When antibiotics were first used to kill bacteria in the 1920s it was thought diseases like tuberculosis and pneumonia would be eradicated. But natural selection kicked in. Large populations and very short breeding times provide the ideal basis for high levels of mutations. An antibiotic needs to kill every single bacteria to be successful. If one mutant bacteria survives it will create more like itself, so developing resistance. Some strains of tuberculosis have developed resistance to every antibiotic used against them, which is one of the reasons why TB is becoming a fatal disease again. A similar principle holds true for pesticides. When DDT was first sprayed on hut walls against malarial mosquitoes in Africa it was a tremendous success. After biting the occupants, the vast majority of the mosquitoes flew to the wall to digest their meal and were killed by contact with the insecticide. However, a tiny percentage flew out through the window and survived. Thus, at a stroke, only survivors bred and resistance developed. The insecticide ensured only the strongest survived so a new one would be needed.

'We are on a conveyor belt of drugs. We cannot get off because it is moving so fast.'

I'd flown in to the Galápagos a few days early to see what else I could do after my cruise. If I was only going to be here once I didn't want to miss anything, but without Darwin I can't imagine that anyone would ever want to visit these desolate and dry islands. The rainfall is so low (less than nine inches a year) there are no rivers and very little drinking water, so the famous Galápagos turtles evolved to survive for a year without water. The climate is determined by the Humboldt Current, a body of cold water which produces temperature inversions as it emerges from the deep ocean near the islands. It creates dry areas on land nearest to it – like the Atacama Desert in Chile and Peru.

All the islands are volcanic and were created from the Cocos and Nazca tectonic plates, which are moving apart: the Nazca plate is moving eastwards towards the Americas at one inch a year and carries all the volcanoes with it. It is believed the islands were created from a mantle plume, a column of hot rock about 60 miles in diameter that rises at about four inches a year from deep within the earth. The same process created the Hawaiian islands. When there's a new fissure, magma forces its way out and the volcanic activity creates a new island. The newest, like Isabela and Fernandina, are a mere one million years old. Fernandina is the most active: ships made detours to watch its 2009 eruption. The oldest islands – Española, Santa Fe and Floreana – are in the west; they're four to five million years old and become dormant as they lose their connection to the core.

We landed on the island of Baltra, a flat featureless blob of rock with spiky dark grey lava stretching out in all directions. The US Air Force built the runway during the Second World War to protect the Panama Canal. An intense heat rebounded off the rocks. There were no trees and no signs of water. Walking the 50 yards to the bus was like walking in an invisible cloud, the air was so hot and humid, a big change from Quito's cool mountain temperatures.

After a short ferry ride to the much larger Santa Cruz island, a low volcano measuring 25 by 20 miles, a bus took us to Puerto Ayora on the other side, where we were to meet our boat, the *Beluga*. Santa Cruz was also raw and inhospitable. The road meandered through barren wastes of a lost world. Stunted and scrubby bushes struggled to find nourishment on the sharp volcanic rocks. The view was the same in all directions, with no point of reference. But as the road climbed through the hills in the centre of the island, green bushes and fields began to appear, thanks to the *garúa*, a mist that hovers over the higher land in winter. Though it never actually rains, the moisture is sufficient to support a wide variety of flora and fauna in the uplands, as well as many small-scale farms. The barren and dry lowlands were a huge problem for the early settlers especially as only Floreana had a reliable artesian spring.

Puerto Ayora, the biggest town on the islands, was much lusher than I expected after the desolate bus ride. Palm trees towered over lime-washed houses. The tropical heat blasted out of the ground and from the sky. I walked in slow motion down the narrow, winding streets and emerged at the port. A small slipway split the tiny harbour, where turquoise fishing boats matched the water. Brown pelicans stood around like pensioners waiting for the post office to open. They ignored me. A large grey marine iguana basked beside a gull and three seals at the water's edge didn't budge as I approached. One casually looked up at me, then went back to sleep.

I was looking forward to a cooling swim at the Galápagos Hotel in Puerto Ayora and an opportunity to soak up more of the islands' history before my cruise departed a couple of days later.

The islands were discovered in 1535 by Tomás de Berlanga, the Bishop of Panama, when his ship drifted off course en route to Peru. He named them 'Las Encantadas' (the Enchanted Islands) and noted the thousands of large *galápagos* (tortoises). The tortoises provided meat and water for hungry sailors. Passing ships loaded hundreds of live giant tortoises into their holds, where they survived for up to a year without eating or drinking; a living fridge which almost sealed their fate.

The Galápagos were not far from the Spanish galleon route between their conquered Incan empire in Peru and their main stronghold in Mexico. England supported pirates and buccaneers who attacked Spanish galleons returning with treasure and these pirates used the Galápagos as a base. Both Sir Henry Morgan and Sir Richard Hawkins, two of England's most famous buccaneers, visited the islands in the sixteenth and seventeenth centuries. That's why each island has a variety of names, the original English one and the new Spanish version, appended following annexation by Ecuador in 1832. Their English names are unmistakable: Indefatigable, Hood and Binloe (after a pirate).

The pirates had long gone when American adventurer Forrest Nelson first landed on the islands in 1951. He returned several times and then in 1961 built the Galápagos Hotel (the first on the islands) with his own hands, casting the concrete blocks on site and using anything else that he could find. The hotel still has a wonderful Robinson Crusoe feel. Big glass windows looked out over the clear blue water where sail boats bobbed in the bay. A hammock hung in one corner almost in reach of the bar. The wooden furniture was heavy and built to last. Faded photos of Forrest Nelson's original boat, the *Nellie Brush*, hung from the walls. Members of his family still run the hotel.

Needing a store of books for my week on the *Beluga*, I walked to the Darwin Research Station and selected *The Galápagos Phat Guide* by Antonio Adrian and *My Father's Island* by Johanna Angermeyer. The reviews for the *Guide* were persuasive: "'It is the best guide on the Galápagos natural history ever! Informative, witty and clear, three thumbs up!" The author's mother.'

The story related in *My Father's Island* turned out to be a real-life Galápagos mystery. It began in 1929, when a Dr Friedrich Ritter and his mistress Dore abandoned their respective spouses in Germany and settled on Floreana island, the only one with a reliable spring. Like many Germans at the time, they emigrated to escape the fascists. Dr Ritter was a dentist; as he and Dore were the only inhabitants of a remote island, he had all his teeth replaced by stainless steel ones – the original 'Jaws' from James Bond. Their idyll was rudely interrupted in 1932 by the arrival of newlyweds Margret and Heinz Wittmer, also from Germany, who were practising nudists and lived with their two children in a corrugated zinc hut on the coast at Black Beach (still occupied by her descendants). Next came Baroness Eloise Bosquet de Wagner Wehrborn, who arrived with her lovers Lorenz and Philippson from Austria, declared herself empress of Floreana and expected to be treated accordingly. Lorenz was rapidly demoted to a lowly servant and used to escape to the Wittmers for relief. In 1934 Dr Ritter suddenly died from eating bad chicken, even though he proclaimed himself a vegetarian. Next, Lorenz went exploring on Marchena island (Binloe) but became shipwrecked and died from dehydration, which was confirmed when his mummified body was found. The Baroness and Philippson left on a friend's yacht for Tahiti but were never seen again. These disasters occurred in such quick succession that the Wittmers were suspected of foul play but no evidence was ever found.

The following year, in 1935, four Angermeyer brothers arrived on Santa Cruz island in a yacht they had sailed all the way from Germany. Their mother had sold their house, bought the boat and sent them off to a new life in the Galápagos, to also escape the Nazis. The Angermeyers' descendants still live on Santa Cruz and run a cruise business and a restaurant at the eponymous Angermeyer Point. The restaurant came highly recommended so I took a water taxi to the Point, 500 yards from Puerto Ayora harbour, and sat at a table on the wooden decking overlooking the bay. A beautiful blue-hulled ocean-going yacht with twin masts lay at anchor 200 yards away. White buildings poked above the trees behind the harbour. A large gull watched as I savoured my smoked fish and lobster thermidor, washed down by a cold Chardonnay. The sun dropped behind the island and the cool sea breeze kept the mosquitoes away.

The *Beluga* set sail the following evening. We were to visit seven islands, spending a day on each and travelling to the next one at night. Also on board were Dale and Lynne, the Scottish honeymooners whom I'd met at Kapawi Ecolodge; US advertising execs Mike and Marci, travelling with their son, Jake, and three New York friends; and a very serious couple from Switzerland who hardly said a word to anyone, including each other, the whole week. Two more guests were to join us on Isabela. Our guide was Sylvia; small and Swiss, she hid her sense of humour well.

My cabin was on the port side at the rear of the main deck. I had a window over the stern and a larger one on the port side, two bunk beds all to myself and my own bathroom. The next morning I woke to see a grey island off the port side – North Seymour. Zodiacs dropped us at the black beach from where we followed the marked path round the headland. The black basalt was warm underfoot, even at 10 a.m. A male frigate bird glided overhead, his jet-black wings stark against the blue sky and his enormous bright red gular (throat) pouch inflated like a balloon, a beacon to females below. Frigates are about the size of a chicken, but their thin wings are over six feet long. They are masters of the air and steal food from other birds such as boobies. Down at ground level, two male frigates sat close together in a heather-like bush, their wings outstretched and their pouches puffed to full capacity. Random black feathers stippled the edges of their scarlet pouches like wayward stubble. Their black wing feathers sparkled in the sun and their long beaks curved down at the end like a tin opener.

Honks and a whiff of guano led us to the mesmerising spectacle of hundreds of blue-footed boobies engaged in their famous courtship dance. Elongating their white chests and necks, pointing their long, straight beaks to the sky, the males waddled around ostentatiously, flashing their famous turquoise feet in a comically exaggerated goosestep designed to get the girls' attention. As they slowly circled their chosen female, they'd lean slightly back and to one side so as to raise their spectacular blue feet just that little bit higher. It wasn't the size of your equipment that mattered, only the colour of your feet. The exact right shade of blue could drive a girl wild. In which case she would turn away, stretch her neck, stare at the sky and honk. The male then responded with a low whistle and some sky-pointing: facing the female, he'd open his wings, raise his tail feathers and stretch his neck up so everything pointed at the sky. As the dance progressed they would start to sky-point in unison, honking and whistling and then mimicking each other's every turn.

As we stood among them, the boobies courted, cavorted and sky-pointed all around us. They paid us no heed: if a pair were courting in the middle of the path we had to walk around them. The more flamboyant among them used rocks as podiums. Others sat on nests, walked slowly about or gazed into the distance. With no predators none of them feared humans. The constant honks and whistles was one the funniest things I had ever seen. I caught Mike's eye behind me. He stretched out his elbows like wings, flashed a foot, pushed his nose into the air and honked.

Both sexes choose mates based on feet colour, and constantly monitor any changes in the shade. In one experiment where some males' feet were temporarily dyed darker blue, the females' second eggs were much smaller than the first. The Boobies' eyes are very sensitive to the blue part of the spectrum so can distinguish subtleties (and hence healthier partners) beyond ours. Blue is an unusual colour in animals. The boobies use a structure of collagen fibres to produce a darker blue and combine it with a yellow pigment that's generated from their food. The healthier the bird, the more pigment is created, resulting in feet that are a brighter blue.

During his three weeks of research on the Galápagos, Darwin concentrated on the smaller and less glamorous birds – the finches – but made the schoolboy error of failing to label which island his specimens came from. He also missed the significance of a comment from the islands' Vice-Governor, Mr Lawson, who declared that 'tortoises differed from the different islands', and that he could with certainty tell from which island any one was brought. Darwin was only able to make inter-island comparisons by using other naturalists' collections once he returned home to England. His inadequately labelled collection of Galápagos finches was a case in point. Only one species of finch arrived on the Galápagos from South America. Isolated and without competition for thousands of years it evolved into fourteen different species, each of which has a unique beak the right size and shape for the food it eats: fruit, insects, cactus or seeds. These are what are now known as Darwin's finches, an example of natural selection at work. Darwin used them to explain how new species evolve to fill the available niches. This type of evolution is now called adaptive radiation.

On his return to England in 1836, Darwin settled into the comfortable life of a gentleman and never went abroad again. Over the next two decades he formulated his ideas and developed his theories on evolution and natural selection. By mid-1858 he had written a quarter of a million words of a three-volume work called *Natural Selection*. But he was too scared to publicise his findings, afraid of angering the Church with his challenge to the Christian view that God created the world and all the species in it in six days. He decided to have his book published posthumously. Then on 18 June 1858 a letter from another Englishman, Alfred Russel Wallace, jolted Darwin out of his reticence. It enclosed a manuscript, 'The Tendency of Varieties to Depart Indefinitely from the Original Type', which Wallace asked Darwin, his trusted correspondent, to publish for him since he was in the Malay Archipelago on a collecting expedition. The manuscript expounded the same theory of natural selection. A shocked Darwin wrote to his friend Lyell: 'he could not have made a better short abstract! Even his terms now stand as heads of my chapters!' Wallace had had the same idea at the same time but there are no prizes for second place in the world of science. Unlike Darwin,

Wallace had to work for a living and collected animals from exotic locations that he sold to gentlemen collectors and museums at home.

There is doubt surrounding the date Darwin claimed to have received Wallace's letter and suspicion he incorporated some of Wallace's work in his chapter on natural selection. Whatever the truth, Darwin was forced to act. At a meeting of the Linnean Society in London on 1 July 1858 Darwin duly presented 'a set of excerpts cobbled together from his own unpublished drafts and correspondence', carefully pointing out he had been working on this subject for twenty years. Wallace's paper was read out afterwards.

Darwin published *On the Origin of Species* in 1859 and, suffering from nausea, quickly escaped to a remote spa on the Yorkshire moors. The newspapers concluded that man had evolved from apes and that Darwin denied man's immortality, but he never defended his ideas in public. Thus the world now flocks to the Galápagos Islands, and not to the Wallace Line in the Indonesian Archipelago.

Española is the southernmost and geologically oldest of the Galápagos Islands. Landing at Punta Suarez, we followed the path up to the headland and along its crest. Like all the islands it seemed mostly made up of the jagged *makatea*, razor-sharp volcanic rock whose edges cut the soles of my shoes, but this one had a cover of low scrub and thin bushes and was carpeted in birds: waved albatrosses stayed seated on the path as we walked around them, masked boobies (blue-footed boobies with grey feet) nested on the cliffs below, and swallow-tailed gulls soared beneath us. A Galápagos hawk flew low over my head, wings outstretched, gliding on the wind. I stopped to watch him as he followed the crest to the bay ahead. He wheeled around and came back on a parallel course inland, over the plants and grasses. The air hummed with insects. The Galápagos hawk flew a figure-of-eight circuit. His piercing yellow eyes scanned the ground for lava lizards and giant centipedes. The sun illuminated the brown ripples radiating out of his tail feathers. It was fascinating to watch but we weren't allowed to dawdle: tourist boats stick to a schedule so they don't all arrive at one beach at the same time, and Sylvia was certainly not one to let rules be broken. She wouldn't even countenance mild dissent.

Learning that our next stop was to be so-called Post Office Bay, I suggested to Sylvia we could sail past and do something more interesting. In 1793 a British ship left a wooden barrel on Floreana island as an international post box. Homeward-bound ships would call in and collect any mail addressed to their countries. No stamp required. I wasn't in the least interested in looking at an old barrel stuffed with tourist postcards. I hadn't any photos of letter boxes at home and saw no need to start now. I did a quick survey and discovered that none of my fellow passengers wanted to go there either. But that made no difference to Sylvia. Like naughty schoolchildren we piled in to the Zodiacs and cast furtive glances at each other while Sylvia droned on about the boring barrel. Ten minutes later we trudged back to the dinghies and the salvation of a cool beer. I wished Antonio Adrian had been our guide. In his *Galápagos Phat Guide* he offers a list of handy tips for guides on how to answer a tourist who points at an empty space and asks 'What's that?' For something that was on the ground, he advises: 'Things that get away fast in the Galápagos are insects, reptiles, birds or money'. If it was something in the sea: 'If it came from above, probably a bird. If it came from below, probably a fish.' And finally, if it was something in the air: 'probably a bird'.

At Isabela the next day we went snorkelling but were warned not to get too close to the sea lions on the beach. I rolled into the warm water off the side of the Zodiac and swam slowly towards the rocks just offshore. It was a different world underwater. Bright yellow and electric blue fish with black vertical lines drifted back and forth with the current as each wave passed overhead. 'Look at the leetle fishes,' said my inner Jacques Cousteau, who always appears when I snorkel.

A small sea lion with brown skin pirouetted underneath me, a juvenile. He acrobatically twisted and turned, then looked straight at me as if to say: 'I bet you can't do that.' I dived down, somersaulted and blew bubbles out of my nose. The sea lion replied with a double twist, pike and roll. I responded but couldn't match his grace and agility. A few of his friends joined in. They seemed to know exactly how far I could reach and how close they could come without touching me. As an experiment I made an exaggerated splash crawl across the water, which attracted even more sea lions. Several stared at me as they approached, before turning and darting past me. The tempo increased as they got excited. I continued to roll and somersault, playing with them on my own ungainly terms but outclassed by their extraordinary athleticism and acceleration. With two flicks of the tail they could shoot forward like a bullet. Two had a mock battle, rotating like a Catherine wheel as each tried to bite the other's tail. Two others were trying to bite each other's noses until they locked jaws in a sea lion kiss.

A large male appeared nearby. He was a lot bigger than the ones I'd been playing with and I shivered. I checked where the Zodiac and the other swimmers were. Two male sea lions were having a serious fight on the beach. Sand flew like dust as they hammered into each other, using their shoulders like demented sumo wrestlers. Smaller sea lions scrambled to get out of the way as the two hulks slammed into each other with a sickening thud.

'Jerome!' called Sylvia suddenly. 'Swim away from the beach, there are some males near you.'

I looked down and saw two big males and several smaller sea lions around me. I was scared and immediately started to swim back towards the Zodiac, but they followed me. Safely on board again, it seemed I hadn't been in for a major mauling after all. 'They bite people's flippers and nip their toes when they get over-excited,' said Sylvia.

As by far the biggest of the islands, Isabela – shaped like a Wellington boot 80 miles tall, with a 'foot' 45 miles long – suffers the lion's share of the environmental problems caused by local fishing and farming practices and by tourism. Over-fishing by unlicensed boats is a particular concern, especially of sea cucumbers – strange, long brown creatures that ingest the sand like earthworms and evade predators by getting rid of their internal organs then growing new ones. Fishing bans are hard to enforce because many boats are owned by politicians or their friends. The fishermen are poor and live in Puerto Villamil on Isabela, out of sight of the tourists.

The popularity of the islands has also harmed the land animals. All food is imported from the mainland and this has led to a parasitic fly larvae spreading from chickens to Darwin's finches, wild birds being infected by the canary pox virus and penguins being hit by avian malaria. Goats are another big problem. They eat everything, can climb trees and out-compete the native flora and fauna. There are also feral cats, dogs and rats. Many attempts have been made to kill all the goats but Isabela is a big island. If the authorities clear the goats from one area others come in to replace them.

A walk through the lava fields of Punta Moreno on Isabela showed the dangerous side of the islands. Sylvia warned us not to leave the path because ten feet away from it the lava field looks the same in every direction and you get dehydrated very quickly. Even though it was only mid-morning, intense heat radiated off the black lava. Everything did indeed look the same. I lost all sense of direction as soon as the *Beluga* was out of sight, even though the hillocks of lava were only a few feet over my head. I climbed one for a better view but couldn't see the boat. It was scary. I'd already cut my hand on the *makatea* that poked into the sky and felt the points claw at the soles of my shoes. It was a maze, a cauldron under the sun on an alien planet. We found our way back by following the painted markers. Sylvia recounted a chilling tale before dinner:

'Several years ago the USA and Ecuadorian armies had an exercise to hike across Isabela and be picked up by the boats a few days later,' she said. 'They never arrived. The sharp *makatea* rocks cut their boots to pieces. The Ecuadorians stopped but the Americans continued. All the Americans died. The Ecuadorians were rescued by ship a few days later when no one emerged from the other side.'

As all the islands looked so similar, whether we landed on a beach or one of the occasional jetties, I suggested to Sylvia that we were

121

perpetually visiting the same island and that we just circumnavigated it every night. She was not amused.

To be fair, the birds and animals were different on each island – as Darwin also observed, but failed to note down at the time. Fernandina, for example, has a colony of large marine iguanas, the only lizard that forages for food in the sea. Prehistoric and surprisingly fast, they spend most of their time motionless. They live off seaweed, which means they eat a lot of salt, but can't excrete it in the usual way. Instead, every thirty seconds or so they snort a white a jet of salt out of their nostrils. There is huge variability between marine iguanas living on different islands. Some can grow to twice the size of those on a neighbouring island, with the greatest difference between those on Genovesa and Isabela: 2 lb versus 25 lb. This is especially surprising as they eat in the sea and have the same predators, mainly hawks, owls and snakes. The current view is that it reflects trade-offs between sexual and natural selection. Sexual selection favours larger body sizes (the females select larger males), but the largest animals of each island die first during El Niño-related famines when the food supply is greatly diminished. They are also the only adult vertebrate that regularly shrinks in body size, by losing bone mass, and then grows again. They do this to more easily survive harsh conditions: during an El Niño event, for example, they shrink up to 15 per cent.

Darwin believed it took thousands of years for a new species to evolve, but we now know evolution is fast. Just how fast was discovered on Daphne Major, a small island to the north of Santa Cruz. Peter and Rosemary Grant had studied the island's population of medium ground finches for many years but a severe drought in 1977 drastically reduced the number of seeds available for them to eat. The finches had to switch from their usual small, soft seeds to larger harder ones that required a larger and more powerful beak. The smaller-beaked birds either died off or were too ill to reproduce so the following year the average beak size increased by 10 per cent, a huge rate of evolutionary change.

New research shows that evolutionary change can happen even faster and may not even take a generation. For example, every time we have a feeling of love billions of molecules flood into our system. These chemical and electrical signals are transported by RNA, the messenger molecules, to and from the cells containing our DNA, which can change an inactive gene to active and vice versa. This new field, epigenetics, holds that our thoughts and experiences can actually change what genes are expressed and thus what we pass on to future generations. Evidence from Överkalix, a remote town in northern Sweden, shows that 'a famine at critical times in the lives of the grandparents can affect the life expectancy of the grandchildren'.

How had I changed on my trip this far? I'd certainly got used to meeting many complete strangers every day and treating them as friends, never hesitating to embarrass myself with my awful Spanish. In fact, the sooner I made people laugh, the sooner and more helpful they became. My survival strategies had become second nature: food safety during the day – I never ate lunch if I couldn't find somewhere that both looked and smelt good – and shelter then food at day's end. I was relying much more on instincts, trusting my heart more than my head (though it hadn't worked with Rosa). Every day I answered hundreds of questions – where, what, why, when and how? – and constantly evaluated and re-evaluated my decisions. The indecision of Mexico and Central America had been replaced by knowing I was doing the right thing, doing something I'd always wanted to do: visiting the Galápagos Islands. Perhaps sowing the seed of a greater confidence and determination.

I was really starting to enjoy my trip but was envious of the families and couples on the boat. I really wished I was not travelling alone, but knew it was better to travel solo than not at all. My genes were telling me they wanted to continue and wanted to leave someone behind. For me, travelling was a substitute for being in a stable relationship, but was furthering the species really the only purpose of life?

The Nobel physicist Richard Feynman, who worked on the Manhattan Project to develop the first atomic bomb during the

Second World War, was often asked meaning-of-life questions like: 'If you're so clever, why are we here?' His response resonated a great deal with me. It went something like this: 'Many people waste a lot of their time and worry a lot about questions that don't have an answer. For example, "Is there a god?" ... My answer to "what is the purpose of life?" is "does it really matter?"' As a scientist he argued that each person should look at the facts, make up their own mind and believe in things they wanted to believe in. We are 'lost in a mysterious universe without having any purpose'. The most important thing is to enjoy yourself, be happy and treat others as you'd like to be treated. You never know when your life will end. Live every day as if it was your last because one day it will be.

On our last night on the *Beluga*, Mike and I nursed beers on the top deck as the sun set over Bartholomé island.

'I'd love to do what you're doing, riding about on a motorbike, going wherever your mood takes you.'

'I'd much rather be married with kids like you. I am only doing this as the next best thing. The grass is always greener.'

'Ah, but the secret is to be happy on your own lawn.'

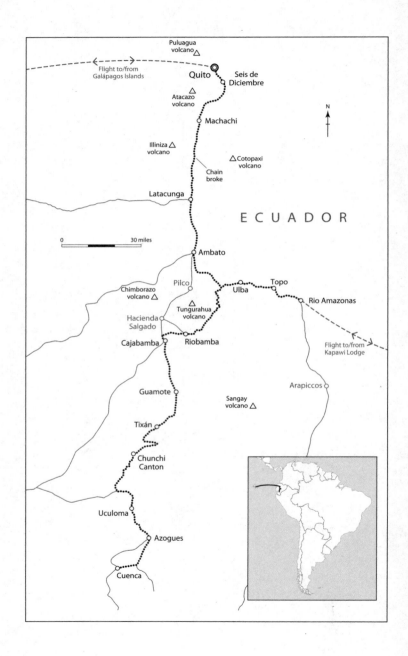

13

Riding into a Sandwich

The room swayed gently as water dripped off my hair and on to my notebook. It was strange being back on dry land in Quito after ten days at sea. My trousers clung to my legs, soaked from the short walk to the restaurant, which buzzed with excitement away from the cold rain outside. It was time to think about moving on. Time to address my favourite topic: how to take less kit. Everyone knows about travelling light. Less is more. There's a big difference between what you want and what you need. What could I send home, or even better, give away? In my mind I often ran through the contents of each pannier and my top box. Did I really need my tent when I was staying in hotels? If not, I could get rid of the ground sheet, poles, pegs and sleeping bag too. And if I wasn't camping I didn't need my stove, pans or fuel bottle either. Now was a good time to send stuff home, but I kept my tent. My big weakness was books. Unable to walk past a bookshop, the fantastic Libri Mundi in Quito added six books to my library: two on the Galápagos, two on the Incas and two Footprint guides on Peru and Bolivia. I was glad I wasn't cycling.

I hadn't thought about my bicycle at all in the Galápagos. My stomach tightened as I called Rosa again.

'I think Eduardo has your money,' she told me, 'but he said he did not. Two days ago I see the man who bought it riding it in town. He paid Eduardo $2,900. Eduardo is not an honest man. He knows you are not coming back.'

Now what was I to do? Fly back to Valle? The longer this went on, the further away I'd be and the less chance I'd have of ever getting my money. A return flight to Mexico City plus taxis and hotels would blow another $600, with no guarantee of success, and what if he refused to hand it over? To go back felt like throwing even more money away and I'm no good at confrontation. I can't think fast enough on my feet. It was now late April and Peru was so close. It pulled me south like a magnet and I didn't resist.

The next day I left for Cuenca down the so-called Avenue of the Volcanoes, a 200-mile-long valley between the major Cordillera ranges. The previously smooth and rounded hills of Central America were gone. Jagged ridges, gullies and steeper slopes promised more ahead. The Andes. The spine stretches the whole length of South America from Venezuela in the north to Chile and Argentina in the south. Five thousand five hundred miles of mountains. I'd follow it to Ushuaia at the very end of Tierra del Fuego. Ricardo had advised me to leave Quito early to get to Cuenca in one day, but I had forgotten why and left late. Hills emerged on all sides and mountains soon dwarfed me and my bike. It would be cold on the many passes. After only half an hour, just pass Machachi, a white point on the skyline was my first real taste of the Andes: Cotopaxi, a perfect yet menacing cone against a blue sky. It grew out of the earth like a huge wart. At over 19,000 feet it is the world's highest continually active volcano. Snow dribbled off the top like runny icing on a cake while sheep grazed in the fields beside the road.

A few minutes later I stopped at a police checkpoint. They waved me through and as I accelerated away the power snapped off and the engine raced. I whipped in the clutch. With no drive in any gear I feared the gearbox had gone. Baffled, I put my bike on the centre stand to work out what was wrong. The chain had fallen off. I must have put the joining link on incorrectly at Armando's. The chain lay in the middle of the road near the checkpoint. Elated to have the hot chain in my hands, I walked back past the cars queuing for the checkpoint and waggled it, smiling at the waiting drivers. They smiled and waved back. I was so happy I knew I could fix it. I pushed my bike into the petrol station on the other side of the road, got a new connecting link from my spares and refitted the chain. The split link wouldn't fit, even after many blows with an improvised hammer. What was wrong? It was the master link for my old KTM I'd used on my last African trip. This chain was a bit wider. I'd have to weld the new link on. The attendant told me the nearest welding machine was five miles away.

Would the plate stay on? I didn't have another connecting link. I rode slowly and coasted downhill. Luckily it was still in place when I reached the *soldar* man. Jorge had a thin moustache and a grey base-ball cap on backwards. Over his shoulder his new kitchen had a sink, a table and chairs but the walls were bare concrete blocks. It didn't yet have a door. He brought out his arc welding machine and pushed the bare wires into a wall socket. A few quick sparks and it was done. I'd replace it in Cuenca. Jorge refused any payment so I gave him a bottle of wine I'd bought for dinner with Jodie in Cuenca. It didn't look like I'd reach Cuenca before dark now.

My bike flew under the radar twisting and turning through valleys sliding and strafing past trucks and cars. The trees thinned out as more and more fields appeared until a distant spire emerged above a hill. The white church dominated the village and looked far too big for such a small place. Dusty streets talked of unfulfilled dreams. I longed for biscuits but there were no shops. Ten minutes later a shop materialised, a single-storey white building that seemed rooted to the rock on which it stood. Heavy iron bars protected the windows. Five women dressed in black with red shawls sat on a bench outside. Their black bowler hats bobbed and bounced as they chatted to each other. I couldn't understand a single word they said. They could have been talking Quechua, an ancient Andean language which predates the Incas by several centuries. One looked up and smiled welcomingly as I walked into the shop. Inside, blue packets of Oreo biscuits lined the shelves but I went for the local alternative. I longed to chat to the women but felt intrusive and sat at the other end of the porch, dangling my legs over the side. I wanted to take their photos but who was I to capture their souls in my camera and ride away, never to be seen again? I tried to imagine how I'd feel being accosted by a tourist leaving Waitrose with my shopping. 'Oh, wow, look at that!' says the Ecuadorian tourist, pointing at me and my trolley. 'I must take a photo.' My reticence stopped me from taking any photos of people in South America. I took photos 'with my mind' instead. I can't remember many of them now.

As soon as I got back on my bike I remembered Ricardo's advice about riding to Cuenca. He'd said I had to be past the town of Riobamba before 11 a.m. After that the mists descended on the mountains and the whole ascent would be in heavy fog and rain. It was now 2.30 p.m., with only 140 miles to Cuenca. As I climbed through a broad valley of brown and bright green fields the clouds sat on the hilltops. A few miles west but completely obscured by the clouds lay Chimborazo, another volcano and at 20,700 feet the highest point in Ecuador. Only pure white clouds floated high above Riobamba. There was no fog at all. Maybe I'd be lucky. Railway tracks crisscrossed the valley as they climbed out of town. The cool clear air and rugged scenery reminded me of the Alps. I stopped to put on a sweater and wondered if the railway was on the list of 'Incredible Railway Journeys' as it clung to the edge of a cliff. I moved towards the clouds. Suddenly around a corner fluffy fingers of mist poked into the valley below. I stopped and watch the mist roll in like smoke, filling in gaps in the trees and rolling ever higher. The clouds above and mists below were squeezing the blue sky out. I was riding into a sandwich. I stopped again a few minutes later. Everything was white save two forested islands floating in an ocean of white cloud.

The temperature dropped as l rode into the mist. Drizzle flecked my visor. It got progressively worse. The tarmac turned to brown dirt. The mist became fog, a thick, wet fog like a blanket, a white night, so thick I slowed to 10 mph. A never-ending series of curves sliced through the side of the mountain, in and out of invisible ravines. Vehicles suddenly appeared with no warning. Many drove at scary speeds and few had any lights on. One light-less truck drove down the middle of the road with bales sticking out over both sides. I constantly wiped my visor to see straight. I stopped on the edge of the road at 8,000 feet and looked over the edge. The treeless grassy slope was far steeper than Cotopaxi's cone and disappeared into the fog. You'd never stop until you reached the bottom.

My fingers felt the cold despite my heated grips. Was water pooling in my crotch again? Knowing that my balls could be flooded with freezing cold water didn't help my concentration. No matter how uncomfortable it was I had to keep both hands on the handlebars. Just keep going until things warmed up again. It felt cold and damp but the dam held. Gore-Tex is great. Especially when you remember to do your flies up. Ricardo had been right. The fog and rain stayed for hours and only cleared near Cuenca.

Dusk was falling as I approached Cuenca, the third largest city in Ecuador, and the road split into a dual carriageway. I followed the driver of a black SUV who seemed to know where he was going until he suddenly slowed – his brake lights didn't work – and turned left up a tiny, minor road. OK, maybe he didn't know where he was going. Ten seconds later it was clear he did. In the dim light huge lumps of concrete blocked both lanes. I turned round quickly and followed him again. The single-track road zigzagged up through the hills between stone walls like a Welsh country lane. The darkness made it easy to catch him up. Lights glowed in house windows. His headlights were a beacon to follow until we emerged on the dual carriageway again.

Trying to find a hotel in the dark was a nightmare. None of the signs were lit so I soon lost the way to Centro. Tired, cold and wet after 240 miles I stopped to ask for directions yet again. Finally I found Jodie's *hostal* but it was full. The next *hostal* had no parking. On the other side of the road a row of flags hung over the street. Another hotel, but much too expensive for me. My hotels don't have flags. While I pondered what to do next a man with short black hair, wire-rim glasses and a short greying beard asked me where I was going. He spoke perfect English and his name was Nico Merchán. He told me he had three KTMs and several other motorbikes. His name rang a bell but I couldn't remember why. Another man joined us from the hotel with all the flags, the Santa Lucia. They clearly knew each other and shook hands before rattling away in Spanish. Fernando was the manager of the hotel and also had perfect English. I explained that I was looking for a cheap hotel and that my budget was $20.

'Try the one across the street, one block down.' It was the one I'd been looking for but had missed in the dark. I was desperate for a pee. I followed the Santa Lucia's doorman inside and asked him what the rate was. Beyond the foyer a central atrium with ten tables with crimson table cloths matched the dark wooden balconies above. A large palm grew in the far corner.

'$75.' No wonder it had so many flags. I was tired, my stomach rumbled and I longed for a hot shower. The hotel Fernando recommended didn't have any parking, so I asked him if he could do a room for $25? He thought for a bit.

'Yes.'

In my experience there are two types of luck. Luck with people and luck with things. I was doing well with both and wondered why. Was I sending out a sign, an invitational or intuitive force field?

The hotel had originally been built as the family home of the first governor of Azuay province. Heavy furniture, beautifully decorated high ceilings and architraves filled every room. Most had large four-poster beds. My room on the third floor had satellite TV, a mini-bar, coffee and tea, really hot water and a bath. I sank into the blissful water. Perhaps if I never went downstairs they might forget I was here? Bugger the budget.

The next evening I caught up with Jodie. She'd already been in Cuenca for a few days after chilling out in Costa Rica with her brother for two weeks. She'd booked two weeks one-to-one teaching at a language school to improve her already excellent Spanish. Over her four months on the road she'd picked it up entirely by ear and worried about the finer points of subjunctives. I didn't even know what they were and had only one tense. Apparently musicians are natural linguists so it was comforting to know why my Spanish was so bad.

Jodie had taken six days to cycle the 240 miles from Quito to Cuenca. My experience was nothing compared to the vertical climbs and the wind, rain and fog she'd had to deal with, as well as the reckless and often light-less buses, trucks and cars. All that with forty kilos in her panniers, the same as me. She was doing this day after day, all the way to Ushuaia in the south.

The following day I left the hotel on a few errands to find hundreds of people streaming past and the street closed to traffic. I asked the nearest policeman what was happening. 'Miss Universo,' he replied inscrutably. Fernando filled me in, explaining that the Miss Universe parade would be passing through the streets shortly. 'You are lucky!' he grinned.

I rushed back to my room, grabbed my cameras and followed the crowds. The whole city was there, filling all sides of the square, shoulder to shoulder, small children perched on parents' shoulders, others sitting in the branches of trees, hanging out of office windows and balancing on the edge of the roofs. We waited and waited. Finally, to huge applause, a brown dog walked down the empty street with his head held high. He looked like he was smiling.

Suddenly a wave of noise flowed over the square. A male jazz band in panama hats and bright yellow tunics over white shirts led the parade. Some of the crowd danced and sang in the carnival atmosphere. Next came the local regional beauties, riding side-saddle. Dressed in long-sleeved white blouses and small panama hats, they rode horses like mediaeval jousters, their saddles garlanded in flowers and their legs hidden beneath white sheets. Another barrage of cheers heralded the arrival of the waving and smiling soon-to-be-ex Miss World, driving past in an open jeep, followed by Misses Costa Rica, Angola and Italy in white t-shirts and black trousers. A sea of smiling faces, black hair and waving arms urged them on. The contestants waved and smiled at the crowds who waved and shouted back for them to *Mirar! Mirar!* (Look! Look!) so they could take a photo. Minders mingled with the women, keeping over-excited locals at bay.

The parade climaxed with a far more colourful local parade. I had no idea who she represented, but one woman in a bikini had two coils of a large sausage over her breasts. A closer inspection showed it to be a coiled snake with its head poking out the centre. Finally a band of pan pipers in black tunics and the ubiquitous white shirts waltzed past, the police removed the rope and the crowds filled the street behind them.

The next day I remembered that Ricardo had given me a contact in Cuenca. It was Nico Merchán, owner of *El Mercurio*, the city newspaper – and, by chance, the man who'd talked to me outside my hotel a few days earlier. We met up and he kindly invited me on a ride in the mountains in two days' time.

Looking over my bike in the car park next day I noticed two loose spokes. Eventually I found a guy to tighten them. Then he tightened all of the others. It didn't seem right.

'Do you know what you are doing?'

'Oh yes,' he replied, and for good measure he also tightened the triple clamp bolts, which clamp the top of the forks and essentially hold the front wheel in place.

I met Nico the next morning, but as I followed him through town the handlebars wobbled. Going faster made it worse. I stood up and looked at my front wheel over the fairing. It wobbled like mad from side to side. The mechanic I had found had completely cocked it up. Brilliant. It was a Sunday morning. Nico called his own professional wheel builder and took me to his workshop. He arrived a few minutes later, removed the spokes, and then relaced my wheel. KTM spokes are much thicker than normal spokes, which may have led the wheel builder to over-tighten them. I'm sure he didn't mean me any harm.

Still stressing over my 'unsold' bicycle back in Valle de Bravo, it occurred to me to call the manufacturer of my bicycle, Santa Cruz in California. Mariano Gon, the export manager, was sympathetic and said he would make enquiries, get the other side of the story, and that I should call him back in a few days.

Meanwhile, I enjoyed exploring Cuenca. It's a beautiful city. It felt like a town, full of narrow, leafy and cobbled streets and magnificent pastel churches. With four universities it is considered the cultural capital of Ecuador, 'the Athens of the Andes'. It was also my last chance to buy a panama hat. All panama hats are made in Ecuador. They were exported to Panama for the workers on the Panama Canal, who liked them because they were so light. President Roosevelt visited the construction site and returned to the US with one. The newspapers called it a 'panama hat' and that was that. They are made from the fibres of the toquilla palm, which only grows on the shadowed slopes of certain valleys around Manabí on the coast. The best ones are from Montecristi and can take a over a month to make. Cuenca has its own weavers who make an alternative and cheaper version. I bought a 'folder' one that slid into a tube. Incredibly light and highly impractical on a motorbike, it was beautifully made. I lost it within a week. It would have been perfect for Jodie.

14

INDIANA JONES

Once out of Cuenca the excitement, freedom and joy of the road swept through me again. Vilcabamba was only 160 miles away through farmed valleys where palm trees hung over whitewashed farmhouses with terracotta tiles. Bright green fields shone vibrantly. It was May and the flowers were blooming. As I crested the last col, Vilcabamba opened up below, a green bowl surrounded by rounded peaks. A wonderful feeling of peace came over me as my spirit slid out and floated over the valley, urging me to stay a while.

The hedgerows and fields burst with yellow and red *Achiras*. The air was warm and inviting. The valley has its own microclimate that keeps temperatures high and the air moist. After only a few hours my resolve to head straight into Peru slipped away. One night became three. Hostal Izhcayluma lay on the road south out of town. Afternoon patches of mist hugged the opposite slopes. Crops sparkled in the sun. Birds and bees continually visited the white, pink and orange cosmeas in the garden. Time slowed. On the second day, a gentle freewheel on a borrowed bicycle down to the village for lunch took up the whole day. The longer I stayed the longer I wanted to stay.

Manfred, the German owner of the *hostal*, said many people felt as I did, which was clearly good for business. He had arrived as a backpacker, then returned to build the *hostal* from scratch and was now here for life – which could well be until he was a hundred.

Vilcabamba has a famously high number of centenarians, attracting scientists from many countries to study the 'Valley of Longevity', though no conclusions have yet been reached.

I eventually left because Peru was only 50 miles away. I could be there in a couple of hours. The rough single-track dirt road corkscrewed between deep hedgerows like a Devon lane. I stopped in a village that didn't exist on my map to check my route. Sweating in the 30°C heat I couldn't go fast enough on such a narrow road to get a cooling breeze. Giant palms, fruit trees and houses with bricks the colour of dried mud lined the road as it climbed out of the valley. Everyone used the road as a workshop or warehouse as it was the only flat land available. Black plastic sheets covered in brown beans lay in the road to dry. A stone at each corner stopped the corners lifting and moving the beans about. Winding through the low hills and tall trees was like riding through a jungle.

Half an hour later I stopped at the head of a deep V-shaped wooded valley, too steep for fields and not a house in sight, locked in by the high hills and distant mountains. Behind me a brown scar threaded in and out of the contours like stitches on a wave. Only a line of telegraph poles gave any hope of life further on. The recently graded road smelt of moist brown earth. Hot, humid and tropical. I opened the vents on my jacket again. Another hour and I reached Zumba, the last village in Ecuador, only 40 miles from Vilcabamba. The first houses had tin roofs, were made of wood and sat on logs a foot off the ground. It didn't look like they had electricity. Chickens wandered about and a pig scratched in the yard. One shop with a red wall had only two shelves of household items. It looked like a hard life. Two men sat on their porch, out of the noonday sun. I greeted them and asked about their crop. They were father and son. I followed the father down the side of the house and peered over a stone wall into a field too steep for any tractor. Taller fruit trees shaded the coffee bushes, but there was no discernible pattern like the neat rows you get with mechanised farming. He pointed to a coffee bush covered in red and green berries and explained the painstaking process. First they pulled at the branches, as if milking a cow, to shake the ripe red berries off the bush and on to a sheet on the ground, then they removed the husks by hand and laid the beans out in the sun to dry. Each sheet would have about five kilos of coffee and took two hours to pick.

The man's son brought a cherry (coffee berry) over and deftly removed the husk to reveal the green coffee bean inside. As I readied to leave the father gave me four tangerines. I thanked him and gave them a packet of biscuits in return. They wouldn't take the whole packet, only two biscuits each. I regretted I hadn't asked their names.

A mile outside the village the road narrowed again to a dirt track hemmed in by fields high with corn. Hardly wide enough for a small lorry and rarely straight for more than 50 yards, it felt too small to be a border road, but I was sure I hadn't missed any turnings and wondered what to do. Five cows blocked the road around the next bend. I killed my motor and waited as they slowly passed, covering me in clouds of their sweet breath.

Jodie had told me that the border crossing here involved being ferried across the river on a raft of old planks and leaky oil drums. I loved the idea of such an Indiana Jones entry into Peru. At the top of the valley just outside Zumba a white wooden barrier blocked the road. Two guards emerged from their hut. The road continued south towards Peru beyond the barrier but another track, blocked by another barrier, disappeared off to the right. Without stopping to think, I asked which was the road to Peru and regretted doing so immediately afterwards.

'Turn right,' said the friendlier guard as he pointed to the unlikely looking track.

It didn't look right. My GPS showed it headed west, following a ridge which dropped over the horizon, whereas straight on seemed the sensible option. Ever the gullible tourist, I imagined them having hysterics and money changing hands as I headed off to the coast on a road that turned into a goat track up a dead-end valley. I couldn't see over the high hedges. I felt worse with every mile along the ridge, until the road turned left and descended via a series of switchbacks.

Maybe I should trust my instincts more. One more crest. A glimpse of a river in the valley below flashed through a break in the green tunnel. The Río Marañón. A few minutes later my heart sank. Border flags fluttered over a three-lane bridge gleaming white in the sun. It arched high over the water, dwarfed the buildings on both sides and shattered my dreams of an Indiana Jones entrance.

Two Ecuadorians had crossed an hour earlier in a 1998 Land Rover and only three vehicles had crossed the day before. The Customs and Immigration officials at La Balsa (Spanish for 'raft', so it must have been a ferry crossing) were so friendly I felt obliged to chat, hang around and queue for something, but there wasn't anyone else to queue with. The friendliest and fastest border crossing ever was full of smiling faces. No one pestered me to change money from Ecuador's US dollars to Peru's soles. In twenty minutes I rode into Peru grinning inanely, happy and overjoyed on another post-border high.

Within an hour I rode into Jaén down a tree-lined concrete dual carriageway between concrete office blocks and flats. There was no trace of colonial architecture here. Red tuk tuks filled the air with clouds of blue smoke. I found an ATM and collected a pile of soles. On my return, two members of the *policia nacional*, in green uniforms and day-glow Sam Brownes, were standing beside my bike. Mr Nasty had a flat cap, shades and a big gap between his front teeth, Mr Nice had a white pith helmet and a round smiley face. Mr Nasty waggled his finger at me and pointed at the yellow line on the side of the road. I smiled, shrugged my shoulders and said I had no idea what they were on about, quickly and in English. Mr Nasty had another go and brought out his notebook. Mr Nice looked a little embarrassed. Emboldened by being in Peru and wanting to get to Chachapoyas before dark, I had no hesitation resorting to bribery. They were as delighted with the last of my biscuits (two each) as I was to be back on a tarred road.

On the outskirts of town my stomach cried out for food and I stopped at a little café. Biscuits and drinks filled the shelves and three Formica tables and chairs lined the wall opposite the counter. I ordered my first Inca Kola. It was the colour of wee and tasted like a sickly sweet and scented bubblegum. Peruvians love the stuff and it's been the national drink ever since it was launched in 1935. It was invented by an English expat named José Robinson Lindley, who had set up home in Lima with his wife, Martha. They sold homemade carbonated drinks from their small shop. Through local contacts Lindley learnt of an ancient drink based on the herb lemon verbena. He experimented with many different ingredients until hitting the recipe that became Inca Kola. Cleverly marketed as a national Peruvian drink that complemented food better than either Coke or Pepsi, it became the market leader. In a world first, McDonald's forced Coke to let Inca Kola be sold in its restaurants throughout Peru. Unable to beat it, Coke bought 50 per cent of Inca Kola in 1999 for $300 million.

The café proprietress, Teresa, returned with a plate of steaming chicken and potatoes in a tomato sauce. I wished I could have taken some with me. We were joined by her husband, Alberto, and their son, Eduardo, who was well over six feet tall. They came from a small village but had moved to Jaén so Eduardo could go to a good school and get a better education. Teresa told me he was an engineer with América Móvil, the biggest Peruvian cellphone company, and beamed at him with a mother's pride.

'It's also better to get old here where there is a hospital,' she said. 'We don't want to grow old in a village.'

Just outside Jaén I crossed the Río Marañón a second time and entered a different landscape. The valleys became broader, flatter and more fertile. The river meandered beside small fields where rice paddies shone like emerald fire, an even brighter green than Costa Rica. I caught up with a white Toyota Hiace which suddenly slowed, without indicating or showing any brake lights, and drove into the river. The water just covered his tyres. Stunned, I watched as he emerged with a red bucket and started to wash his van.

Although Machu Picchu was the next big thing on my list, the thought of being one of the five hundred tourists who walk the Inca

Trail every day put me off. I imagined a long line slowly trudging up a steep mountain pass, held back by the slowest. In a surprising moment of forward planning I'd found out that remote northern Peru had more and larger ruins than its southern rival. I especially wanted to see the ancient fortress at Kuelap, which is bigger and far older than Machu Picchu. That was why I wanted to go to Chachapoyas.

Soon bare brown mountains replaced the broad green fields of Jaén and squeezed the valley into ever steeper and narrower contortions, like a giant accordion. The road changed colour ahead, the tar disappeared into a narrow, dusty and treeless gorge. I felt vulnerable and unwelcome. Where was Chachapoyas? Would I get there before dark? The crow-flies distance on my GPS was small but I had underestimated how much longer it would take to get up and over the Andes.

Two orange traffic cones made me slow before a corner where a small river flowed across the road on a bed of pebbles. I turned up a canyon and followed the river. The canyon walls grew steeper and closer together. Through my helmet I heard water crashing and cascading over the rocks. The river completely filled the bottom of the canyon so the road cut through the canyon wall, leaving a huge overhang of rock above my head. Perhaps it wasn't such a great place to stop. The water thundered over the rocks below.

With dusk descending, I rode into Chachapoyas, capital of the Amazonas Department, where colonial buildings with terracotta roofs surrounded the Plaza de Armas. Founded in 1538 by Alonso de Alvarado, it is the oldest Spanish city east of the Andes. The massive valleys and gorges of the Andes have protected its colonial heritage. The vast Amazon basin is only 30 miles away. Few tourists come here, which may explain why the locals were friendly if slightly wary. I checked into the Casa Vieja. Its large double wooden doors opened on to a courtyard where bougainvillaea climbed the wooden columns and fish swam in the four small ponds. A central fountain twinkled.

The next morning at breakfast I couldn't help but notice the brand of strawberry jam: Fanny. A few days later I found some Fanny tuna chunks and wondered if it was a family name or had another origin.

Dick, the son of the hotel owner, alerted me to a crack in my bike's top triple clamp, which holds the front forks in place. I'd just ridden the most dangerous road I'd ever been on (though it was nothing compared to what was to come). I couldn't ride it now. My spoke tightener must have over-tightened it in Cuenca. I checked the other bolts and slackened them all off a bit. It was scary but why worry when nothing had happened? I called Diego Maranzana at KTM Peru in Lima but he didn't have a new triple clamp so I ordered one from the ever efficient Sommer in Germany. It would be in Lima in three days.

While on the phone I called Rosa again. She told me Eduardo was very angry because Santa Cruz had spoken to him. I called Eduardo. He was indeed angry.

'Why do you make trouble with Santa Cruz? They say bad things about me.'

'You said you didn't have my money but you do. Perhaps now you will give my money to Rosa.'

That evening I met tour company owners Charles and Tina Motley in a bar while toasting my first night in Peru. Charles captivated me with tantalising tales of the Chachapoyan civilisation, the 'cloud people' who dominated this remote mountainous region of northeastern Peru for at least a thousand years from AD 600, some six hundred years before the Incas established their capital at Cuzco. Countless Chachapoyan ruins lay buried in the high, cloud-blanketed forest, he explained, many of them still undiscovered in the dense, often inaccessible jungle. Apparently the only way to see them was on foot, with mule support, and even that wasn't always possible.

Images of hidden valleys, of me hacking my way through sweaty jungle amid the hum of cicadas, of hiking historic Inca pathways festooned with creepers and then finding mysterious ruins never seen before filled my mind. Indy was back. I was hooked.

Charles recommended I sign up for his Gran Vilaya Expedition, which included the centuries-old mummies at Karajía, a three-day donkey trek through an alluvial tarn, hiking to the ancient hilltop ruin of Cacahuasha, and a day at the Kuelap fortress. An English couple, John and Dianne, had just returned from the same trip and were buzzing with enthusiasm. 'It was fantastic,' said Dianne, 'the scenery kept changing – grassy valleys, dense jungle, cloud forest. Now we're worried we might be disappointed by the Inca Trail.' She looked completely knackered, while John, who seemed incredibly fit, looked as fresh as the proverbial daisy.

Charles introduced me to Araceli, who would be my guide. She was barely five foot high and plump with dark eyes and black curly hair. She said all the right things but I wasn't convinced. Somehow her words didn't ring true.

'I am archaeologist,' she proclaimed. 'I studied in Lima and I will be your *cocinera* [cook]. It will take three or four days to arrange but tomorrow we can visit the mummies of Karajía. Bring binoculars if you have them.'

The rocky path to the Karajía site descended between small fields of corn which swayed in the gentle breeze. It dipped out of sight ahead, then rose up the other side of the valley. We moved aside for two donkeys trudging up the hill laden with firewood, followed by a small boy in a dirty green t-shirt and grey shorts, carrying a stick in his hand. The path steepened before suddenly revealing a narrow gorge about 100 yards wide. We scrambled down between the trees and walked along the loose scree under the cliff, 100 feet above the stream. A copper-coloured cliff flycatcher flashed its wings and flew away.

'There are more than fifty tombs here and all but three or four were looted by the locals,' said Araceli. 'There are many artefacts in the houses of the villagers. We want to put them all in a museum but the villagers won't let us have them.'

We rounded a corner and were confronted by a large sandy cliff. 'What can you see?'

It took me a while to spot the six sarcophagi decorated with ochre face-paint, necklaces and tunics on a ledge halfway up the cliff. They were unlike anything I'd ever seen. Thin elongated heads balanced atop armless conical bodies, like oval biscuits perched on flared lollipop sticks. The sarcophagi were nine feet tall and the mummies – of Chachapoya chiefs – would have been placed inside in a foetal position. Because Karajía is so inaccessible the sarcophagi had remained intact long after most others, but eventually they'd been broken open at the back and any precious items robbed, leaving only vertical sticks and plaster. Two human skulls stared over the top of the sarcophagi.

'The skulls were from old enemies of the chiefs and put there to frighten people away,' Araceli speculated. Being a guide must be great fun. You can say anything you like and the gullible tourists nod appreciatively. Another tourist told me the skulls had been put there by the robbers, to scare the locals away.

There were several other sarcophagi, their single faces tucked into smaller ledges not high enough for the body. They were hard to spot at first as they blended into the cliff so well.

Back up in the village Araceli insisted on showing us the local museum.

'If we visit they are less likely to rob the graves for themselves.'

The 'museum' was an old shed with a wooden table and two shelves. A brown skeleton in a foetal position sat on a rock in the corner. Skin and sinew stretched over bits of the bones. It looked like bits from several skeletons as the skull was a completely different colour. Two sarcophagi heads with a skull on each stood on a wooden table in front of pieces of faded red cloth.

'The mummies wear their finest clothes and jewellery.' Rather than the locals fleece the graves I felt fleeced by my $1 'tour' of the museum.

Three days later we drove to the start of our Gran Vilaya trek, via mountains that towered above us and where the valleys were so deep you only saw the bottom when crossing the river. Fields were rare and clung to slopes and tiny ledges. All the cultivation was done by hand. Many slopes were too steep for trees, and every so often cliffs exposed bare rock. The dirt road was never straight for long, it constantly turned and zigzagged up and over every pass and hillside. The sheer scale of the scenery made me feel tiny and insignificant. It was humbling. No wonder there were so few visitors. We started climbing again and then came to a halt at a dip in the road blocked by two men and three mules.

'This is the end of the road,' said Araceli.

On John and Dianne's advice I had booked an extra horse for my trek, so I could ride when hiking got too tiring. But these 'horses' looked like mules to me.

'"Horse" and "mule": the word is the same here,' soothed Araceli as she introduced me to Nelson, the charismatic muleteer, and his second, Juan. Ever the trusting tourist, I let it slide on the first day. But I was apprehensive. It had been raining ever since I'd arrived in Chachapoyas, I had a dose of the runs and the last time I'd ridden a horse I'd fallen off. I didn't relish the prospect of being cold and wet, riding an animal I couldn't control across high passes with sheer drops and continuously having to jump off for another shit in the woods. I'd brought an extra supply of loo rolls just in case and had opted for Araceli's plain Western menu rather than spicy Peruvian dishes.

The track, recently graded, followed the crest of the hill, a raw scar through the bushes and trees. It was already gouged with ruts from the frequent heavy rains. After only two miles it dipped into the Belen Valley, our first night's camp and the reason I had wanted to do this trek. Charles' brochure described it as 'a silted glacial tarn with a meandering river'. Hemmed in by low, treeless and rounded hills, a river coiled across the flat grassy valley floor like a vast python. A shaft of sunlight cut through a gap in the clouds and lit up five black cows grazing near one of the bends. Nelson and Juan put the tents up while the sun sparkled off the water. In a few millennia the valley would be full of oxbow lakes.

The cows wandered over and one stopped ten yards away from me. One thought about it for a moment then came closer. Either I smelt nice or she just fancied me. She stopped right in front of me and started to lick my knees. I wasn't sure what to do. It was just too funny. I tried to distract her by offering a bunch of clover. She wasn't interested. She started licking further up my leg towards my crotch. Perhaps she wanted to give me a blow job. At 8,000 feet, I hadn't had one that high before. I like trying new things but there are limits. I bent forward to stop any further advances and she started licking my hair. She had big eyelashes and her breath was hot and sweet. It was getting out of hand.

I wandered over to where Araceli had taken one hour, and half a litre of gasoline, to get the fire going.

'We eat steak tonight.'

It gave off a strange odour and took my 'good *cocinera*' another hour to cook. Luckily we ate in the dark. It smelt like dog food and didn't taste much better, but it's amazing what you can eat when you are hungry. I asked what it was.

'This is a Peruvian dish available in many restaurants all over Peru.'

I wondered how many were still in business and how many diners had died. I soon began to also question Araceli's organisational skills. She had packed four head torches but two of them were dead and the other two had feeble beams and no spare batteries. I decided to go with the flow and enjoy every cock-up – just as long as there was enough loo paper. I hoped I'd survive her cooking as I hadn't brought any biscuits.

The next day started with a mooing competition. My new admirer had spread the word during the night. The girls started at five and kept it up solidly for two hours. It made me laugh. They knew we were going to have breakfast and they wanted some, preferably all of it. Juan had a full-time job running about trying to scare them away. At one point, during a particularly melodious passage, I thought they were about to start rapping.

Araceli was having trouble lighting the fire again.

'There are too many cows about.'

After half an hour she presented me with an egg. I cut the top off and the white poured out over the plate.

'How long did you boil it for?'

'Seven minutes,' came the confident reply.

We weren't very high – barely 8,000 feet – so I made a mental note: she can't count. Nelson and I looked at each and started to laugh.

'Araceli, please let me do it,' I said.

'No, I am your guide. I will do your *huevos*.'

I resigned myself to going with the flow again. She boiled the second one for ten minutes. After three of those there would be no need for Imodium.

The next morning we crossed the river and hiked up out of the valley. Bushes and tangled undergrowth encroached on the track as we climbed towards the rounded hilltop. The track must have been ancient as it had the most extraordinary corrugations. Ruts deeper than a Wellington boot filled the whole width of the path. Grass grew out of the ridges and all the troughs were filled with water. I took long strides to take two ridges at a time. Araceli walked in the troughs because she wasn't co-ordinated enough to walk on the ridges, which came up above her knees. It must have been hard going for her as her legs weren't very long. The corrugations were made by the mules.

After a surprisingly non-fatal lunch we hiked towards the clouds on a muddy path through a tropical garden of pink and yellow flowers, ferns, bamboo and orchids. This was a proper rainforest. The mist hung heavily around us and the warm, damp air smelt of decaying leaves as another stretch of water-filled corrugations appeared. It was as if a giant tank had clawed its way up the steep path. A mule carrying a wooden box lashed with old brown rope approached us from the other direction. Four more heavily laden mules came around the corner. The last carried two long planks of wood guided by the muleteer at the back. Nelson and he greeted each other warmly and chatted as we continued on.

'He is a relation of Nelson and this is an old Inca road,' said Aracelli.

We were in the middle of nowhere. Where were they going? Was this part of La Gran Ruta Inca, the 4,300-mile road from the south of Columbia to central Chile that united the Inca Empire?

'Yes, it was built by the Incas.'

Through the tangled undergrowth I spotted a wall, some 20 feet high and covered in lichen high up on my right.

'Yes, that wall was built by the Incas, but this route was made by the Chachapoyans, the first people to live in this area.'

The Chachapoyans fought the Incas and the Spanish from their high forest strongholds and were one of the last kingdoms to succumb to the Incas in around 1470. Chachapoyans still live in remote and inaccessible areas of northern Peru. Indeed, there are an unusually high proportion of fair-skinned, blonde natives who do not have any European ancestry.

Three passes later we arrived at the first fields we'd seen. A single-room hut stood on the top of the hill. A young girl emerged then disappeared when she saw us. Torrejón lived there without electricity or water with her granddaughter Maria, two days' walk from the nearest road. She had lived there all her life and was looking after Maria while her parents were in Chachapoyas selling the vegetables they grew in their fields. We walked over to their neighbour's house, which had two small rooms. Mercedes put the black kettle on her fire and gave us tea. We supplied the snacks.

The next morning we set off for the ancient hilltop site of Cacahuasha, buried in jungle so thick that the ruins are impossible to spot from the air. You have to walk.

We crossed a fast-flowing stream on a carefully felled tree. The two thin sapling handrails moved uncomfortably. Out of the cloud forest, we climbed through the dense jungle along a narrow path. Ferns, orchids and bromeliads brushed past with every step. Little sunlight reached the ground as the canopy was so thick. Mud oozed beneath my feet. After an hour and a half up ever steeper slopes a low wall four feet high suddenly appeared on my left. A few minutes later we came across another 20-foot-high wall. Defensive walls built by the ancient Chachapoyans, according to Araceli. Further up, an even higher wall appeared. I took another drink from my water bottle as a rivulet of sweat ran down my face. It was getting difficult to follow the path. It had become so steep and slippery that I looked for handholds.

'Only about four or five tourists come here every year,' said Nelson, 'sometimes none at all.'

The path petered out altogether. Nelson sliced through overhanging creepers with his machete. Every branch dripped with orchids and bromeliads. It was impossible to see very far ahead as the vegetation was so dense. My admiration for the American explorers Hiram Bingham and Gene Savoy increased ten-fold. Hiram Bingham was the man who discovered Machu Picchu; Gene Savoy discovered both Cacahuasha, where we were headed, and Vilcabamba, the so-called last refuge of the Incas in Peru (600 miles south from the lovely valley of the same name I'd stayed in in Ecuador). It was amazing they ever found anything at all. You could walk past a vast city only five yards away without ever knowing it was there.

My shirt stuck to my back. Imperceptibly the plants and creepers thinned and I realised we were at the top. We had reached Cacahuasha. Several circular platforms about three feet high and covered in moss and dead leaves were dotted about the hilltop.

'Each platform contained four dwellings,' said Araceli. 'There are forty of these platforms here, so, with an average of four people per family and four families on each, the village's population was about six hundred.'

There was hardly anything left of the highest building. The walls had crumbled into piles of moss and rock. But a large circular grinding stone lay in the centre. Araceli knelt on the ground and asked us to join her. She produced some of the previous night's wine and gave each of us three coca leaves. One by one we took a sip of wine, made a silent wish and buried the leaves in the ground.

According to Gene Savoy, Cacahuasha was part of a vast 'city' he called Gran Vilaya, a network of over 24,000 round, oval and walled stone structures that spread over 100 square miles. He argued that a high civilisation (like the Chachapoyans) had existed here in the jungle interior as well as on the coast and in the high Andes (like Machu Picchu).

Savoy was once dubbed the 'real' Indiana Jones by *People* magazine. He was a charismatic figure with long shoulder-length hair and a Zapata moustache. Inspired by Hiram Bingham's 1952 story of his discovery of Machu Picchu, *Lost City of the Incas*, Savoy moved from Reno, Nevada to Lima, Peru. In the late 1950s he married a wealthy Peruvian lady, fathered a son, Jamil, and settled his family in Yungay, a town below the spectacular Cordillera Blanca mountains 200 miles north of Lima. Sadly the Savoy family and most of the other inhabitants of Yungay were to suffer a terrible tragedy in 1970, which I was to learn more about when I visited the town a few weeks later. Savoy obtained a job with the *Peruvian Times*, created the Andean Explorers Club with himself as its chief (and only) explorer and through great showmanship persuaded people to fund his expeditions.

He was looking for many things in the Peruvian jungle: the Fountain of Youth, the treasure of El Dorado, proof that Solomon's gold had come from South America, and the ancient roots of a universal religion. A complex character, he was deeply religious and subsequently founded the International Community of Christ. What brought him to Chachapoyas was his belief that 'the jungle was not on the fringes of Peruvian culture but at its very centre'. In his view academics were overly concerned with the mountains, to the detriment of jungle culture. There has always been much antagonism between explorers and archaeologists. The former feel looked down on by 'qualified' academics but the latter depend on explorers to find the ruins in the first place. Through his drive and force of personality Gene Savoy created his own cult and discovered the real 'lost Inca city' of Vilcabamba in 1964. He discovered Gran Vilaya a year later and one of Nelson's relations was on that expedition.

There should have been a fabulous view down the length of the valley but it was impossible to see anything through the tangled web of trees. No wonder ruins were so hard to find. In this climate the jungle grew so fast you could almost hear it moving. I asked Nelson if I could borrow his machete while he had lunch.

'Start from the bottom and work your way back up,' he said, looking slightly embarrassed.

He opened a small pouch, placed several leaves into his mouth and started chewing. I dropped over the ledge and hacked away at the saplings but soon got carried away. This was not the place to lop off a leg. The nearest road was a day's hike away, and the nearest hospital a five-hour drive from there, assuming there was a car at the end of the road. I settled into a slower, safer rhythm. Although I was having a lot of fun I wasn't making much progress. I looked up to see Nelson standing nearby, his eyes shining brightly from the coca. I gave him his machete. Suddenly he transformed into a Whirling Dervish. Small trees and branches fell at his feet as he sliced, slashed and scythed his way through the timber. The air filled with the sweet smell of sap and fresh leaves, mingled with jungle juices. He soon cleared a huge area, revealing the valley below. The forest dropped almost vertically away. The ridges faded into the distance forcing the river to zigzag through the fingers. Everything was green, with no houses, village or any sign of life at all. We stood on the summit and soaked up the view, the same view the Chachapoyans had enjoyed hundreds if not thousands of years ago.

Late in the afternoon we crossed another massive trunk over a river into Vista Hermosa, Nelson's village. With no road there were no cars or even bicycles there. Mules were the fastest goods carriers. Nor was there electricity, shops or a post office. A patchwork of brown footpaths linked the houses. On the opposite hillside a scar zigzagged through the forest where the trees had been felled, waiting for the bulldozers and the new road. It would transform the village economy, enabling them to sell surplus food and coffee in Chachapoyas, something that was not profitable when it took two days to get there on a mule.

Nelson's house had been built several generations earlier. Made of rough-cut stone, it had a wooden balcony running the length of the three

A grasshopper omelette, Valle de Bravo, Mexico

Bike on a bike, Valle de Bravo, Mexico

Butterfly sounds at Campario Mariposa Monarchica Reser
Anangueo, Mexi

The monarchs of Campario Mariposa Monarchica Reserv
Anangueo, Mexi

Clavadistas, Acapulco, Mexico

Neto's silver bracelet workshop
Taxco, Mexico

The Sixaola Bridge between Costa Rica and Panama

Cartagena, Columbia

One of the funniest thing·
saw on my whole tri·
A blue-footed boob·
Española, Galápagos Islan·

Marine iguanas, Fernandina, Galápagos Islan·

Land iguana, North Seymour, Galápagos Islands

The 'soldar man' and sons:
I wish I'd asked them their names. Near Cotopaxi, Ecuador

Jodie cycled through this for a day at 8,000 feet. On the road to Cuenca, Ecuad

'The valleys are so deep it can take a while just to fir where they left the road' – the Chachapoyas to Celendín Road, Pe

Kariajia sarcophagi and skulls, Chachapoyas, Peru

Nelson, the Whirling Dervish, and Maria in Vista Hermosa, Peru

Chachapoyan Mummy Museum
Leymebamba, Peru

Huacas de Moche, Trujillo, Pe

Local road above Caraz, Pe

On the road to Nazca, Peru: the pilgrim who preferred money to food

The *Puya raimondii* tree flowers once every 100 years then dies, Caraz, Peru

Richard and Jane at Machu Picchu, Peru

Getting my bike blessed ...

... in Copacabana, Bolivia

Local fishermen, Copacabana, Bolivia

I smelt it before I saw it: on the road to Lima, Peru

A truly odd experience: riding Bolivia's Atocha river 'road', which is only open for part of the year

Butch Cassidy and Sundance country: Atocha to Tupiza, Boliv

Late-night chain shopping with Juan, Hernán and Danie
west of Resistencia, Argentin

Saints of the south: Marcos, Gustavo and Sebastian of SM Motos Río Gallegos Argentina

Matt Pope and Mount Fitzroy El Chaltén, Argentina

'My farm is just over there': Atilio Mendez, just off Ruta 40, Argentina

Riding into a cattle grid in no-man's land on the Argentina–Chile bord

Like the poster on my childhood bedroom wall. Carretera Austral, Chi

Monkey puzzle trees and Volcán Lanín, Paso Tromen, Chile

Deviation, Paso Tromen, Chile

Victor, Juan and Irwin, crew of the *Dr Hans Steffen* ferry Carretera Austral, Chile

With fifteen *moai*, Ahu Tongariki is the largest on Easter Island

The fattest is the heaviest of the standing *moai* at 87 tor
Ahu Tongariki, Easter Islan

bedrooms on the first floor. The kitchen, storeroom and guest and grand-mother's bedroom were on the ground floor. I took my first shower in three days in the garden behind a thin screen of split bamboo. Nelson's family came to listen and laugh as I yelled each time I ducked into the cold water which came from a spring up the hill. Refreshed, we moved inside to watch Araceli cook. The kitchen had only one small window and a dirt floor. The walls were black from years of wood smoke and the room had a strong smoky smell like Lapsang Souchong tea. The stove was a steel grating over wooden logs which glowed under a big pot. I sat at the one table, made from an old door laid flat, while Araceli added more wood. The single oil lamp produced a thick coil of smoke which drifted towards the chimney over the hearth.

Nelson's wife and sister chattered and giggled constantly, casting frequent glances at Araceli. I wondered what the scratches and squeaks were. A minute later a white guinea pig scuttled across the floor. Six more *cuy* lived under the table. They're a delicacy, bred for food and apparently at their best at about nine months old. They taste like gamey chicken but require lots of fiddling about to get all the meat as they're not exactly over-endowed with muscles.

That night's taste sensation was 'fried chicken and rice'. Which took just under an hour to cook. I cut into the chicken leg and under the dim light of my head torch saw blood ooze across my plate.

'Araceli, it is raw.'

The other women in the kitchen smiled silently and watched Araceli.

'It's the wood. It is wet.'

The fire was roaring away behind her. Two chickens wandered in from outside, pecked twice, thought it wasn't a good place to be and went out again. Fifteen minutes later something dark and crispy appeared on my plate.

Later that night, there was a knock on my door. It was Nelson.

'What would you like for breakfast?'

I giggled. It was like planning a midnight feast while our parents were away.

'Huevos y pan tostada, por favor.'

After Nelson's wonderful breakfast we hiked up to the trailhead where the pickup was waiting to take us to Kuelap. Araceli arrived an hour later on my 'horse'.

'My shoes are broken,' she said.

Nelson mimed a trip and another tumble, a huge grin across his face. I said a sad farewell to him and Juan and tipped them both. Back in Chachapoyas I gave the woman in Charles' office three English primers and asked her to give them to Nelson.

On the way to Kuelap we stopped off at Gocta Falls. This region is so remote that the 2,530-foot-high waterfall was only 'discovered' in February 2006, although it had of course always been known to the locals. They kept it quiet because legend said a blonde siren would capture anyone who visited the lake at the bottom of the falls. It is listed as anywhere between the fifth and sixteenth highest waterfall in the world.

The fortress of Kuelap is the jewel of northern Peru and is relatively unknown because it's so hard to get to. The first dirt road was only cut into the area in the 1970s and before that it took two months' trekking on ancient tracks to get there from the coast. Kuelap is much larger and more mysterious than Machu Picchu and twice as old as the Inca Empire. It dates from AD 500, whereas Machu Picchu was not even started until the 1460s, nearly a thousand years later. It is the largest man-made structure in South America and is estimated to contain three times as much stone as Khufu (Cheops), Egypt's largest pyramid. Historians believe that the Chachapoyans built it to stop the invasion of the advancing Huari from Bolivia.

Like all Chachapoyan citadels, Kuelap rests on the end of a massive V-shaped promontory. It cuts north–south into the Utcabamba River, a superb defensive peak 10,000 feet above sea level. Although the fortress is only two miles from the river, the mountain is so high and the terrain so severe it takes over an hour to drive to it. It's in the climatic zone known as la *ceja de la selva*, the eyebrow of the

Amazon. Above the *ceja* it freezes at night, resulting in the bare grassland of the *cordillera*.

Kuelap made every English castle I'd ever seen look like a toy. It dominated the promontory like an entrance to Mordor in *Lord of the Rings*. One side of the cliff was so precipitous no defences were required. On the other side the first defensive wall was 70 feet high and over 1,100 yards long. There were four levels of walls within and each was between 20 and 40 feet high. Nearly all the walls had been restored except for one part incongruously covered in blue plastic sheeting. Despite the altitude, orchids and bromeliads covered the stonework and trees filled the open spaces inside the fortress. The three entrances were mere slits, wide enough for only one person at a time. There were many defensive towers around the top, in one of which archaeologists found over 2,500 limestone sling stones.

The citadel was once home to around three thousand people (three times as many as Machu Picchu) and among the four hundred stone buildings that littered the site were circular platforms for houses just like the ones at Cacahuasha. The homes of higher-ranking people had more ornate bases with patterned stone. Around one corner a face was carved into the rock at knee height, but another photographed in 1893 had disappeared.

Apart from the archaeologists and restorers working in various corners of the citadel, I had the whole site to myself until I met two other tourists, an English couple. I was enjoying speaking English until I discovered they were missionaries. The way missionaries destroy indigenous cultures, trading on healthcare and salvation, makes my blood boil. These ones gave out free umbrellas, Wellington boots and basic medical care in exchange for prayers and a foreign god. Who wouldn't sing a few songs for a longer life? I wished they'd just stay at home and convert their own countrymen.

We returned to Chachapoyas late that night. I loved the novelty of being driven, leaving me to admire the scenery the whole time, something I could never do on my bike.

The next morning the Plaza de Armas was packed with people. It was Carnival Week of the Amazonas Department and each of the twenty-one local districts was set to parade in local dress through the town square, past the judges sitting in the shade of a green awning. The star judges were Señorita Turismo in her long gold dress and Señorita Regional in a long white one. They began by comparing their tiaras. After the first five sets of performers had passed by they started reading newspapers.

Every district got two minutes in front of the judges and local dignitaries. Eight-year-old boys in black suits and red cummerbunds partnered girls in multilayered red and pink skirts that flew out as they twirled. A hunting dance performed by five young men dressed in fawn sacks and hats with toucan beaks stuck on the front climaxed when they put their arms around each other's shoulders and pecked their quarry to death with their beaks. Another district's representatives wore individually decorated pink hats; the most creative was adorned with red and blue ribbons, beaded necklaces and three spoons and forks sticking up like aerials. A group of young hunters followed. Two of them carried a pole on their shoulders with a boy covered in a black jaguar skin slung underneath. The jaguar descended from the pole and danced in front of the judges to music that gradually increased in tempo. Finally three young men carried in a twenty-foot pole bearing a large carved head like the sarcophagi at Karajía. They stopped opposite where I was standing and raised it up. The whole square fell silent and bowed their heads in a sea of black until music shattered the spell.

After all the floats had passed a sudden yell went up from the opposite side of the square. Smoke floated across in the breeze. People screamed and rushed out of the way as a *vaca loca*, a 'mad cow' sculpture made from bamboo and paper, rushed through the crowd, covered in exploding fireworks, shooting streamers and bangers. It was nice to know they had mad cows a long time before we did.

The following day the new triple clamp for my bike still hadn't arrived. It had taken only three days to get from Germany to Lima but was still in Lima Customs a week later. DHL wanted $110 Customs duty (half the cost price) and another $25 in clearance fees. Despite pleading phone calls to DHL they wouldn't budge. Stuck in a small town 400 miles away, I wasn't going anywhere soon.

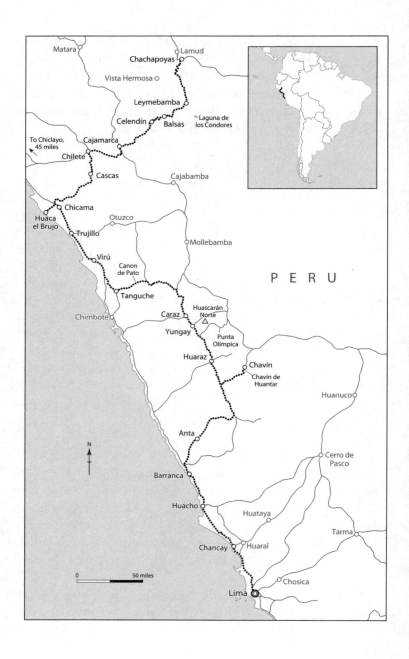

15

THE WEDDING MARCH

I called Diego Maranzana, the KTM importer in Lima, and explained my situation. Two days later he told me that he'd got the duty reduced from $100 to $20 but that the triple clamp would still take at least three days to get to me. DHL didn't deliver to Chachapoyas very often.

When the triple clamp finally arrived I fitted it with the help of a mechanic called Abel. He was a friend of Dick's, the hotel owner's son who'd spotted the crack in the first place. Abel was disappointed I hadn't let him repair the original instead of spending hundreds of dollars and many days waiting for a new one. Although I'm sure he could have had a go at repairing it, the consequences of the front wheel collapsing didn't bear thinking about.

With the new triple clamp fitted I cast an eye over my bike to see if anything else was wrong. One of the pannier frame bolts was loose. Vibrations can loosen bolts if they're not Loctited so I wasn't concerned. I tried tightening it but it just spun round. It had sheared off, leaving a stub sticking out of the frame. Luckily Abel drilled it out and retapped the thread using another bolt. A quick test ride revealed the speedo wasn't working. Why do things always come in threes? I found the loose wire. Free at last.

Which route should I take to Lima? The longer but faster tarred low valley road via Chiclayo or the slower but much more direct and more exciting mountain road to Celendín and Cajamarca? Charles Motley, the owner of Chachapoyas Tours, helped me make up my mind, warning me that he never sent his clients via Cajamarca. Minibuses regularly went over the edge on that road, he told me. 'It's not unusual to have an accident every month. The bus often takes twenty hours from Cajamarca, so the driver's tired. The valleys are so deep it can take a while just to find where they left the road.' All his clients came via Chiclayo. It wasn't only the roads that were dangerous. The airport at Chiclayo had been closed since a plane had crashed there two years earlier, killing forty-eight people. Landing without radar in bad weather in the middle of a cloud forest among huge mountains had proved impossible.

Another good tip from Charles was to go and visit the Chachapoyan Mummy Museum in Leymebamba. In late 1996 farmhands felling timber above Laguna de los Cóndores (Condor Lake) spotted a tomb in a cliff on the opposite side of the lake. It took them a whole day just to reach it. When they eventually scrambled up to the ledge 300 feet above the water they discovered not one but a whole row of burial houses with mummies everywhere. The site had lain untouched for five hundred years. They slashed the mummies open over the next few months, looking for treasure. Word of their find soon spread and a stream of visitors began to arrive from Leymebamba – only 12 miles away but a two-day trek by mule – to see it for themselves.

The authorities in Lima heard of the discovery and prevented further looting. A purpose-built museum was constructed two miles south of Leymebamba with a grant from Austria. It contained over two hundred mummies, many of them still intact, as well as a vast array of items recovered from the burial houses, including large quantities of Chachapoyan textiles, ceramics and *quipus* (the Inca record-keeping device). The Inca established the mummification technique and the use of *quipus* when they conquered the Chachapoyans.

The mummies needed an air-conditioned environment to protect them from the high humidity in Leymebamba. I was glad the museum was at the original site so the locals could benefit from their heritage. That's where museums should be, not thousands of miles away in rich countries where the original descendants have no hope of ever seeing them.

One mummy, bound in a foetal position in a display case, reminded me of Tintin's *The Seven Crystal Balls* just before the 'cleansing fire' hurtles down the chimney and returns the mummy of Rascar Capac to 'his true element'. Hergé had an extraordinary eye for detail, helped by a collection of thousands of cuttings and photographs. He continually added to it, never knowing when an article might come in useful. His files included a photograph of a Peruvian mummy in exactly the same position. Later in the story things are looking rather grim because the Incas are about to burn Tintin, Captain Haddock and Professor Calculus to death on a funeral pyre. While they wait for the sun to rise the Incas perform a dance with a huge snake. This was based on a drawing from a *National Geographic Magazine*. All the blocks in the walls of the Temple of the Sun had exquisite, perfectly formed joins, just like those in Cuzco and Machu Picchu.

The mummies in the Leymebamba museum were round and surprisingly compact, only about three feet high, as if they might fit inside each other like Russian dolls. They were bound up into as small a size as possible and covered in alpaca and llama cloth tied with string. Where the mummies had been broken open, the revealed textiles often had beautiful, intricate designs in a wide range of colours. It was incredible that such fragile materials had survived in a cloud forest climate for so long. The Chachapoyans clearly had advanced embalming skills and selected sites protected from the rain.

Other surprises emerged from the unique find. It had generally been held that the pre-Columbian Americas were a healthy, idyllic paradise until the Europeans arrived with weapons and disease. But in 2000 Gerry Conlogue and Bill Hennessy from Quinnipiac University in Hamden, Connecticut x-rayed 205 mummies and found evidence of many illnesses. They were interviewed by William Mullen of the *Chicago Tribune*:

> Very few villagers were living past the age of forty. Twelve per cent of the villagers were bent over with hunchbacks due to tuberculosis of the spine. Perhaps 50 per cent or

more of the villagers had less severe TB in the lungs. Though most adults were only in their twenties and thirties, 11 per cent of them suffered from arthritis. Most adults had terrible teeth or none at all and both men and women suffered from scoliosis, a condition of crooked spines. It was thought that because they were so remote, the Chachapoyans would be nearly disease-free. We were surprised at the large percentage of mummies who had an infectious disease process in the spine and lungs which resembled tuberculosis. It was thought the Spanish conquerors brought TB to South America, and these mummies predate them.

The museum also housed a collection of *quipus*, the Inca record-keeping device, a precursor to writing. A *quipu* is a cord from which a number of smaller and shorter cords hang and was key to how the Incas controlled their dominions. *Quipu* means 'knot' in Quechua, the Inca language, and the numbers were easy to understand as they were in base 10. There were known positions on the cord which corresponded to 1s, 10s, 100s and 1,000s. The last digit was always nearest the free end.

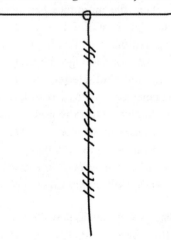

A *quipu* showing 374 items

Intriguingly, *quipus* were a lot more complex than that: different coloured cords had different meanings, and the meaning depended on the context of the message. Yellow might mean corn if relating to the storage of food or gold in relation to money. Some sixty different colours were used. Furthermore additional cords were inserted into a knot which may have had knots and cords of its own. Some of the largest ones were several feet long and contained about two thousand cords. A large one would easily make a skirt if wrapped around your waist.

Quipucamayocs created and read the *quipus* and they were crucial to the running of the Inca Empire. Information was collected and summarised then sent to the Inca, the supreme ruler. New orders were received in the same way. The Incas needed a very efficient system for the empire extended 2,500 miles from Quito in the north to central Chile in the south. A *quipu* could travel up to 200 miles a day, carried by a runner on the Inca roads for 1.25 miles to the next hut where a fresh runner awaited. As a former accountant I find *quipus* fascinating as apparently one artefact contains the concept of debit and credit – the foundation of double-entry bookkeeping. Only about seven hundred *quipus* survive. The Spanish destroyed all *quipus* they found as part of their policy to eradicate the indigenous culture and replace it with Catholicism. Any form of communication they didn't understand was viewed as a threat and ruthlessly suppressed.

I took the exciting mountain road to Celendín and headed up into the mountains from Leymebamba, leaving the cloud forest behind. The lush green forests thinned out into bare, brown, scrub-covered hillsides that signalled the lack of rain. Riding deep down between close valley walls made me feel hemmed in, almost claustrophobic, until climbing out and cresting a col revealed several successive ranges melting into the distance. As the road weaved through myriad valleys and over several passes, the temperature and vegetation constantly changed with height. In a few places the road cut across an almost vertical mountainside so steep I couldn't see the bottom. There were no barriers or any namby-pamby safety features at all. I parked my bike as close to the edge as I dared and walked back to take a photo. Dust billowed out behind a minibus in the distance as the driver hoped for a stage win on the Peruvian Mountain Minibus Rally. He flashed his lights to show he'd seen me but it still took him over a minute to reach me. He hooted and several arms shot out the side as he went past. I was pleased I wasn't one of his passengers.

A few hours later I crested Abra Barro Negro, another cold and windy pass at 12,000 feet, only to see a thin string zigzag up the other side of the valley through a distant haze. The mountain plunged thousands of feet to a verdant river valley below, the bright green a huge contrast to the brown, dusty and dry mountains. I wondered how long it would take to reach the opposite height.

Two hours. Log houses with outside toilets stood beside small fields on steep slopes. One pale blue toilet shone in stark contrast to the dark brown soil and green fields. The land became increasingly fertile as I descended. The Marañón River slices through the valley, flows north, then loops round to the east and feeds the mighty Amazon. At the bottom, fields full of corn and trees laden with oranges covered the tiny floodplain wedged between the giant slopes. The hot air felt thick with fertile freshness, a hidden oasis in the mountain desert. The concrete suspension bridge at Balsas was 9,000 feet below and 20°C hotter than the top of the pass. The valley is one and a half times deeper than the Grand Canyon in the US.

After eventually climbing up the other side, the road became a tightrope over the roof of the earth. My concentration compressed, my nerves tingled and my mind accelerated. It didn't take long to learn to never look away on corners. I couldn't take my eyes off the road for even a moment. Celendín was only 50 miles from Chachapoyas as the crow flies but 110 miles by road. The bus was supposed to take twelve hours and I did it in six. An exhilarating rollercoaster of a single-track dirt road with sheer drops, vast views, huge climbs and descents, serious switchbacks and blind corners all spiced with a few manic locals coming the other way. Total sating of the soul. A beer never tasted so sweet as when I arrived buzzing but exhausted in Celendín.

The next morning I started on the final descent through Cajamarca towards the coast and passed into the lee side of the Andes. Hillsides of bare rock hemmed dried-up riverbeds meandering and cutting their way down to the coast. Only a line of bushes and trees showed where the river sometimes flowed amongst the rocks and sand. Suddenly a blaze of green fields and trees erupted from the earth. Terraced rice paddies hugged the left side of the valley beside the road. A welcome shock after wondering how the locals survived out here. The hills got gradually lower and rounder with each passing mile until the valley became so wide and flat it was hard to see one at all.

I loved the amazing friendliness of the people in the mountains and the almost complete absence of tourists and was secretly dreading reaching Cuzco and Machu Picchu. Cajamarca brought me back to earth: traffic jams, car horns, blaring music and people everywhere. The rider of a slow-moving and overladen motorbike ahead had very fat legs. I hadn't seen any really fat people in Peru. Then I realised there were too many legs. Four. Four legs on each side. Mama, papa and the two *niños*. The whole family on a blue 50 cc motorbike.

It reminded me of my first motorbike, well, not exactly a motorbike, it was a Puch moped with 50 cc of pure power. I used it to commute 20 miles into the City of London every day while doing my accountancy articles, sometimes reaching the dizzy speed of 30 mph. I loved the freedom and jousting with the traffic. As a moped it had bicycle pedals to help on steep hills, but I also used them for quick getaways at traffic lights. My commute soon became the highlight of my day and I got more satisfaction and enjoyment from my moped than I ever did from work. Bitten by the bike bug.

A dual carriageway and two roundabouts in the centre of Cajamarca caught me by surprise. I didn't wait to see who was supposed to give way to whom and shot through the gap in the traffic and was away before any of the drivers realised I'd ever been there.

The Panamericana Norte on the Pacific coast was an even greater shock. A dead-straight road bisected the featureless wastes of a moon-like arid grey desert. It never rained here (due to the Humboldt Current). Patches of sand had blown on to the edges of Ruta 1N. Yellow taxis, traffic lights and poverty in Trujillo. The grey desert morphed into brown then snapped into a thin strip of orange flowers fed by ancient irrigation systems and hidden underground rivers that flowed down from the mountains. Then it switched back to desert again. The contrast made the desert feel even more hostile. I longed to be back in the mountains.

It took me a while to find the *hostal* run by Michael White and Clare Bravo in the suburbs of Trujillo. Michael is a former chartered accountant turned tour guide. His area of expertise is Peruvian pre-Columbian (pre-European) civilisations, from the Chavín, whose highly developed culture dominated the region between 900 and 200 BC, to the Chimú, who were conquered by the Incas in around 1465. He agreed to take me to some important local sites, or *huacas* (places, people or things believed by pre-Columbian peoples such as the Moche to be endowed with supernatural power). We were to begin with the Huacas del Moche, three miles southwest of the city.

Leaving the city boundary was like entering another world. Trujillo is built on a flat plain, with not a hill or even hillock in sight. Suddenly the buildings stopped and bare fields revealed a totally unexpected sight. Two huge ragged mounds stood 500 yards apart, rounded and worn like melted chocolate. Sand blanketed everything so it looked like a cross between a building site and a windswept beach. Without a guide I wouldn't have known what they were, but they had, according to Michael, once been two large pyramids made of about fifty million adobe bricks – the Huaca del Sol (Temple of the Sun) and the Huaca de la Luna (Moon) – built by the Moche people between 100 BC and 650 AD It appears that the Huaca del Sol was the political centre of the Moche kingdom and the Huaca del Luna the religious centre. The Huaca del Sol was the largest manmade structure in the western hemisphere, measuring

150 feet high. That is, before the Spanish washed half of it away by diverting the river to get at the gold inside. Only about one third of the structure remains.

When the Moche lived there, this wasn't a desert. They created a vast network of irrigation canals from streams flowing down from the Andes and grew maize, beans and other vegetables. They produced food surpluses to feed urban artisans like potters and metalworkers and it is thought the Moche network of roads and system of way stations was an inspiration for the Incas. The Moche were master potters and expert craftsman. Each valley or river tended to be a separate city-state and each had its own artistic style. The societies were based on slavery. Human sacrifice was common, as shown by the discovery of the remains of thirty-four males near the base of La Luna. The reliefs and paintings on La Luna were in very good condition, having been protected from the wind and sun by being buried under many feet of sand. One wall was covered in large diamond squares, each of which had a square face with large white eyes and a red nose, hair like a breaking wave and was surrounded by two-eyed heads just like those in the Space Invaders computer game. Maybe the game was invented by a Peruvian descendant.

It was common to build directly on the previous structure so it's thought there were at least six successive buildings on top of the original La Luna. We walked past trenches being dug by archaeologists in faded blue overalls, past crumbling walls and into a shack with a corrugated iron roof. Two archaeologists sat on foam mattresses as they carefully brushed the wall with their dry paint brushes. One wore a black 'Lexus' baseball cap, blue t-shirt and jeans, the other a tracksuit with a red stripe. The babble of an excited commentator emanated from their battered radio held together with tape. Nearby, one section of La Luna had been completely excavated to reveal five rows of red, white and blue friezes rising 35 feet above our heads. It was extraordinary that such vivid colours could survive for over two thousand years.

Next stop was Chan Chan, only three miles from Trujillo. From a distance it looked like yet more sandy wastes rolling to the sea. Apparently centres were built near the coast to minimise the loss of farmland. Chan Chan was the capital of the Chimú kingdom, which lasted from AD 1100 to 1470. It is the largest adobe city in the world. Nine great compounds covered 14 square miles and probably supported a population of fifty thousand. Each compound was built by a different Chimú king who would construct a new palace and tomb once he acceded to the throne.

It wasn't long before the scale of the city became apparent. I stood on a wall and saw nothing but walls and courtyards in every direction. The city obtained its water from some one hundred and fifty walk-in wells. The water table was maintained at an artificially high level by irrigation further up the valley. It still worked. A large pond fringed with green reeds was the only sign of life on the whole site.

Michael's keen eye, expert knowledge and vivid imagination were invaluable at the next site, Huaca el Bruja, 20 miles northwest of Trujillo, which he said was seldom visited. In any case, advance permission had to be sought as it was an active archaeological site. The approach road over the moonscape was dotted with hundreds of pits like baby bomb craters.

'Those are gravediggers' test trenches,' Michael explained. 'If the *huaqueros* [grave robbers] find something they carry on. If they find nothing they try again somewhere else.'

We were the only tourists in a square mile of ruins. An off-white mound like an old spoil heap of quarry tailings shimmered in the distance. It was the only feature for miles around. Beside the kiosk where Michael bought our tickets lay a viringo, the world's ugliest dog. I'm a dog lover but found it hard to warm to him. The same size as an Alsatian, his dark brown-grey body was completely hairless. Only a few wispy black strands stuck out of the centre of his head like a balding Mohican.

We walked towards the sea. A sandy mound covered in high corrugated-iron roofs supported on wooden poles protected the archaeologists from the sun. They were working on a badly damaged stepped pyramid from the Moche period, apparently, dating from some time between 100 BC and AD 650. To me it looked like a cross between *Raiders of the Lost Ark* and mine workings. I wouldn't have been surprised to see someone panning for gold. Once my eyes adjusted to the gloom a row of relief plaster figures in blue and red stretched 20 feet down the wall. A red-painted character held a sacrificial knife in one hand and a decapitated head in the other. Moche society was brutal and normally they sacrificed captured warriors.

The murals were discovered by *huaqueros*, who fortunately reported their finds in 1990 to a local banker interested in archaeology. Imagine tearing through the desert like Indiana Jones and discovering gold buried deep in ancient pyramids, unseen by the human eye for thousands of years. Grave-robbing is still a Peruvian national hobby and word spreads fast. In 1987 police stopped two *huaqueros* near Chiclayo, which led to the greatest discovery ever made in the western hemisphere. The tomb of the Lord of Sipán contained huge amounts of gold, silver, ceramics and jewels, as well as the bones of dogs and llamas. The Sipán museum is near Chiclayo 100 miles northwest but I hadn't read that section of my guidebook in time and didn't want to go there now. 'There are so many ruins in Peru there isn't enough money or manpower to investigate them all,' Michael said. 'If the authorities were lucky enough to stumble on these two men imagine how many there are the *huaqueros* loot unimpeded. A *huaquero* could make so much money through one such find he'd be set up for life.'

Leaving the coast and Indy behind, I headed back into the mountains. In Quito Ricardo Rocco had recommended the ride through Cañón del Pato, an apparently wonderful road through a narrow canyon, with thirty-six tunnels and many bridges.

Taking Ricardo's advice, I looked for the shortcut, a private mining-company road 20 miles south of Virú. I stopped at the gate to speak to the guard. He was so delighted with the packet of biscuits I offered him he let me through. This was total desert. Bare rock, bleached and surgically clean. No trees, no grass, no sign of water or rain, only bleak grey rock bouncing back the heat. The mountains grew around me until I was hemmed in by immense folds of rock in all shades of brown. A short while later I turned north into a small canyon, past a fountain of rock whose strata leapt vertically out of the ground only to curve around in a perfect arch and pour back into the earth.

I emerged on the banks of the Rio Santa, where several rivulets meandered through the gravel beds. It would be scary at peak flow. The river narrowed as I climbed. I handed over some more biscuits to the gatekeeper at the end of the private road. I crunched into the first two potholes, which were impossible to see under the vertical sun, but my KTM's long travel suspension soaked up the smaller bumps. Dark brown and purple valley walls closed in until the river disappeared from view. This was Cañón del Pato. Water crashed through the invisible rocks when I stopped for a rest. Where did the single-track road go? There was surely no room through the tiny gap ahead. A thin tunnel filled with dust and dirt cut straight through the rock. There were no smooth or polished surfaces inside, just jagged edges left by explosives. Drill holes peppered the walls like a colander. None of the thirty-six tunnels were lit and the centre line was a pile of rocks and powder. A 4 × 4 had just emerged from the second tunnel and I stopped quickly inside because the dust and sudden switch to darkness made it impossible to see. Looking back through the tunnel a few minutes later the sun sliced through a rock window and lit up my dancing dust. I stood on the foot pegs to go faster and increase my stability. My bike rocked back and forth as the wheels bounced off the bumps. I accelerated and the rear wheel spun, squirting rocks and grit behind me. A little voice whispered 'Don't crash' as I rode the adrenaline wave through tunnels, around blind corners, with no barriers between me and the big drops into the writhing river below.

Gradually the sides of the canyon inched away until wide enough to allow small terraced fields and the first trees since Trujillo. I stopped for water in a small village hidden in an oasis of trees.

The mountains closed back in. Purple and black streaks rose vertically through the twisted strata. Vast towers of rock dwarfed three cyclists on the other side of the valley. They seemed relieved to stop for a chat. Lisa and Martin, two Germans, were on a post-university pre-work cycling holiday. Kate was from Australia and on her first trip overseas. They were all headed for Ushuaia for Christmas. It was going to be crowded there. I had already met four other cyclists aiming to be there at the same time. I hoped they'd booked a space. It would be a bit of a downer to have spent an entire year getting there only to be told there was no room at the inn and to please come back next year instead. The trio were only managing 3 mph in the canyon, and so were covering a lot less ground than their usual 40 or 50 miles a day. We agreed to meet in Caraz, a few hours' ride for me but two days' uphill slog for them.

Caraz is in the heart of the Cordillera Blanca, which has Peru's highest mountains, twenty of them over 16,000 feet. Hostal Chamanna was hidden a mile out of town down a rutted lane past dilapidated terraced houses built right on to the road. I knocked on a small wooden door built into the bigger barn doors. The garden was a riot of palms, ferns, red and yellow flowers and large white lilies blooming around a large lawn. Snow-capped peaks and Huascarán Norte, at over 22,000 feet the highest mountain in Peru, cut across the skyline above the walls. Inside it was a different world. Neatness and order and I was transported back to the Germany of the *hostal*'s owner. Ute was in her late forties with slightly greying blonde hair. She had come to Caraz for her husband's work and stayed behind after he left. She seemed a little strange.

The full breakfast next morning was so big I couldn't eat it all. A jug of fresh orange juice, melon, half an avocado, salami, a basket of eight croissants, fried eggs, chocolate cake and delicious fresh coffee. As I walked past the kitchen, Ute warned me not to go into town that day.

'There are big crowds in town,' she advised. 'They are looking for the mayor and they are angry.'

'Why, what's happened?'

'This is a poor area and the locals have discovered the mayor has built himself a big house in Lima with money that should have been used to improve the town. They want to kill him but he is hiding in Lima. Yesterday the crowd ransacked his house and burnt tyres in the main square. Two months ago the same thing happened in Llave but the mayor was not so lucky. The crowd found him and lynched him.'

Martin, Lisa and Kate arrived in the afternoon. Martin agreed that Ute was a bit odd. 'Maybe she has been here too long on her own,' he said. Finding out that breakfast was $10, I decided to move to the backpackers in town. I told Ute I was going into town to get some money to pay her.

'You cannot go on your motorbike. You must leave it here.'

'Why? I'm only going on my bike. I still have all my kit here.'

'If you take it I will call the police.'

I got my cash and moved into a backpackers in the centre of town. It was neater and cleaner than I'd expected. A small square with palm trees and green grass surrounded by shops and a bar. The smell of wood smoke filled the air.

The next day dawned clear and bright and I set off up the mountain to find the *Puya raimondii*, an extraordinary plant that was discovered by Antonio Raimondi in 1860. Born in Milan in 1826, Raimondi emigrated to Peru to be closer to the natural history which fascinated him. The 'Modern Discoverer of Peru' then spent nineteen years systematically travelling all over the country and writing about everything he found. His range of interests was vast: archaeology, botany, chemistry, history, geology, palaeontology. He was even an accomplished artist and drew many of the plants he found.

The tropical Andes is the richest and most diverse region on Earth and contains about a sixth of all plant life in less than 1 per cent of the world's land area. Different types of vegetation grow in specific altitude ranges. The *Puya raimondii* only exist at altitudes over 14,000 feet, 3,000 feet above the valley floor. The road was an adventure of its own, a great feat of engineering. Up close it looked impossible but I zigzagged up a sheer cliff face and doubled back in crevasses too tight for a truck. The *Puya raimondii* was unmistakeable. A stout trunk filled out into a big skirt like a fat girl's bottom. Large, spiky leaves hung down all around it and from the centre a twenty-foot spike pierced the sky. A little further on the road emerged on to a plateau. It was a surreal sight. *Puya raimondii* dotted the treeless landscape like triffids on the march. The plant holds several records: it takes a hundred years to mature, flowers once and then slowly dies. The flowers form on the spike which, at up to 30 feet high, is the tallest in the world. The spike bursts into as many as twenty thousand white flowers, another record for a single plant. Reassuringly it is related to the pineapple.

The engine cut out on the way down and wouldn't restart. Suspecting a sooty spark plug from the high altitude, I found I'd left my tools behind in Caraz. A man in a bright yellow t-shirt and jeans appeared from a field below. Sandor understood my mime for a pair of pliers and ran back to his house. He returned five minutes later sweating profusely so I gave him the rest of my water. The spark plug was black. I cleaned it off with leaves and my t-shirt. It started first time and I limped back down the hill as I revved the engine constantly to stop it happening again.

Gertie Rutten's fáfé had the best lattes in town and a pretty barista. Lola. We chatted, and clicked. Perhaps I should stay a little longer in Caraz. We met after work on a bench under a palm tree at the Plaza de Armas. She had a lovely smile which flashed through her dark eyes as she saw me. Lola's younger sister came as a chaperone. We wandered back to my *hostal* and sat in the garden in the evening sun. Later I walked Lola back to her house. As we wound our way through the streets crowded with stalls selling fruit, flowers and balls of bright coloured wool I heard comments made by the locals. I began to realise they were directed at Lola. I felt the tension in the air as the word was spat out.

'Puta!'

173

'What are they saying?' I asked.

'They're saying I'm a bad girl because I want to marry a foreigner and not a Peruvian. But I don't care, because they are stupid people.'

'But you have to live here. Calling them stupid won't make it any easier.'

'All they can see is what exists here. They don't realise what is happening even in Lima and they just don't care. I can't wait to get away from this place. I hate it.'

The following night she insisted I walk her home again and the same vitriol poured out. It wasn't pleasant but she ignored it. We took a different route and approached a church.

'Let's go in,' she said.

As we walked down the aisle she started humming the Wedding March.

'Dah, de, dah, dah. Dah, de, dah, dah.'

'I want to get married here,' she said.

'Who to?' I asked innocently.

'You,' she replied.

It was time to go.

Yungay is a small town eight miles southeast of Caraz. It was here that Gene Savoy, the American explorer who discovered the 'city' of Gran Vilaya near Chachapoyas in northern Peru, settled his family in 1962.

The town has a much-documented tragic past. On 31 May 1970 an earthquake triggered a massive landslide from Huascarán Norte, Peru's highest mountain. Estimates put the 'piece' that broke off at half a mile wide and over a mile long – big enough to be a mountain anywhere else. The mountainside plummeted towards Yungay. Many people were inside watching an international football match on television. Three minutes later it tore through the town at about 120 mph and buried everything under 30 feet of rock and rubble. Twenty-five thousand men, women and children were killed, including Savoy's three-year-old son, Jamil. Following the tragedy, Savoy, a deeply religious man, came to believe that his son's birth had been the second coming of Christ. This concept formed the core of his numerous religious books, writings and church doctrines and he founded a New Age Christian church, with himself as minister.

The only survivors were the children who happened to be at the football stadium watching a circus and those people who were at or who managed to get up to the town's graveyard in time. The site has since been declared a national cemetery. Only the old church tower was rebuilt; the 'new' Yungay was reconstructed a few miles away. Under a pure blue sky I walked through lines of stones laid out to mark the streets. Former houses are now simple gardens filled with thousands of red and yellow roses which swayed gently in the breeze. Relatives erected memorials where whole families were killed. Four palm trees protruded through the rubble in the Plaza de Armas but only one was still alive. On a small hill above town a huge white statue of Christ stood on a blue globe with his right foot pointing to South America. His outstretched arms were open towards the murderous mountain. It made me angry. How could anyone believe in the goodness and benevolence of a deity after the death of twenty-five thousand innocent people?

In the complete silence, amid the scent of beautiful flowers beneath the towering mass of Huascarán, I imagined the sounds of laughter and bustle of a busy town, the noise of children playing in the streets. Then the sudden avalanche of destruction seconds later. I crossed a small stream that gurgled and rippled its way down the hill and bent to smell a red rose. The sweet scent made the tragedy even more unbearable. Suddenly, overwhelmed by grief and sadness, a lump formed in my throat and tears rolled down my cheeks.

I was too upset to ride over Punta Olimpica, the highest pass in Peru at 16,000 feet, so took the easy route to Chavín instead. The ubiquitous single-track road turned west and wove back and forth, ever higher, through wisps of cloud and patches of snow that soon blanketed the ground, leaving only the road snow-free. I shivered constantly in the freezing air, having not bothered to stop and put on my down jacket. A solid wall of grey rock appeared around a bend and I rode into an unlit and narrow tunnel at 15,000 feet. It was hard to see potholes on the wet unmetalled road in the dark. Freezing water poured from the ceiling and some splashed down my neck. Blocks of ice glinted on the centre line. I crunched slowly along a wheel track, trying hard not to get pushed offline, before emerging into a warmer, snowless and much narrower valley.

Chavín de Huántar is a small fortress temple of the Chavín cult, the earliest civilisation in pre-Columbian Peru. Very little is known about them as they had no writing, but their civilisation is thought to have lasted from about 900 to 200 BC The highlight of the ruins is a low, flat-topped pyramid. Steps descended through the pyramid and a maze of poorly lit tunnels before emerging at a narrow slit too small to squeeze through. Through the gap a thin carved obelisk extended upwards out of sight. It was covered in strange markings, animals that were unlike others I'd ever seen: snakes, tigers and crocodiles, human forms with hair made of snakes and two great fangs in the upper jaw. This was the El Lanzón monolith, a representation of the principal god of the Chavín cult, hidden deep in the heart of the pyramid.

The on-site museum had some other interesting carved tablets and stone heads but I was annoyed to find, having taken the trouble to visit the actual place, that the best pieces were in other museums hundreds and even thousands of miles away. Chief among these was the one known as the Raimondi Stone, now in the National Museum in Lima. It was named after Antonio Raimondi (he of the strange *Puya raimondii* trees). He came across it at the home of a local farmer, Timoteo Espinoza, who was using the exquisitely carved six-foot-long monolith as his kitchen table. Its carvings depict the Staff-Bearing God and his huge headdress of snakes. The artists used a technique known as 'contour rivalry', which reveals different images when viewed from different positions. From one side it looks like a scary god holding two staffs with a headdress of snakes, but from the other the god is a smiling reptile with a headdress of smiling fanged faces. The image has an extraordinary power and must have been terrifying in the flickering firelight of thousands of years ago. It still resonates in the modern age, as Pablo Picasso indicated. 'Of all of the ancient cultures I admire,' said the Spanish artist, 'that of Chavín amazes me the most. Actually, it has been the inspiration behind most of my art.' One reason for the Chavíns' strange and tormented designs could be that their shamans used the San Pedro cactus for its hallucinogenic properties. Chavín de Huántar is also known as San Pedro de Chavín.

The Quechua name for a monolith translates as 'stone of power'. A new football team in Huancayo, near Lima, was mystified to receive a large order for football shirts from England after a piece about them appeared in *The Sun* newspaper. The team had no idea why they were in demand. 'It is very strange,' one of them was reported as saying. 'Everyone in Britain seems to think we have a funny name.' The team was called 'Deportivo Wanka' – 'Team Stone Power'.

By midday I was descending a mountain pass halfway to Lima. The air had that purity, crispness and clarity that only comes with altitude. The sun shone in a cloudless sky and the warmth seeped into my soul as I descended towards the coast, but I desperately needed to pee. I'd been looking for a suitable place but there were no turn-offs and the verges were too steep to stop. Rounding a corner a crash barrier offered the perfect support. I leant my bike against it and took my helmet off. The ground was dusty so I put it on top of a pannier. It was Sunday morning and there was no traffic. I finished my pee but, as I turned, my backpack pushed my helmet over the barrier. In stunned silence I watched my helmet disappear over the cliff into the valley below. It reappeared a few seconds later, hundreds of feet below, and continued to bounce and smash its way down the scree. I willed it to stop, but it didn't. The slope was too steep and there was nothing in its way, nothing but bare rocks on a forty-five-degree slope.

It was surreal watching my helmet plummet down the hill. To my huge relief it eventually stopped beside a bush. I was 200 miles from Lima. I thought about riding on without it but I had nothing to protect my eyes. I had to try and find it. I changed into my hiking boots, left my water backpack on my bike and set off. It would surely be easier than searching for my wallet on the hard shoulder of a Texan interstate. All I had to do was walk down the slope and pick it up.

A gully a few hundred yards back up the hill meant I could avoid the cliff, but it was steeper and more difficult than I'd expected. The ground was covered in loose rocks and rubble left behind when they made the road. Rocks kept sliding away from under me. Even the largest moved unexpectedly. This was not a good place to twist my ankle or break a leg. I wore my motorcycle jacket because I didn't want to leave my money and passport unattended on my bike. It was hot under the midday sun. I took off my sweater and tied it round my waist. I was soon thirsty but had no water. I slipped several times on the scree. I crouched lower and used the branches to steady myself but they kept snapping off. After scrambling down for ten minutes I thought I was in the right position but couldn't see my bike above me. Two rock screes fanned out down the slope. I scrambled up, down and across both of them, expecting to see my helmet at any time.

After half an hour's searching my legs were getting tired from the constant workout. If I could see my helmet from my bike why couldn't I see my bike from down here? I was thirsty and needed a rest. After an hour I was beginning to think I should give up. No one knew I was here. The only clue was my bike parked up on the road. My legs ached and I was getting extremely thirsty. I pushed through some more branches and as I did so, a branch catapulted back, caught my glasses and flicked them off. I felt a surge of panic and whizzed round to try and see where they landed. I can't see without them. At minus eight I'm really short-sighted. Luckily I saw the gold reflecting in the sunlight a few yards away. I climbed a big rock to get a better view.

Nothing. That was it. I'd had a go but failed. I'd just have to ride slowly to Lima and buy another helmet. My little voice told me to have one last look. I went further up the other scree, almost crawling to stop myself slipping or tripping over. My heart leapt. There it was! Elated, I picked it up, threaded my arm through the visor hole and immediately started up the hill. It got steeper and I was tired. I needed continual handholds, but, with my left arm threaded through my helmet, I couldn't keep my balance. I climbed a few more yards and looked up. It got even steeper. I turned and went back down. There were fields in the bottom of the valley. Fields meant paths.

I slid down on my bum, saving my aching legs, and my spirits rose when I saw a small spade-width channel cut into the slope carrying sparkling water to the fields. I longed to sate my thirst but didn't risk it, even though my mouth felt like gravel and my lips were stuck together. An hour later, exhausted, I reached the road and thumbed a lift back to my bike. Everything was exactly where I had left it. Nothing was missing. I donned my battered helmet and headed south for Lima.

Overjoyed at reaching the coastal Panamericana and excited at meeting my Brit biker friends Richard and Jane again in Lima, I overtook a taxi in the centre of Huacho. My loud exhaust made a policeman look up and he ran to his motorbike. He'd never catch me on his smaller machine but I played safe and slowed down. He came alongside and waved me down. He looked angry. I pulled over and took off my helmet. He babbled in Spanish before calming down.

The wise words of Australian Harley-Davidson traveller Peter Forwood popped into my head: 'Make it their problem. You have all the time in the world so just start talking. Be really polite and just keep talking until they realise it's actually their problem not yours.'

'Show me your driver's licence.'

I gave him a colour photocopy. He theatrically whipped out his book of offences. There were two columns beside each offence. The figures beside the speeding one said $300 and $150.

'You must pay this,' he pointed to the $300 figure, 'in US dollars at the police station in Barranca.' Barranca was 25 miles north. I didn't believe it could be that much. Confusingly they also used the '$' character for soles. I shrugged.

'I am very sorry but I didn't know what the speed limit was and I don't have any money.'

He babbled away again. It rapidly became apparent that I could get a big discount and avoid travelling 25 miles in the wrong direction if I paid him in cash right now.

I kept repeating that I didn't have any money and the price kept dropping.

$150, $100, $50.

Even though I still had a long way to go I tried to look as unhurried and relaxed as possible.

'$30.'

He still had my driving licence.

'I am not going to pay anything,' I said.

He changed his tack from angry cop to nice cop.

'Are we friends?'

'Oh yes',I assured him, 'we are friends.'

'There is a restaurant over there where they sell chicken and rice.'

I felt a momentary pang of guilt before my resolve returned.

'No.'

'They have coffee.'

'No, nothing. I have no money.'

I felt even more guilty, but if I gave in he'd stop every tourist. In a last desperate attempt he turned on the hopeful puppy eyes.

'A Coke?'

'No.'

He sighed, gave me back my licence and asked me about my bike and my trip. I answered politely and rode away as quickly as possible. I felt a strange mix of triumph and guilt at the same time.

I cruised the final miles into Lima. Bare brown hills and mountains hazy in the heat and dust. No sign of life at all. No trees, shrubs or bushes, not even a blade of grass until a line of trees marked the irrigation ditches. A green mist appeared on the horizon. A vast carpet of grass pushed out of the desert floor. Wherever water appeared the lushness and vibrant greens exploded into colour. Basking in my triumph over the policeman I continued south. Fifty miles from the city a new dual carriageway climbed up through featureless hills beside the sea until I caught the wonderful fragrance of fresh flowers. Where was it coming from? There was nothing here. No houses or farms, nothing. I sped up to enjoy the flip-flop through the curves. The scent got stronger. An old pickup limped along in the distance. The rear deck was a blaze of white, yellow, red and purple chrysanthemums, stacked several feet high and facing out on every side.

Diego Maranzana welcomed me into his office in Miraflores in the heart of Lima. He oozed the charm of a natural salesman. He owned Sportmotorcycles, the KTM importer, but had no workshop or mechanics of his own. Owners did their own servicing or got a local shop to do the work for them. I paid him for the new yoke he'd sent me in Chachapoyas and asked him to recommend a mechanic. One of the bolts holding the pannier frames had sheared again and needed replacing.

I am nervous letting anyone near my bike. Ernesto looked a little shifty in his greasy blue overalls. My Spanish was not up to explaining everything but with Diego's help he soon nodded his head in agreement. He could start the following morning, not the best sign of a mechanic in demand, but I was impatient to get going.

At 10 a.m. I wandered into the small paved area behind the showroom to find no Ernesto and the whole of the rear of my bike missing. He'd completely removed the panniers, seat, footrests and rear sub-frame. The wiring loom lay splayed out on the ground. Angry and annoyed, I hoped he hadn't damaged any of the electrical components when taking them off and prayed that he'd remember how to route the cables through the frame. If he got it wrong they'd chafe and short out. All he'd needed to do was remove the pannier frames and drill the bolt out again as Abel had done in Chachapoyas, but it was too late now.

Ernesto reappeared after his lunch at 3 p.m. with the fixed sub-frame. I made my feelings clear but soon back-pedalled when his eyes flashed in anger. He was doing his best so I left him to get on with it. Diego called me to say it was ready at 5 p.m. the next day. Sure enough my bike looked normal again and everything worked: the engine, indicators and brake lights. I just hoped he'd got the wiring loom routed correctly. How long would it take to find out?

The Gringo Trail is a well-trodden path through South America. Everyone visits the same sights. I stayed at the same hotel as Richard and Jane, last seen in the Turtle's Head in Quito. One evening over pisco sours I asked Jane if she'd ever asked a banana a question. For some strange reason both Jane and Richard looked at me as if I was slightly mad and exchanged a quick, knowing glance between themselves. It was the 'clearly bonkers but let's humour him' look.

'No, how do you ask a banana a question?'

'Ask anything you like but it must have a "yes" or "no" answer as bananas aren't very bright. Think of a question but don't tell me what it is or it won't work. Ready?'

'Yes.'

Using a sharp knife I cut off the last sliver from the stalk-less end.

'It's a "no",' I said and showed them the small black blob in the centre of the white flesh. 'If it's a "yes" you see a distinct "y" shape.'

'It's bollocks, it doesn't work at all,' said Jane.

'What do you mean?' I said, astounded a banana could lie.

'Well you said ask the banana a question so I asked "Are you a banana?" and it said "no".'

Before leaving Lima I called the export manager of Santa Cruz, my bicycle manufacturer, in California. He told me Eduardo had just got the money for my bike. At last. All I had to do now was get Rosa to send it to me. Suddenly Cuzco and Machu Picchu seemed a lot nearer. I left Lima with a growing sense of excitement and headed for the famous Nazca lines.

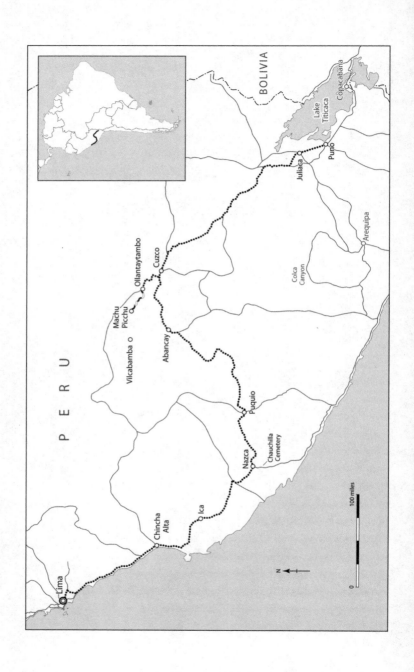

16

FLYING THE AERIAL HELTER-SKELTER

A ribbon of tar burnt a black line through the desert. On the right a huge white outcrop like a burger bun was so bright I had to squint just to look at it. Low hills wavered in the haze. No buildings, no life, nothing existed out here. It was like riding across another planet. I wouldn't have been surprised to see an astronaut bounce across the horizon in slow motion. It was even more extreme and inhospitable than the Panamericana Norte north of Lima. There was hardly any traffic. The only colour came from the dotted yellow line down the centre of the road. Twenty miles from Palpa I crested a small rise under the blazing sun. Two purple figures were walking on the side of the road, the only living things in the whole desert. One was carrying something.

His name was Ramírez and he was carrying a huge wooden cross on his shoulder. The crossbar was taller than he was. A small wheel stopped the end from dragging along the ground. A purple 'Lima' bandana kept his long black hair out of his face and a pile of cloth four inches deep spread the load over his right shoulder. I wondered how often he changed shoulders. He looked relieved to stop for a rest. He wore a white t-shirt, brown trousers and trainers under his purple robe.

'Tiennes agua?'

I gave him some water. Ramírez was on a pilgrimage to carry the cross from one end of Peru to other, a distance of 1,500 miles. His friend carried a small satchel, two bottles of water and two oranges in a plastic bag. Ramírez told me they had no money. They depended on people giving them food, drink and a bed for the night.

A red lorry honked as it went past. I gave Ramírez the rest of my packet of biscuits but he clearly wanted money. He was cross and I heard him complain as I rode away: 'No quiero comida … quiero plata.' I don't want food … I want money.

It is strange how deserts seem so clean. The heat sterilises and purifies. I opened my legs to get a cooling breeze. The black line arrowed across the desert floor and disappeared into liquid pools in the mirage ahead. Fifty miles to Nazca. A fog of heat hung in the air like dust. It dampened my sight but not the desert. The sky merged into the sand. The horizon had vanished. Nothing to see, nothing to do but ride the line. I sped up to banish the boredom. Thirty miles. Twenty miles. The excitement of a corner and a chance to lean over. A hill and another corner. Joy unbounded. A sweeping succession as I descended into more warmth. I accelerated hard on a long straight and the engine nearly died.

I revved hard, the power surged back but rough and uneven, coughing and spluttering. What was going on? Could I make the top of the hill? The engine only worked at full throttle or not at all. I tried desperately not to stall as I doubted I'd be able to restart it. As I descended into Nazca everything changed. Green potato fields shone beneath bleached and heavily gullied bare hills. I continually revved the engine madly and got strange looks from the locals but managed not to stall it. I stopped at the first hotel I found. The silence was a relief and I slumped down in a chair.

Richard and Jane were drinking pisco sours in the bar!

'JB! We heard you coming. These are the best in town,' declared Jane as she offered me a slug. They had arrived from Lima two days earlier.

'There's something wrong with my bike. It won't run at all. It's full throttle or nothing. I have to wring its neck to get any response at all.'

'My dear boy,' said Richard, 'worry about that tomorrow. It's happy hour.'

'We can't decide what to have next,' added Jane. 'Another pisco or try something new.'

'It's not easy being an overland biker, is it?'

'Awful,' said Richard.

'It is a bit of a struggle,' giggled Jane as she slid deeper into her third pisco sour. 'I sometimes wonder how we manage.'

Another gruelling day on the road, beside the pool, soaking up the sun and being extremely busy doing absolutely nothing. This was not the sort of thing a novice should attempt on their own and needed careful training. I could have no better guides, no better role models, than R & J. Who else could have spent three weeks in Lima being 'extremely busy' but still only visiting one museum and making one trip to the coast? Real experts make everything look easy. R & J were artists.

The next morning, feeling slightly hung over but fortified by *huevos rancheros*, I took the seat off my bike, removed the Keihin carburettor and dismantled it in my room. When I removed the top the needle stayed in the bottom. It should have been attached. The circlip had come off. Relieved at such a simple solution, I replaced it with my spare one. The constant vibrations must have worn it away. I'd also noticed that the tyres I used, Pirelli MT90s, weren't lasting nearly as long as normal. Perhaps riding for many hours a day was accelerating the wear rate of everything.

A quick test ride proved my bike was happy again and I set off for the Chauchilla cemeteries. Following Jane's instructions, I turned off the Arequipa road and into the desert, ignoring the fact that there was no sign. Well-graded at first, the desert track deteriorated as it followed a gully into the hills. A wide, flat valley opened up between hills streaked with red, grey and green minerals, like the writing in a stick of rock. The track disappeared. I couldn't see any wheel marks at all. I doubled back to find another track. Perhaps not one of Peru's most popular sites. I was full of admiration for Jane's navigational skills. Perhaps women really are superior at map reading after all? Through another brown gully and out on to another plain. Feeling much more confident simply because the track was straight and easy to follow, I reached the low hills in the distance and rode into a small canyon, twisting between the coloured rocks and then turned sharply right.

Into a wall of rock. The road ended at a small cliff beside a battered red 4 × 4. A man in a blue shirt and jeans with 'Consorcio' written down his left leg was looking at me in a rather surprised fashion. I waved a greeting and managed to get off my bike without falling off.

'Buenos días!'

Emilio introduced me to his three companions, Christian, Pibe and Lucio. I shook their hands like visiting royalty. Pibe and Lucio wore red scarves over their mouths to filter out the dust. They were mining copper. Emilio walked towards the 4 × 4 and beckoned me to follow him. A mound of green malachite glinted in the evening sun on a large black plastic sheet. Intrigued, and recalling my year studying Cornish tin and copper mines at university, I asked Emilio if I could have a look in his mine.

'Si, claro.'

He gave me a spare acetylene lamp and we entered the adit cut directly into the side of the cliff. We could easily stand upright. The adit was surprisingly wide too and wonderfully cool. After 30 yards we turned a corner and he pointed to the top corner of the wall. I couldn't see anything at all, just the same buff-coloured rock. Emilio threw some water on it from a bottle and a thick vein turned a vibrant green. He told me that it was hard work but safer than mining gold like their friends did near Arequipa, using mercury to dissolve out the gold. The copper miners were happier with less money and a much lower risk of poisoning themselves.

Copper, gold, silver and even platinum have been mined in Peru since pre-Columbian times. The Incas worked all of them, even platinum, which has a very high melting point. They achieved this by mixing it with gold dust. The Spanish called platinum *platina del pinto* because it looked like silver. They threw large quantities into the sea to stop it becoming a cheap imitation of silver. Emilio and his partners were only doing what their forebears had done over the millennia. I thanked them and headed back to Nazca. As I rode back down the main road I saw the sign to the cemetery I'd missed earlier.

I got there just in time. After taking my entrance fee at the Chauchilla hut the cashier locked up and wandered off, carrying the day's takings in a battered black tin box. The site was totally flat and featureless like a beach. I sank a little in the sand with every step.

A four-foot-deep grave lay under a tin roof. Three bodies in a foetal position, their ribs and bones white, huddled against the long wall. Bits of ragged red cloth sat on their shoulders. Two of the skulls had full heads of brown hair. The scalps looked like orange peel that had been peeled away in one piece. The hair looked entirely normal, though could probably have done with a good wash and some conditioner. The bodies never decayed in the dry desert. They had remained buried or in open graves here with their hair and clothes intact for hundreds of years.

A path marked by small stones led me from grave to grave. At each, crooked timbers like driftwood supported a corrugated iron roof to protect the mummies from the sun. Many small mounds of sand off the path showed another grave missed or robbed.

Several of the mummies wore bandanas and clothes draped around their shattered torsos. All the corpses were sitting in a foetal position like the Leymebamba mummies, as if they were trying to fit in the smallest space. Some graves contained a collection of bones scattered haphazardly on the floor, while others were carefully arranged. In one, an incongruous corpse had been created from spare arms, legs and a head from different bodies. Nothing matched. The *huaqueros* had picked the site dry and left only bones.

But who were these people? Did they create the lines?

The Nazca Lines are hundreds of drawings of plants and animals created by the Nazca people over two thousand years ago; scraped out of the ground like crop circles, they measure up to five miles long and range between one and ten feet wide. The Monkey, for example, is 360 feet long and impossible to see at ground level. The best, but most expensive way to see them is by helicopter. As usual Jane had done her research. It was advisable to go early in the morning, she said, before the thermals got too strong. 'The flights are bumpy with many tight turns,' she read, 'and many people are airsick.'

'I'll have a big breakfast,' I said. 'I'm sure one shouldn't sail on an empty stomach.'

'My dear boy,' exclaimed Richard, 'do you think that's wise?'

I sat next to the pilot. The three others sat in the back. The pilot handed round the sick bags, then pointed at my feet.

'Keep your feet away from the pedals and stick.'

He started the engine, we took off, made a gentle turn and flew northwest over the desert. It seemed pretty tame to me.

'First we fly over a drawing so you can take pictures out the left side, then I turn around and do the same for the right side. The Man, left side, ready, now!'

The plane yawed way over forty-five degrees. A huge motif hundreds of feet tall filled the side of the hill. Safety belts were tightened and cameras clicked and whirred. It was all over in an instant when we flicked over into a high g-force right turn. My stomach compressed and my head spun as I hoped the wings wouldn't fall off. I had no idea where we were but got my camera ready.

'Man, right side, ready, now!'

I peered through my viewfinder and kept the button pressed; eight free digital photos poured into life every second. I'd never have taken so many if I was still using film.

'Now we see the Spider.'

A short horizontal hop and the same routine. I think it must have been a female spider, as it was so huge. I thought of the male *Tidarren* spiders: males are only 1 per cent the size of females but each of their sexual organs accounts for 10 per cent of their body weight. They chew off one of their genitals before mating so they can run faster. The female likes to eat her lover.

Flying the aerial helter-skelter, I soon lost count of how many designs we saw. The most memorable were the Astronaut, Bird and Monkey. The Astronaut covered the flank of one hill and looked like an overweight ET from Spielberg's film. I stared at the horizon whenever it flashed across the windscreen in my attempt to not throw up but wasn't helped by the unmistakeable smell which wafted from behind. Just as I couldn't stand it any more and grabbed my bag we suddenly levelled off and headed back to the airport.

The lines were 'discovered' in the 1920s when planes first flew over the Nazca Desert. Passengers reported seeing 'primitive landing strips' on the ground below. Maria Reiche, a German mathematician, arrived in the 1930s and spent the rest of her life mapping and restoring the lines. Known as 'the Lady of the Lines,' she believed they were a sophisticated astronomical calendar. But it was Erich von Däniken who really put them on the map in his book *Chariots of the Gods?: Was God an Astronaut?*, which I read at school. It was full of photos explaining what the various designs meant and I remembered wishing I could see them for myself. Von Däniken (the same man who interpreted the Mayan carving at Palenque in Mexico as being an ancient 'astronaut in his rocket') believed 'our forefathers received visits from the universe in the remote past,' and used the Nazca Lines as evidence. 'The lines were laid out to say to the gods: "Land Here! Everything has been prepared as you ordered."'

There are hundreds of lines spread over some 170 square miles west of Nazca and they've been categorised as one of two types: about seventy of them are 'biomorphs', that is an animal or plant design, and the rest of them, some nine hundred in all, are classed simply as 'geoglyphs', images made on the land surface by using rocks or cuts in the ground. The Pelican is 935 feet long and the Condor is 450 feet. I believe the Lady of the Lines named many of them but there is still so much that is unknown. Many of the designs incorporate a hand-like design with prominent 'fingers', which Däniken saw as very significant. Perhaps his flights of fancy were fuelled by a few extra substances. Underneath a photo of a 'hand' he noted: 'This is very reminiscent of the aircraft parking bays on a modern airport.'

Though the meanings of the images are open to question, it is generally agreed that the lines are thousands of years old and that they were created by three different peoples: the Paracas (900–200 BC), the Nazca (200 BC to AD 600) and the Huari (AD 630–1000). They played an important role in the ritual life of pre-Columbian societies. As I'd seen at the Huacas del Moche in Trujillo, 500 miles to the north, a *huaca* was a person, place or thing with supernatural power. Important Incan *huacas* were joined together with lines. The Incas had a system for recording time called the *ceque* (ray). These *ceques* were radial lines that spread out from Cuzco, the Inca capital, like spokes on a wheel, with the Coricancha temple at the centre. There were forty-one *ceque* lines which were marked by *huacas* along their lengths. The *ceque* system bound the religious, social, organisational and astronomical systems together. The lines may also indicate some of the extensive network of underground canals that channelled water from subterranean aquifers to the fields. Some of these canals are still used today. The lines have been preserved because it never rains and the winds keep the lines clean. The real reason behind them may never be known. They are an enigma.

Heading east out of Nazca a few days later, I climbed through the contours as they twisted and turned through rounded valleys and bare rock. So little vegetation and so much rock. A land of limited life and contrasts. A small white grave with a blue cross told a terrible tale on a sharp corner. A world of four colours: the bright blue sky, the newly laid black road and its yellow lines and the light brown rock.

Strangely, the temperature rose as I got higher. It's normally the other way round. From 16°C in Nazca at 2,000 feet it was 23°C only 1,000 feet higher. It always seemed to be colder at sea level in Peru. Unfortunately, that was as warm as it got. I hoped the 340 miles to Cuzco would be an easy day's ride but my IMO soon suggested otherwise.

Normally passes were fun. You wound your way up, getting colder and colder, basked in a wonderful view or hurried through clouds or rain and descended into the welcoming warmth. It went horribly wrong on the way to Cuzco. I crested the second col but a third appeared in the distance. I put on my sweater. A new colour. Black. A black mountain was my next col. Tufts of grass in little valleys gave me hope that I would soon be descending. But I never did. Snow appeared on the mountain tops and gusts of wind started blowing me about. I put on my down jacket. Brown, white and black llamas grazed beside the road. All had pink ribbons in their ears. Every time I got to the 'top' another peak appeared a few miles away. It never stopped. The pattern repeated like a stuck record. This was the altiplano. It got windier and I got colder, even though I wore all my layers – a t-shirt, long-sleeved shirt, sweater, down jacket, biking jacket, silk gloves inside winter ones – and had the heated grips on the 'toast' setting. More snow. After half an hour there was no end in sight. How long could this go on? Despite the heated grips my fingers started to hurt. I'd never make Cuzco. My first taste of the altiplano was 100 miles between 13,000 feet and 15,000 feet before finally descending into the warmth of Abancay just before dusk.

The next morning I needed to stop for a pee on the way up and out of Abancay. The road squirrelled back and forth up the mountain but I couldn't find anywhere flat enough to stop. Just in time I pulled into a viewpoint overlooking the town, flipped the side stand out and leant the bike over. There was a funny noise and my bike kept on leaning. I jumped off as it crashed to the ground again. Petrol poured out the breather pipe while the engine ticked over. I killed the engine and tried to pick it up.

It was on a down slope and much too heavy. Graunching gears made me look up as a green lorry ground past at walking pace. I waved at the driver, pointing to my bike and hoping he'd help me pick it up. He changed down another gear and for a split second I thought he would stop, but he just crawled past, staring straight ahead. I had to empty all my panniers and top box to heave it upright. The side stand lay on the ground. One side of the bracket had sheared off from fatigue. It was going to be fun finding a hotel in Cuzco. I used the side stand every time I stopped. With a 39-inch seat I couldn't get off without it. I'd have to lean it against walls and lamp posts.

Cuzco is in a natural bowl and the first hotel I tried lay on a steep cobbled and cambered street. Putting my foot down to turn around I found only air. I leapt off and my bike crashed to the ground. Two passers-by ran to help the useless gringo pick his bike up.

Bike journalist Dan Walsh and Richard and Jane were in town so we met for a drink at the Norton Rats Tavern, the local Mecca for motorcyclists. Owned by bike-loving Brit Jeffrey Powers, it served real beer and pub food. A cheeseburger never tasted so good as on a balcony overlooking the Plaza de Armas. Dan brought two other bikers along, Pete and Gary. Pete was relaxed, affable and amusing but Gary was something else. He claimed he was a pilot from Texas and that he wrote for several travel magazines but nothing he said rang true. It was like having a drink with Darth Vader. He oozed negativity and created a suffocating atmosphere. Anytime anyone made a positive, encouraging or funny statement he found something wrong with it and dragged the mood down again. Things became increasingly awkward and tense and when he eventually left the whole table sighed with relief.

Dan harangued me again for always being in a rush: 'Slow down, Rabbit! Slow down.' It was OK for him. His regular feature for *Bike* magazine paid for the rest of his month. But he had a point. I rushed from place to place in order to keep my mortgage down. I still couldn't shake off the feeling I was spending my future. Even as a not-very-good former chartered accountant I knew that wasn't a wise thing to do.

Despite its amazing treasures, Cuzco was too crowded with tourists to hold my attention for long. From the twelfth century until 1534 it was the capital of the Inca Empire and 'centre of the universe'. The Incas had conquered more than twenty-one different tribes and incorporated more than twelve million subjects into their system without the wheel or by riding on animals (they only used the llama as a pack animal). When the king ('the Inca') died, his possessions and palaces were sealed up and the new king built a new palace of his own. That's why the centre of the city is so extraordinary, being full of grand Inca residences. Tourists thronged the streets of the modern city, snapping shots of small boys holding llamas; an Indian in a red-and-gold Inca tunic walked past carrying a staff. I longed for the low-key Chachapoyas.

My next stop was Machu Picchu, the 'Lost City of the Incas', high in the mountains 50 miles northwest of Cuzco. I'd hoped to do the famous hike along the Inca Trail to get there. The 26-mile trail threads its way on Inca paving stones and paths through mountains, misty cloud forest and subtropical jungle tunnels to the ruined city complex, which sits on a ridge below the peak of Huayna Picchu. But with numbers limited to 500 tourists a day, hikes were fully booked for five weeks ahead – the first time my 'turn up and get a discount' approach had failed.

Instead I decided to learn more about the two great explorers who brought Machu Picchu to the world's attention – Hiram Bingham and Gene Savoy.

Hiram Bingham was an ambitious history lecturer at Yale University. His first expedition in 1906 traced the route taken a century earlier by the Venezuelan soldier and statesman Simón Bolívar (1783–1830). Bolívar had led the revolutions against Spanish rule in South America, liberating Venezuela, Columbia, Ecuador, Peru and Bolivia, and Bingham followed in his footsteps.

In the years that followed, Bingham returned several times to Peru, getting support from wealthy friends at Yale and *National Geographic Magazine* and following leads about a place called Huayna Picchu, which was rumoured to have superb ruins. As usual the locals had known it was there all along and were growing food on some of the Inca terraces. What he found under the jungle growth was a small town with temples, palaces and buildings of intricate stonework like the Temple of the Three Windows, a room 35 feet by 14 feet with three trapezoidal windows, the largest in Inca architecture. There were also hundreds more terraces fed by aqueducts built into the incredibly steep slopes. His spectacular piece in *National Geographic Magazine* (which included the magazine's first ever fold-out photographs) was published in 1913 and made him famous. He took another thirty-five years to publish his book, *Lost City of the Incas*, in which he made his findings support his premise that Machu Picchu was the 'last Inca capital' – the last before they finally succumbed to the Spanish. Their last refuge was actually Vilcabamba but Bingham didn't let this get in the way of his story. He said it was Machu Picchu simply because it was so dramatic. However, the discovery of further ruins throughout the region show that Machu Picchu was just one of a series of fortified sites along the Inca road, the Inca equivalent of a summer palace in a beautiful spot. Just like Hampton Court.

Gene Savoy found the true 'Last City', Vilcabamba, at Espíritu Pampa, 50 miles southwest of Machu Picchu, in 1964. Ironically Bingham had found a small Inca settlement in almost exactly the same place fifty years earlier but dismissed it because it wasn't big enough for the lost city of Vilcabamba he was searching for and stumbled on Machu Picchu instead. Savoy explored the jungle beyond Bingham's initial discovery and found out how large Espíritu Pampa really was. Other historians have since confirmed the site was the great last city of the Incas, the so-called Vilcabamba deep in the jungle where they retreated in their final days after the Spanish Conquest.

I wanted to climb Huayna Picchu, the pinnacle that dominates all photos of Machu Picchu, and see the sun both rise and set over the ruins. The easiest way was to stay at the Sanctuary Lodge just outside the entrance gate to the Machu Picchu site. I negotiated a discount and justified the expense because I would probably only be here once in my life. I could always regret it later. I wondered if my spending habits had anything to do with my money worries. Staying in the Lodge meant I could remain inside the ruins until 9 p.m. rather than 6 p.m. when everyone else had to leave and also get in at 6 a.m., before the first bus arrived at 7 a.m. Unfortunately, when I looked out my window at 5 a.m. mist covered everything. My dream of watching the sun rise over the ruins slipped back to bed.

Several people advised me not to climb Huayna Picchu in the wet. The path up the sheer 1,000 foot outcrop is very narrow and steep in places and can get really slippery. On one side of the main site the terraces drop precipitously over the edge before plunging 1,300 feet to the Urubamba River below. The hotel manager told me that five to ten tourists are severely injured or die every year at Machu Picchu, with most of the accidents happening on Huayna Picchu.

I signed the Huayna entrance book at 9 a.m. and set off. The path wound around the edge of a steep drop into the valley hundreds of feet below. My head spun as vertigo kicked in. The path plunged down about 100 feet across a narrow ridge before it climbed to the top. Now that I was here I could see how steep it was. Each step increased my anxiety. I only hiked for ten minutes before I gave up. I signed myself back in with the comment: 'Too scared'. My resolve had also been affected by the news that a French woman had disappeared at 6.30 p.m. the previous night. I met her three friends who were anxiously shouting out her name while a guard called for assistance on his radio. She was still missing the following morning.

The ingenuity of the Incas was extraordinary. There were several paths to Machu Picchu, one of which was defended by the Inca Bridge. Poles were laid across a twenty-foot gap which were removed for protection. But what a gap. The path was a natural cleft halfway up a vertical rock face several hundred feet high. I was glad the path to the Inca Bridge had collapsed just around the corner so I couldn't go any further. Only the previous week a Canadian birdwatcher had died when she was looking through binoculars at a rare bird and took a step backwards to get a better view.

I tried again at 6 a.m. the following morning but cloud covered everything. The weather changed so quickly. The previous day started cloudy, became sunny, cloudy again, sunny, light drizzle, pissing rain and a cloudless sunset. Four seasons in one day. This was, apparently, normal.

Sometimes when you've wanted to see something for so long the reality is a dull disappointment, but not here. I understood why Bingham proclaimed the ruins the Last City of the Inca. The site is simply spectacular. Huayna Picchu rises like a fortress lighthouse at one end of a long finger of rock, the saddle of Machu Picchu, around which the Urubamba River flows first one way, and then back down the other side. Every glance in every direction overwhelms your senses; views across the Urubamba valley to forests on the other side, down vertical cliffs to the river below and over the roofless buildings glowing in the sun.

Wandering through the ruins I could see, however, why Machu Picchu wasn't the last Inca stronghold. The water supply was too easily cut off, which is one of the reasons it was thought to have been abandoned. I reflected on how sad it was that the Incas, an advanced civilisation, were destroyed by Spanish greed and disease. The Incas worked gold, silver and platinum and were the first to vulcanise rubber. They discovered quinine was an antidote to malaria. They were aware of the dangers of radioactive elements and forbade the use of *aya kachi* (stones or salts of the dead), until they could be used safely. *Erythroxylon* (coca) was used by the Incas when Pizarro, their Spanish conqueror, arrived. However it was too important for the common Indians. It was only after the Spanish destroyed the Incas that they made it available to the masses and its abuse became common.

The population of the Inca Empire at the time of the Spanish conquest in 1532 is estimated to have been about twelve million. But during the first century of Spanish rule the Indian population declined by almost 80 per cent to just over two million – due to over-work, malnutrition, and the introduction of diseases like smallpox and measles. Peru's first accurate census in 1791 showed the impact of Hispanic dominance of the Incas: the population had further declined to just over one million. The population gradually increased after Independence in 1824, but it was not until the mid-1960s that the population of Peru recovered to its Incan height – more than three hundred years to replace the population lost in the first century of Spanish domination.

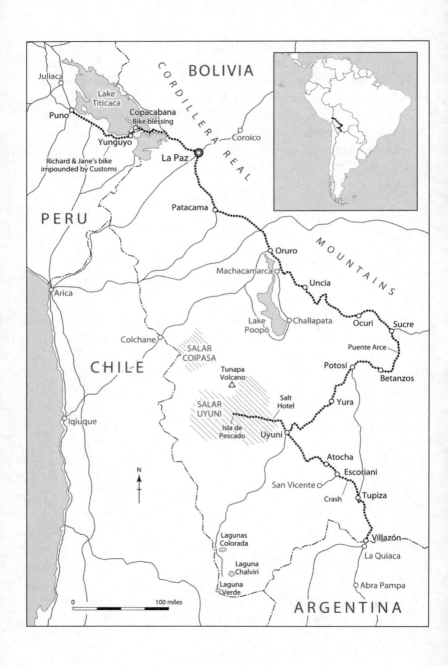

17

A BLESSING

'Welcome to Bolivia,' smiled the Customs officer as he handed back my bike's papers. 'We have all the best parts of the lake. We have the Titis while the Peruvians have all the Caca.'

Excited at being in a new country, I entered my age as '106' instead of my usual '102' in the large Immigration ledger. I never had any idea why this information was needed so always entered a daft date. No one had ever noticed.

Lake Titicaca glowed a deep blue and the thin grey line of the high Andes split the horizon. The most sacred lake in the Andes has had a mystical power for thousands of years. To the Incas it was closely bound up with their creation myth. Viracocha, the Sun God, sent the founders of the Inca dynasty, Manco Capac and Mama Huaca, to come to life on the Isla del Sol, an island in its waters. I weaved 20 miles around the shore below low hills to Copacabana. Whitewashed buildings and red roof tiles gave it a Mediterranean feel. A row of yellow pedalos lay on the beach. 'Batman 10' waited to go into action, while a clutch of white fishing boats bobbed at anchor. The slow holiday atmosphere made me want to stay a while. The moist air was a relief after the dry plains of the altiplano. Sounds of the town crept into my helmet. Music from a bar on the corner. The crunch of feet on the road, voices of passers-by. A dog barked and a child screamed. Cerro Calvario (Cavalry Hill) rose up beside the water like a small volcano and watched over the town.

A large cross on its summit was silhouetted against the clear sky. The government built fourteen smaller Stations of the Cross on the summit to enhance the town's tourist potential. Copacabana means 'Lookout of the Blue' in Quechua and the famous beach in Rio de Janeiro, Brazil is named after this one.

I settled into Hostal La Cúpula on the hill beneath Cerro Calvario. Tin roofs sparkled like glass around the rim of the Peruvian side of the lake before the sky turned orange. As I sat in the terraced garden looking out over the lake, enjoying the new-country buzz, Dave, an English backpacker, joined me for a beer. He had just done the Inca Trail and was nearing the end of his six-month trip. He was looking forward to getting home.

'Whatever you do don't drink the water in Bolivia,' he said. 'I thought I'd acclimatise more quickly but spent five days in hospital.'

'What happened?'

'I got typhoid.'

Just before going back inside Dave asked, 'What are you running away from?'

I didn't think I was running away from anything. I hoped I was running towards someone. I recalled the moment when a married friend with two young children was asked, 'When was the last time you were happy?' That one question made him realise he was miserable in his marriage and he started to turn his life around. I had indeed run away from life in London, which had quickly seemed boring after the constant excitement of my previous motorcycle trip. I was lonely now but life on the road was intoxicating. I was certainly running up an ever increasing mortgage. Was I also running to satiate a shallow need for speed?

Ricardo Rocco's advice popped into my mind: Get my bike blessed. Copacabana Cathedral ran a sideline in issuing special policies not available from one's local insurer. The *hostal* manager advised me to get to the cathedral for that day's two o'clock blessing as there would be a lot more people and much longer queues the following day, a Sunday.

'Don't forget the flowers, fireworks and champagne,' he added.

I rode through town, passing Quechua women in trilbies and blue shawls with bundles over their shoulders and a couple of men in panama hats. A black dog lay asleep in the middle of the road and a small boy tried to hit him with stones. Litter and potholes mingled in a side street. A poster on the corner of the square announced that Roy and the Gentiles were playing in the Coliseo next week. In the Plaza Dos de Febrero giant cacti with white trumpet flowers looked tiny against the massive bulk of the cathedral.

The cathedral was much too big for such a small town tucked away in a secluded bay of Lake Titicaca. Completed in 1619, it was built to house the vast numbers of pilgrims who came to see the four-foot-high black wooden sculpture of the Virgin Mary carved by Francisco Tito Yupanqui, a grandson of an Inca. Soon after the image was placed inside the cathedral miracles started to occur – such as people getting the house they'd prayed for – and Copacabana soon became a place of pilgrimage. The Virgen de Copacabana was made the patron saint of Bolivia.

My thoughts were more amused than spiritual as I parked in front of the cathedral. The *ch'alla* (ritual blessing) occurs throughout Bolivia but has been refined to an art form in Copacabana. Looking at all the tacky religious paraphernalia on sale at the crowd of stalls I thought only of the theatricality and regarded paying a church I had no faith in as the entry fee for a little fun. Not for one second did I imagine how significant this moment would turn out to be.

Wanting to participate, I bought some red plastic flowers and cheap firecrackers and then waited my turn in front of the priest in his brown cassock and blue hat. 'Nomine padre, nomine madre,' he intoned, sprinkling holy water over me and my bike. The sky was a brilliant clear blue and there wasn't a cloud in sight. It was a beautiful day for a blessing.

As I sat gazing over the waters of Lake Titicaca in the evening sun I couldn't stop smiling, for having my bike blessed had been exactly the right thing to do. I had acknowledged my bike's central role in my life. When I then decided to name my bike Fred, my father's nickname for me, another piece of the jigsaw fell into place.

My father committed suicide when I was a rebellious sixteen-year-old and away at boarding school. He hanged himself from a tree in the garden. All three of my sisters were living at home. I was so shocked by his death I cut him out completely, angry that he could have done such a thing. Calling my bike Fred was a way to bring him back, to right the wrong of shutting him out for all those years. Perhaps I wanted to share my adventure or show him what I was doing, show him the fun you could have by living for the moment, letting tomorrow take care of itself and not taking life too seriously. For Fred was my freedom. Freedom to travel where, when and how I wanted. Freedom to be who I wanted to be, unfettered by familial or societal pressures. Fred had become a best friend and a rock on whom I depended. Everything I did, everywhere I went and everyone I met I did because of him. Fred made me realise how much I missed my father.

Looking at my maps the following morning, I remembered another of Ricardo's tips: 'Get your Bolivian maps before you get there,' he'd told me. 'Theirs are terrible. Many of the roads don't exist and some of the towns are in the wrong place.'

I'd bought one anyway the day before in Copacabana but Ricardo was right. The roads were broad smooth lines with no indication of how they meandered, nor of elevation changes, distances between towns, minor roads or the relative sizes of the towns and villages. Apart from that it was perfect. Luckily I'd bought a better one in Quito.

So, where next? To the north were the High Andes, where the snow-capped Cordillera Real rose to over 19,500 feet and the Illampu hiking circuit sounded enticing. To the south lay Potosí, Sucre and the Salar Uyuni, a huge salt lake. Then again should I ride 'the world's most dangerous road' to Coroico into the Amazon? Dreaming, dawdling and debating the options with myself it happened again.

Barry Manilow's *Copacabana* blasted into my ears and Lola the show-girl, complete with yellow feathers and low-cut dress, pranced interminably through my mind's eye.

The chorus wouldn't stop. How embarrassing to even know the words.

I'd been vacillating about 'the world's most dangerous road' for quite a while. I wanted to do it for the thrill and the scenery. In only 30 miles it descended 13,000 feet from the dry altiplano through verdant valleys with ever steeper sides until it cut across sheer walls, through several waterfalls, to emerge in a tropical rainforest at Coroico. Why was it dangerous? It is a single-track dirt road with no crash barriers and drops of thousands of feet over the edge. The road is one of the main routes to the northeast and consequently it's used by cars, combis, buses and trucks. Eighty to ninety people die on it every year. The roadside is littered with memorials and shrines. Juan, whose house I'd stayed in in Valle, Mexico, had ridden the road a few years earlier.

'I was riding with a friend,' he told me, 'and I was in the front. There was a big drop on the right where I was supposed to be. The rule is that whichever driver is nearest the cliff passes on that side as he can make sure his wheels don't go over the edge. Bicycles and motorbikes don't count. We have to get out of the way. I went into yet another totally blind left-hand corner and a huge truck suddenly appeared, completely blocking the road. There was nowhere for me to go. My friend said "Goodbye, Juan" and thought I was going to die, either by going over the edge or by crashing into it head on. I was going too fast and didn't think I was going to make it either. But I saw a gap open up on the inside against the cliff. Without braking I just went for it. My friend thought I'd never get through with my panniers sticking out and that I'd be crushed against the wall. I have no idea how I got through. There were scrapes on both sides of my panniers and I never even noticed.'

You can even ride down it on a hired mountain bike. I'd heard of one cyclist who went over the edge and was saved by a tree growing out of the cliff. I wanted to do it for the thrill and to get into the Amazon again but couldn't make up my mind.

Bike journalist Dan Walsh would have been the perfect companion on the Coroico road. Part poet, part raving drunk, his writing was on a totally different level to the rest of the magazine. All his pieces were angst-ridden, emotional roller-coasters. I wasn't surprised his monthly columns took a week to write. Right now he was up against it. He asked if he could borrow my laptop as he had to file his copy the next morning or he'd get fired. He'd have to work through the night to get it finished in time. His bike was in a sorry state so I wondered how much care he would take of my property. He'd never actually owned a bike, they'd always come with the job.

I needn't have worried. He returned my laptop in perfect order and agreed that the world's most dangerous road would make a good next story. We would ride it together.

I knocked on his room the next morning. He was in bed and still pissed from the previous night. He wasn't going anywhere soon.

Half an hour out of Copacabana the road ended at the lake's edge and Barry Manilow's song started up again.

Bare hills rose on the other shore half a mile away. Terraces stacked up behind the brick-and-whitewash houses on the bank. The open barge listed across the Estrecho de Tiquina and looked nowhere near big enough for the blue coach it carried. The coach leaned heavily to the right and down at the front. I thought a coach's engine was always in the back so the barge should have been lower at that end not the other. After twenty minutes the barge returned empty and as I rode on to it the planks of wood moved. They were not fastened to anything, just laid on the barge's ribs. Once underway I started to feel queasy on the tiny waves. My plan to visit Antarctica didn't look good. How would I cope with Drake Passage, home to some of the roughest seas on the planet, if I couldn't cross a puddle like the Estrecho de Tiquina?

A few hours later I stopped at a junction above La Paz. The city filled a natural bowl hemmed in by mountains on all sides. A thick brown haze hung over the metropolis, which sprawled up the sides of the valley like old porridge. Should I go left towards danger and Coroico or right to Sucre and Potosí? What was I waiting for? Shouldn't I feel the fear and do it anyway? The Clash kicked in with 'Should I Stay Or Should I Go?' Gripped by indecisiveness, I stared at my map. Instantly I was back on my first trip in Syria, standing on the Damascus road trying to decide whether to head into the desert to Palmyra or beetle into the security and safety of Lebanon. Back then I'd chickened out and run into Lebanon. So ended my first attempt at riding from London to Cape Town after only three months on the road.

I chickened again. I had been lucky on the Chachapoyas–Celendín road so why tempt fate?

One night in La Paz was enough for me. I felt claustrophobic in the city centre. It was like a grimy high-rise Soho. Narrow streets with soot-covered buildings, crowded pavements and beggars. My hotel was an oasis of relief from the noise, pollution and millions of people crammed into a tiny space. I rode Fred into the foyer and parked beside a huge vase of dilapidated plastic flowers. I woke in the middle of the night with an urgent desire to get out. I left for Sucre at dawn.

My heart flew as I climbed out of the bowl and left La Paz behind. After four hours' riding, Lake Poopó was irresistible, though too far off to see. I wondered where all the Poopó came from. Probably from the petrol they used for fuel. It was shit. I'd just filled up with the lowest-rated petrol I'd ever seen: 85 octane. The lowest at home is 95. No wonder my bike ran so badly. Fred hardly accelerated at all and the altitude made it even worse. There was 30 per cent less oxygen here at 13,000 feet, but with the carburettor delivering the same amount of fuel as at sea level the engine ran very rich. It was like having the choke on all the time. The exhaust was really black from the unburnt fuel and my miles per gallon had plummeted.

Ten minutes later the liquid road rifled across the dry and dusty valley and merged into the sky. Nothing broke the emptiness. No trees or telegraph poles, only miles of bare rock and tufts of spiky grass. I enjoyed the complete lack of traffic and the warm sun on my face. Easy riding. What was that in the haze ahead? Another cyclist?

It was someone walking towards me, pushing something. Pushing a blue trolley in the middle of nowhere, miles from the nearest town. Ian was from the US and was walking from Ushuaia to Alaska, from the bottom of South America to the top of North America. He was wearing an 'Eco-Challenge: the Adventure Race' badge on his wide-brimmed hat. The sun was fierce at that altitude.

He had left Ushuaia carrying a backpack but found that it hurt his back and put a lot of strain on his knees and ankles. A three-wheeled trolley was less painful and could carry a lot of water.

Two bicycle wheels at the back and a small one at the front supported a flat platform and two plastic bins. A small blue pedal bin at the front contained food and cooking gear, a large green bin at the back held all his camping equipment and clothes, and four big bottles of water were strapped on the sides. He had everything he needed.

He averaged 26 miles on the flat with a longest day of 56 miles. Most cyclists I met averaged 50 to 60 miles a day and even in the steepest sections they could maintain a walking pace by using their gears. Ian walked everywhere all the time, but with neither brakes nor steering he couldn't freewheel down hills and had to physically hold the trolley back.

He had already been walking for nearly two years and hoped to get out of South America in another year. Lucid and eloquent, his drive and determination astounded me. I could never take so long to cover such featureless terrain. I'm too impatient. That's why I love biking. No one holds me up. I can go as fast as I like whenever I want. Adapting to a walking pace slows everything down. By walking, Ian had more time to observe and more time to think. I checked out Ian's website (ianwalk.com) when I got to Sucre and he sure can write. I hope he publishes a book.

After La Paz, Sucre was a joy. A spacious colonial city of wide tree-lined avenues and squares. Beautiful orange and pink churches, white colonnaded government buildings. Sucre is the judicial capital of Bolivia. Founded in 1539, it was renamed in 1840 to honour Antonio José de Sucre, a Venezuelan freedom fighter and Simón

Bolívar's most brilliant general. Sucre helped Bolívar – Bolivia's namesake – liberate New Grenada (modern-day Colombia, Panama, Venezuela and Ecuador), Peru and Bolivia from Spanish rule. As I stopped outside the university a well-dressed man in a grey suit approached me. Dionisio was a motorcyclist. We talked about my trip and what he did. He was the Secretary General of the university and he gave me his card.

'Let me know if I can help.'

The kindness shown by complete strangers never ceased to amaze me. I lost count of how often I received something for free. So many people refused to accept any payment or gift in return that I used my own international currency: biscuits. I met so many people every day I had to rely on instinct. If it didn't feel good I'd make excuses and go, but that almost never happened. Gary, the American I'd met in Cuzco, was the scariest person I met on my whole trip.

Trusting Eduardo to sell my bicycle in Valle had been my biggest mistake so far. The constant worry had taken the edge off my trip and I'd spent a lot of money on phone calls. The next day I called Mariano Gon at Santa Cruz Bicycles again.

'Eduardo said he now has the money and gave it to your friend Rosa as you asked.'

At last. All I had to do now was get Rosa to send it to me.

Every day on the road had a theme. Something I thought about while I rode. Across the US it was whether I'd get to the rally on time. In Mexico it was why was I on another trip so soon after the last one? Today it was whether to go down the mine in Potosí, and what route to take out of Bolivia: the high pass into Chile past the spectacular Lagunas Colorada and Verde or the lower road through Butch Cassidy and Sundance country into Argentina? It was difficult deciding where to go and what to see from the many options available. Choices now restricted future options. One thing at a time could ruin the big picture and wreak havoc with joining the dots. It was impossible to do them all. This was traveller's stress. While having lunch at a café the next day I noticed a German on the next table had a new version of my guidebook, so I asked if I could borrow it. While flicking through the early pages I noticed everything had been ticked.

'What do the ticks mean?'

'Those are the things I have seen.'

'But you have seen everything in the guidebook.'

'Ja, if someone has taken the trouble to find out all this information then I will see it.'

Ten miles out of Sucre a huge white sign urged me to use 'Fancesa's Portland Cemento'. Behind it sheltered a faded red pickup mounted with a white campervan body that extended over the windscreen. Its tiny windows made the body look more like a hen-house than somewhere for people to sleep. It looked so incongruous – an angular shoebox plopped on to the pickup's curved lines. The roof, windows and windscreen were covered in wire netting. Patches of rust and grey filler pockmarked the panels, but it wasn't going anywhere. The truck was bricked in up to the sills and the bonnet. Maybe it was an early Bolivian wheel clamp. Perhaps I should be careful where I parked my bike.

Soon I was on the altiplano again. My bike was not running well again and neither was I. Fred coughed and spluttered on the crap Bolivian petrol like an asthmatic miner. I wasn't enjoying Bolivia. I didn't like the food and I always seemed on the edge of the runs. I was going through the motions rather than enjoying every day. I looked forward to getting out of Bolivia and to getting lower.

Twenty minutes later I descended through dry hills of red stone into a small valley and crossed a wide dried-up riverbed. Green bushes dotted the river's edge like stubble. I stopped, stunned at the most beautiful bridge I'd ever seen: Puente Arce spanned the Pilcomayo River like a suspension bridge from Camelot. Twin crenellated towers of red stone stood surrounded by the blue flowers of a jacaranda tree. The cables drooped over the riverbed, supporting a bed of sun-bleached wooden planks barely wide enough for a handcart. All the planks listed to the left as if the cables had stretched more on that side and I expected two knights on white stallions with lances to ride across the bridge.

As I climbed a narrow pass after lunch, beyond the village of Betanzos, a fountain of black smoke belched from an ancient blue lorry crawling up the hill. I opened the throttle and pulled out to overtake but nothing happened. I yelled at Fred to get going but he just coughed and spluttered without accelerating at all. I had to give up, much to the amusement of the driver. He honked his horn and waved out of the window. My engine was misfiring so badly I thought it would cut out. This was not a good place to break down. It got seriously cold at night here. I begged the motor to keep going and by some brutal revving eventually managed to overtake the truck.

It was my fault. Bad planning. I should have brought smaller jets for the carburettor, but my initial research suggested my bike would be good at altitude even though it was set to run at sea level. Clearly my advisers hadn't ridden at 15,000 feet in Bolivia. When I filled up that night I'd had the worst consumption of my whole trip – 31 mpg instead of the usual 54 mpg.

At 13,400 feet, Potosí is the world's highest city. Remote, almost hidden in the Andes, it contains many beautiful colonial build-ings, some with balconies that hung over the pavement like giant window boxes. Looking for a hotel, I stopped in a back street to check my map. Bolivia is one of the poorest countries in South America. Kids in dirty clothes crowded round, eyes wide open at the gringo on his motorbike.

Potosí was founded in 1545 following the discovery of incred-ibly rich silver ore in the mountain that overlooks it. Silver from Cerro Rico (Rich Mountain) funded the Spanish economy and its monarchs' extravagance for two centuries. By the eighteenth century it had a population of 200,000 and was both the largest city in Latin America and one of the largest in the world. A volcano made of silver, it is riddled with ancient mine workings and is open to the public. A trip down the mine would require gifts of dynamite, coca leaves and cigarettes for the miners. Did I really want to spend four hours descending into 40°C heat and bad air while crouching in claustrophobic corridors to see someone at work? I decided to head straight for the wide-open spaces of the 4,000-square-mile Salar Uyuni salt lake instead.

It was a relief to be back on the road. The tarmac gave way to red dirt. Dry, dusty and devoid of life, but every so often a tree with purple flowers shone like a beacon. In another valley bright green willow trees marked the old course of the river which had meandered away. Four distant poplars hinted at a homestead. I crouched below my fairing to reduce the effect of the early-morning chill, which seeped through my jacket in the thin air, a permanent drain on morale and momentum like a leaking battery. As I crested a col hundreds of llamas dotted a wide plain below. A dust devil swept through. Half an hour later I rounded a corner into a wall of brown and black llamas on their way to join the others. The llamadess carried such a big bundle of sticks she was hard to see.

At last I rode on to the Salar Uyuni at 12,000 feet. About eleven thousand years ago Lake Tauca rose to 12,200 feet and lasted for a relatively short one thousand years. When it dried up it left two large puddles, lakes Poopó and Uru Uru, and two major salt pans, the salars of Uyuni and Coipasa. The salt was so blinding I put on my sunglasses. The surface was split into bizarre hexagonal shapes like crazy paving and the hard, abrasive salt crunched under my wheels. I stopped at a hole the size of a tray which was full of water. The salt is only six inches thick and floats on the water. It is thin but immensely strong and supports cars and coaches too.

There were no tracks to the Salt Hotel so I followed my GPS. A small bump appeared on the horizon, then grey walls and a roof of dried grass. The whole place was made of blocks of salt, like a rectangular igloo. No one else was staying there. I had a salt bed. The sitting room had a large salt table and salt benches. The manager and his wife looked miserable and their smiles were brief, but the pan pipe music on the radio was bright and happy and woke me up. Did they have a menu? No. It was sausages from a tin. One bite was enough and I was glad to survive. It was so cold at night I slept in my sleeping bag as well to stay warm. Breakfast. Would I like some sausages from a tin? Did they have eggs? Yes. Fried eggs were my staple start to the day. A good safe food. I had no idea what they did to them but they had a strange taste and made me feel slightly sick. Maybe it was just me. I wanted out of Bolivia.

The Isla del Pescado lay 40 miles west across the salt. The line of mountains on my right descended with each mile until it disappeared. Two colours today: white and blue. There was only the sound of my engine and the crazy-paved crunching under my wheels. The horizon curved. Were my eyes distorting reality or was the lake so big it followed the curvature of the earth? I accelerated, took my hands off the bars and stretched out my arms like wings. I stood up and flew through space in my Spitfire.

Where was the island? Time, distance and speed had no meaning. Time stopped but my wheels were turning. There was nothing but white and blue. At last a black blemish appeared and I relaxed. The black volcanic island was covered in saguaro cacti. I parked my bike and followed the path as it wound through fractured and frozen rock. It was like being back in the Galápagos Islands again. One cactus looked like it was juggling. All it needed was a sombrero. I felt my shortness of breath climbing the hill and another tourist, clearly on a mission, overtook me, sweat dripping off her nose. The island was surrounded by a white ocean. The air was cold but the heat reflected off the rocks like a barbecue. Black, white and blue. To the north Tunapa, a snow-crested volcano, rose out of the black rim. An ant crawled across the salt. It was a coach. Time to go.

Many others could soon be crawling over the salt, for Uyuni's brine contains more than half of the world's lithium. Lithium is used in mobile phone batteries and once electric cars become common demand will soar. However, Bolivia's socialist government is in no rush to extract the lithium, which history shows will only benefit foreign companies – just as happened with their gold, silver, tin, oil and gas.

That night in Uyuni I hesitated while thinking of my route into Chile, via the geysers and coloured lakes of Laguna Colorada and Verde. The Laguna Chalviri beckoned – a barren and surreal landscape of boiling mud holes and the stench of sulphur – but the 16,400-foot pass sealed my fate. Fred was running so badly at 14,000 feet I couldn't risk a breakdown up there on my own.

I wanted to get off the altiplano as soon as possible and head for Argentina. My spirits soared at the thought. The quickest way out was southeast through Villazón. By tomorrow I could be in the lowlands of Argentina, a formerly First World country with beautiful women, safe salads and the best meat in the world.

Back on my bike the next morning I was excited at leaving Bolivia and getting Fred running properly again. I used a seasonal shortcut, a road that was only open for six months of the year. For the other six months it was a river. At first I couldn't make out the embankments as Fred and I flowed across the plain, the smooth surface broken only by vehicle tracks, but soon the banks drew in and we rode into a canyon, a tube of brown rock in brilliant sunshine beneath the merest wisps of cloud. It was the strangest feeling. Like being a fish. In the far distance a peak kissed the belly of a cloud. Gradually the hills moved in and the river meandered more and more as it sidled up towards the mountains. My fear of a flash flood and sense of vulnerability increased as the banks grew higher and I rode deeper into the cleft. Soon I could see nothing but the canyon walls, a kaleidoscope of brown and red rocks, and my sense of dread rose.

A small stream wandered indecisively from side to side. Where had the water come from? How long ago had it fallen and where? How much rain did a flash flood need? Two feet of water would be enough. The cliff walls towered over my head. Small fry in a big pond. They had changed from smooth rounded rocks to jagged edges thrusting out of the ground at crazy angles. The power of the water was obvious from the high cliffs, gouges and overhangs on one side and the sandy beach on the other. Strange shapes and gashes in the bare rock perplexed me. All I could see were the orange and grey walls. How much warning would I get? Maybe 'flash' flood was right. Where was the exit? The cliffs were far too steep to climb. I rode a bit faster but then slowed again. I hadn't seen anyone on this road. I needed to concentrate and get to Villazón in one piece.

A flash of turquoise on the right bank gave an instant reprieve. The bank then disappeared around a corner. I followed the tyre tracks and sighed with relief as they led up the bank and on to a parallel road. A white wall enclosed hundreds of identical white boxes, like dog kennels with bell towers. Two cars were parked beside the gate. A Bolivian woman in a pink baseball cap held a young girl in her arms and walked through the gate. Atocha Cemetery. The hillside was covered in hundreds of graves tightly packed together, rising back up the hill over the uneven ground. All of them faced downhill with a 'steeple' at the back. A cross stood atop each steeple and many were draped in flowers made from old plastic bags. Atocha was a poor mining town. The tombs were all angular, functional concrete coffins. The richer families painted their tombs yellow.

This land of dusty canyons and mines was Butch Cassidy and the Sundance Kid country. In my head someone whistled the theme tune from *The Good, the Bad and the Ugly*. A fusillade of gunshots and suddenly it was all quiet again. Deathly quiet. They died in San Vicente, a tiny mining town 22 miles south of Atocha, after robbing a mining payroll and being identified when they strolled into a nearby village. As usual Hollywood distorted the truth. Apparently, rather than both dying in a hail of bullets, one of the outlaws got severely wounded and was then killed by the other outlaw, who then shot himself. Both were found dead the next morning.

I was soon back on the altiplano again. Welcome to the Empty Quarter. A lone line curled through miles of barren brown dirt. Clouds of dust rose in my wake and the wind carried them away. Dried scrub and small brown bushes like heather disappeared to the horizon. The edges of the single-track dirt road were deep red powder. I had to stay in the tracks. I'd fallen off Fred ten minutes earlier when I'd stopped for a photo and my foot had sunk up to my shin in the powder. I loved the way Fred's suspension soaked up the bumps. With one foot of suspension movement at each end, my bike could do more than I could dream of, even here at 14,000 feet. This is what my KTM Adventure was made for. I was having a ball on the corrugated surface and went a bit faster. I was a god. I could ride anywhere and over anything. Over a crest, distant hills with no names seesawed across the horizon. At one with Fred, I pulverised the dirt and pounded over the altiplano towards Villazón.

I loved being outside, the thrill of speed and of being on my own in the middle of nowhere. There was no hiding here. Adrenaline. I felt a surge of joy at being alive and laughed under my helmet. I was really good at this. I snatched another glance at the distant hills, where the ground haze merged into the clouds above, and felt dwarfed by the beauty of the landscape and the vastness of the world. It was all mine.

And then it wasn't.

Six inches off-line the handlebars snapped sideways but my steering damper held them back. I started to weave, and looked down. Fatal. I panicked and closed the throttle. Even worse. The back end bounced from side to side, the front wheel dug into the ridge and I flew over the bars. I lay still. Nothing hurt. I spat out a mouthful of dirt and got up to see who had been watching, but who could possibly live out here? Fred lay on his side with the rear wheel spinning. Petrol dribbled out of the filler cap. He was wounded. The tank had been pulled off a mounting and my neck was scratched from the sand.

I got out my tools to remove and refit the tank. While tightening the last bolts I suddenly realised I was not alone. A man and two women were watching me intently. Each had a brown blanket wrapped around their shoulders. The man looked bemused. Both the women were carrying large bundles on their backs. I greeted them and they me, with more stares. They accepted my offered biscuits with a nod.

My visor was covered in dirt so I poured some water over it. As the water ran into the ground I caught the horrified looks on their faces, stopped instantly and guiltily offered them the remains of the bottle. Their faces broke into smiles. How could anyone survive out here in the arid climate of the altiplano? The only signs of life were the dried grasses and thin scrub. It must be a harsh existence, constantly battling against the elements. No wonder they looked so appalled when a rich foreigner poured precious water into the ground just to clean his helmet. I shook their rough hands and waved goodbye. I was relieved both Fred and I were still in one piece. I loved Fred. He could do anything, even if I couldn't.

It was a defining moment. The warning was clear: confidence beyond my ability. The view had just been the trigger. From now on, whenever I hit an adrenaline peak or power surge or felt I was incredibly talented I must slow down immediately. I didn't care how many times I fell off when stationary or turning around. All I cared about was not falling off at speed. Had I learnt my lesson?

The graded road cut through sandy soil and thin tufts of grass. Small red buttes rose out of the ground and fallen debris fanned out like a miniature Monument Valley in Utah. I slalomed into the foothills between dried bushes. Everything was brown or red. I hadn't seen another vehicle since Atocha cemetery two hours earlier and was climbing once more. Another crest revealed another line of hills in the distance. I passed 14,000 feet again and 'The Only Way Is Up' popped into my head. I was done for again. Round and round it went. I couldn't stop it, but I didn't care. Soon I'd be off the altiplano and down in Argentina.

I am a long-distance rider. This is my job. This is what I do. Every day I wake up somewhere new, get on Fred and ride. The former loneliness of the long-distance rider has gone. I am no longer alone, because Fred is here. The spirit of my father is here. Michael's words on the last evening in the Galápagos Islands drift back to me. 'Be happy on your own lawn,' he'd said. I am happy now.

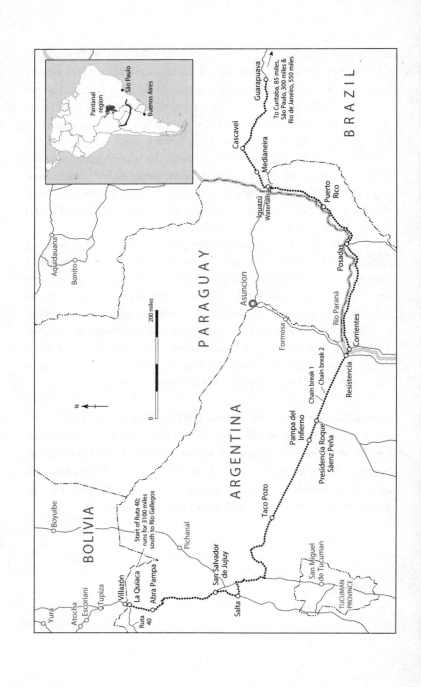

18

Trouble with Fred

The streets of Villazón thronged with so many people it had to be market day. Quechua women in panama hats pushed wheelbarrows past battered pickups lining both sides of the road. One woman in a bright red dress carrying a heavy bundle slung across her back waddled across the street right in front of me without a glance. I threaded my way past the people walking in the road.

My guidebook said that this was a major smuggling route tolerated by both the Bolivian and the Argentinian governments and that I should just go to the front of any queues. A bridge over a river linked the two countries. I squeezed my bike between two overloaded handcarts. It felt like a carnival but the bridge was deserted and blocked by a row of bicycles. Beyond that lay a mound of ashes and another row of bicycles. It looked like a meeting of French farmers.

What was going on?

'Está cerrado.' The border was closed.

Bolivian lorry drivers had barricaded the border in protest at recent fuel price increases. Even worse, they had closed the two other crossings into Argentina as well. No vehicles had entered or left Argentina for five days. I looked at my map. My next stop was to be the spectacular waterfalls of Iguazú, 750 crow-miles east where Paraguay, Brazil and Argentina met. My alternative options would be either to return to Uyuni and do the 16,400-foot pass into Chile I'd just rejected, or to ride north and east across the whole of Paraguay. The Paraguayan route was the shortest: 1,200 miles north to Boyuibe, Bolivia, and across Paraguay to Iguazú – probably four to five days. My original route was two days straight across the Argentinian pampas. I was so frustrated at being so close but so far from all that Argentina had come to represent – fabulous food, warm lowlands, trees and a European lifestyle. I salivated at the thought of lamb chops, steaks washed down with a Sauvignon Blanc hinting of gooseberries and summer fruits.

I wanted to shout at someone. The fuel price hike was nothing to do with me so why should I be affected? But if I had learnt anything on my trip so far it was that patience pays. Friendliness and smiles cost nothing. Smile a lot, be polite, get them laughing at my appalling Spanish and then ask for help. Whenever I'd seen tourists getting angry, it had got them nowhere but one beat nearer CPR. Although the language barrier made it more frustrating, it could work in my favour as a guest in their country. I decided to ask the Chief of Customs for advice on the best route into Argentina. I'd see how it went over a couple of hours and consoled myself that no matter how bad it seemed something good always happened. I'd never been to Paraguay.

The Customs Chief's door was padlocked. I found him in the Police Chief's office. He smiled and invited me to sit down. He had a kind, patient face, grey hair and large smiley brown eyes. We exchanged pleasantries before getting down to business.

'Are they letting tourists across?'

'Si, but you have a moto. All the other tourists have been walking across.'

'Who can I ask to let me through?'

'First see if they let you walk across.'

I thanked him for his help and inched my way on foot through the crowd whose boxes and bundles formed an assault course to the tractor tyre which prevented anyone crossing. I smiled at the man holding it and, as I approached, he wheeled it out of the way. I squeezed through and on to the bridge. I returned a few minutes later and the Chief of Customs pointed out the lorry driver's leader.

The leader's HQ was a rusty Formica table surrounded by locals attempting to do deals.

Trying to keep calm, I asked if I could take my moto into Argentina. He looked me up and down. A 1,200-mile five-day trip teetered on the edge. An extra week of petrol, hotels and food hung on a nod or shake of his head. I yearned to get into paradise over the bridge.

He nodded. I smiled and thanked him profusely. All I had to do now was run the gauntlet of the crowd on my bike.

I asked him if could I ride down his side of the bridge, as the pavement was wider and had a lot fewer people. He didn't even reply. Just waved his hand pointing to the other side of the bridge. I didn't argue. I wanted to get it over with as soon as possible. I asked the Customs Chief to cancel my temporary bike import permit.

'I will wait until you are across the bridge,' he said.

I walked over to the other side and traced out my route. There were only 20 yards of pavement to get through but there were hundreds of people jammed together, standing beside their possessions. I'd have to go very slowly but the noise of my bike might help clear a path. I moved two handcarts out of the way so I could ride up on to the pavement. As soon as I started Fred a crowd folded in behind us and cheered us on. A carnival atmosphere developed from nowhere. Were we going to be the first vehicle across in five days?

People yelled and whistled as I edged through the crowds. I had hoped to slip through unnoticed. I dreaded hearing a big shout as the boss changed his mind. Fred created a path through the sea of people, which opened like a time tunnel. There was some jostling from behind but the pressure from his exhaust kept them away. Realising the atmosphere could change very quickly if something went wrong I inched forwards and smiled at everyone. Ten feet from the tyre barrier a small man with greasy black hair and a crazed look in his eyes suddenly jumped in front of us.

'No, no, no,' he shouted, waving his arms.

Fred's wheel filled the gap between his legs. The man swayed from side to side. He was so drunk he could hardly stay upright.

Hands reached across to pull him away but he furiously threw them off and started to push Fred backwards. Spittle flew out of his mouth as he ranted. I braked but felt the crowd pushing us forward from behind. A quick blip of the throttle gave me some space. The crazy blocked the narrow pavement. The tyre man had already pulled the tractor tyre away but there wasn't enough space to go around him.

If I forced my way through and hurt him it'd be a Bolivian cell for me. Suddenly the Customs Chief wrapped his arms around the guy, picked him up in a bear hug and held him against the railings. I moved forwards, closer and closer to the tyre, but couldn't get through. The gap wasn't wide enough. Then I went backwards. The crazy had broken free and was pulling my bike back. I was so close to freedom. I piled on the revs and let the clutch out a little more. The powerful exhaust hit him square in the face. The crowd stepped back at the noise. I mustn't hurt anyone. It could get ugly very quickly. Somebody shoved the tyre out of the way. I edged forward and Fred accelerated. The Customs Chief had the crazy again. A huge cheer erupted as I slipped through the gap. I punched the air as I rode over the bridge.

Was this Italy? The border guards sat around chatting or sleeping in their Raybans, sharp creases and highly polished black boots. The Customs officer laughed and just shook his head at the chaos over the bridge.

'You are lucky.'

I cruised down the border road into La Quiaca, filled up at the first petrol station and let the smiling owner relieve me of my last Bolivianos. He gave me an appalling rate, but I didn't care, I was so happy to be in Argentina. A culture shock of a different kind. He had a working electronic cash register. The fuel pumps were digital and worked too. Rows of biscuits and bars of chocolate lined the shelves.

The next country always promises something more and something new. I was so glad to get out of Bolivia and never worried about what Argentina would be like. The shops were full even though the country was just emerging from economic meltdown.

> *Food, glorious food!*
> *Hot sausage and mustard!*

There was only one way to turn Oliver off.

My first steak and salad. I savoured every mouthful like a reprieved prisoner. I never got used to Bolivian cooking and knew I'd love Argentinian cuisine. My time in Bolivia had made me appreciate what I took for granted. I met so many people who had nothing yet gladly helped a complete stranger, refusing any offer of reward, even a biscuit. I wondered how much that would change now I was in a First World country.

The difference in living standards was stark. The streets were much wider and more spacious. Returning to super-smooth metalled roads was a delight. I went faster. The buildings were a familiar European design, far more neatly arranged and in much better condition than anything in Bolivia. The electricity and phone wires didn't droop between strangely angled poles but were taut and business-like. My shoulders dropped as the weight slid away. But there were many boarded-up shops, clear reminders that the good times had gone. A legacy of the economic collapse in 2002. Argentina had boomed in the mid-nineties and Buenos Aires became the jewel of South America. Living standards were high and everything was possible. Then a combination of Italian financial skills, greed and corruption bankrupted the country.

Ruta 9 rolled south to Salta via the Quebrada de Humahuaca, an ancient trade route which the Incas had incorporated into their *Qhapaq Ñan*, the main Inca 'highway' that stretched 3,400 miles from Quito, Ecuador, in the north to Mendoza, 600 miles south of Salta. The Quebrada valley, which follows the *Río Grande,* descended through hills of twisted strata whose bands of red, pink, orange and green rock writhed across the surface like huge Loch Ness Monsters.

I loved going down. It got warmer with every inch. I removed my down jacket and changed to summer gloves. My first tree filled my heart with joy. More and larger trees appeared beside the road and in fields. Grass. Everything became lusher until the altiplano was behind me. Green fields full of cows. I stopped beside pens containing hundreds of cattle. Birds swooped through clouds of flies around cows that were farting their way through another day. I took my sweater off and didn't use it again for two months. The warmth was delicious. Moisture hung in the air like a warm bath. I was smiling and so happy to be off the Andes and down in the lowlands. This was Eden compared to the desert dryness, barren rocks and tree-less moonscapes of the altiplano.

In a celebration of trees I stayed on the old Ruta 9 and took the direct but slow road south from Jujuy to Salta towards the only clouds in the sky. The narrow road meandered up the hillside, weaving its way through the indigenous forest. It started to rain. Bliss. My first rain since I'd left Quito late and had ridden through the fog to Cuenca, Ecuador – five months ago. I rode more slowly, wanting it to last, revelling in the smell of wet leaves and rain on the hot tar. I wasn't bothered when it started to rain much harder. I stopped on a corner and photographed Fred against a backdrop of grey clouds and green fields that reminded me of home. I savoured every second through the forest. I felt like crying. The rain ebbed away and the sky cleared as I rode over the pass, bathing in the warmth and sunshine, almost drunk as I descended into Salta.

The colonial city of Salta is a wonderfully mild 3,500 feet above sea level. The pink and white cathedral resembled a large strawberry fruit fool and the thickness and warmth of the air felt like I was bathing in one after the dry and dusty altiplano. I checked in to the Hotel de Virrey and soon found myself falling in love again – with lamb chops and mashed potato. The meat melted on my tongue and the smooth buttery delight made me smile. I could have bathed in that too. Nothing moves the heart more than the realisation of how much you've missed something.

Mike Rutherford's 'Living Years' played in my hotel and made me think of my father.

I know that I'm a prisoner
To all my father held so dear
I know that I'm a hostage
To all his hopes and fears
I just wish I could have told him in the living years.

I thought of what a sporting disappointment I must have been to him. He loved sport and had played rugby for Rosslyn Park as a fly-half and cricket for Surrey as a schoolboy. He built a cricket net in the garden and would bowl to me, for hours on end, but I never liked the game and gave it up as soon as I could. I wished I had known then what I knew now and I wished I had known him.

Salta's magnificent buildings and churches were perfectly preserved, but they had been built on foundations of slaughter and slavery. After the Diaguita rebellion in 1657 the Spanish governor of nearby Tucumán cleared the Calchaquí valleys, taking five thousand prisoners and sending the remaining eleven thousand as 'gifts' to Spanish settlers. These included the Quilmes, a fiercely independent people who had resisted the Spanish (and the Incas before them); in revenge the Spanish made the Quilmes walk 600 miles to a remote area near Buenos Aires. Their numbers were decimated by the forced march, hunger and their treatment in Buenos Aires, so much so that they were considered extinct when the first Argentinean government formed in 1812. Their area of Buenos Aires eventually became the municipality of Quilmes, where the famous brewery of the same name was founded. So if you should ever drink a Quilmes beer, by far the most popular in Argentina, spare a thought for their ancestors.

I didn't want to hang around such tarnished splendour and was eager to move on to Iguazú Falls. It would be an easy two-day ride, via a stop in Resistencia 550 miles away.

Every day started the same. An eager excitement to get going, to beat my record and ride away within an hour of waking, followed by 'Can I find the right road out of town?' A spike of joy when I hit the open road and my soul would seep out to the horizon. Idle thoughts and time to think. What would the day bring? I had to try and remember the things I wanted to see and do before I'd gone past them. And also keep an eye on my GPS to make sure I was always going in the right direction – even if it wasn't the right road.

I would enter the distance to my destination into my IMO trip computer, and wait to be told what time I'd arrive if I didn't stop en route. It was always a downer to see how long it would take just to reach the halfway point. Those negative waves would lap around my feet all morning. The tide would turn as I passed the magic mid point, bringing a ray of sunshine. On a long day lunch was biscuits or nothing at all, depending on supplies. The lowest ebb always came in the middle of the afternoon, the time in the doldrums, the price of what was to come. At some strange magical moment the tide turned again, always with about an hour to go. The end was in sight. The floodwaters propelled me on, the adrenaline kicked in and my speed increased. From then on I loved every second, senses on overdrive, concentration at a peak, constant scanning, reading the road and plotting my course, more graceful arcs through calmer seas. Suddenly there would be only ten miles to go. I'd slow as more people appeared and the traffic increased. I'd stop at the first petrol station, fill up ready for the next day and browse through the guidebook for a city map and a hotel with secure parking for Fred. My routine never changed. This was what I did. This was my job.

My map showed the road from Taco Pozo to Resistencia was dead straight for 300 miles. Perhaps I could swerve from side to side to relieve the boredom? Scrubby bush gave way to ever greener fields and more cattle country. It was completely flat: the Pampas. Two rows of electricity pylons marched beside the road. One was V-shaped and the other a more British style narrow pyramid. The top half of all the pyramid pylons had collapsed and fallen over. Many propped themselves up with their arms and looked drunk. The cables were missing.

Perhaps they were never strung. Had the economic downturn come to this or was it sabotage?

As the tide turned at halfway I felt a slight vibration beneath me and continued up through the gears, changing into top as I passed a Shell station. Another vibration and Fred's engine raced. I pulled the clutch in and coasted to halt. His chain had fallen off again. It lay in the road some distance behind me. A bloke on a moped appeared from nowhere.

'Hello, can I help?' he said in perfect English.

'Buenos días. My chain is there,' I said, pointing back at it. He zoomed off and returned, smiling and holding my hot chain. He pointed back to the Shell garage.

'They will help you.'

I thanked him again and he buzzed away before I could speak again, waving goodbye over his shoulder.

The master link, which joined the two ends of the chain together, was missing. A small circlip held the outside plate on. Eventually it wears too much, falls off and the chain breaks. Suddenly it dawned on me that I'd never replaced the chain after it was welded near Cotopaxi in Ecuador five months earlier. I was so happy it hadn't broken in the wilds of Bolivia.

The manager of the Shell station directed me to a local welder a few hundred yards away. Jorge stopped working on his engine rebuild to help me and introduced me to his daughter, Belen.

Using some of my spare links he welded another plate on. He wouldn't let me give him any money. Not even ten pesos for a beer. I thought the engine was noisier but dismissed it as my normal paranoia and was soon back up to speed and into my normal rhythm. Even though the land was totally flat and the road dead straight I basked in the green scenery. With only an hour of daylight left, I wouldn't make Resistencia before dark. Just as dusk fell, I felt another slight vibration and stupidly carried on at my normal speed.

A minute later the chain broke again. The last village was several miles behind me and there was none in sight. In the gloom I stood on the side of the road with my thumb out, holding the chain in my other hand. The road was busy but no one stopped to help. I knew someone would stop eventually but it might be tomorrow. Would you stop for a biker in the dark? I sent out waves of positive stopping vibes but they didn't work. I was glad I hadn't sent my tent or sleeping bag home even though I hadn't used them since leaving the US.

A car flashed and braked as it went past. I ran after it but it accelerated away. If no one stopped soon I'd push Fred to the fence 50 yards away and pitch my tent nearby. The grass sloped down from the road so it would be easy.

It was pitch dark now. I sat on the ground away from the road trying not to think of sleepy drivers crashing into Fred and ending my trip. Flashing orange lights brought me back as a breakdown truck stopped by my bike – the free breakdown service financed by road tolls. I was so happy to be in Argentina. I showed him Fred's chain. He suggested shortening it and then joining it again without a master link by hammering one of the pins in. Brilliant. He would find a tool to remove two links.

My spirits plummeted the instant he drove off and left me in the dark. He had taken Fred's chain. If he didn't return I was totally buggered. Why had I let him go? It had all happened so quickly but had seemed so sensible. This is not Transylvania. Just chill and relax. What use is a knackered chain to him? He's just trying to help. Things are always so much worse at night. He reappeared twenty minutes later but the chain was too short. He towed me back to the last town. It was half past ten and still hot.

As we pulled off the main road we met the local police, two up on a Honda 125. The pillion carried a repeating shotgun. They rode off to find a bike mechanic. A few minutes later we set off again and followed them to Juan's shop, which was still open. Hernán and Daniel were leaning against the open window drinking beers. Juan's wooden shed was crammed full with second-hand motorcycle parts. He brought out a box of old chains and found one with the right pitch. He wouldn't keep the change. I offered again. No.

'Please accept it for beers and thanks.' He smiled and accepted.

Would I make it to Resistencia, 75 miles away?

'Yes, if you don't stress the chain and only go slowly, no more than 60 mph.'

I kept to 50 mph.

I missed Resistencia in the dark. I only realised when I was on the two-mile-long bridge over the Rio Paraná, the second longest river in South America. Fred and I limped into the outskirts of Corrientes but another 'click' on the first roundabout started the vibration again. I would stay at the first hotel I found, no matter how many stars it had. What joy to break down in Argentina. The signs were lit at night! I turned in at a neon 'Hotel' sign opposite a Shell station, down a drive lined with tall bushes. An attendant waved me through the entrance gate straight into Room 9's parking space. The moment I stopped he closed the long curtains behind me. I looked at Fred's chain. One of the side plates had come loose. Lady Luck again. But why the closed curtain?

How long did I want to stay? One night. He looked surprised. The television pumped mindless music. I went to turn it off but stopped dead in my tracks. Two very pretty women were sitting on a stud and wobbling about. The loud music almost drowned out the moans and groans. I could unload my bike later. But the novelty soon wore off so I changed channel. There was only one. It was sex, sex or sex. It was 1 a.m. on a Sunday. Didn't Catholics have rules about this sort of thing?

I had checked in to a Love Hotel. One-storey buildings on the edge of town designed to allow you to arrive and depart as inconspicuously as possible. Most guests paid by the hour. The sheets were clean and the water hot, but they had the smallest towels. I couldn't turn the TV off so pulled the plug out. A strange piece of equipment sat in the corner of the room. It looked like something in a fitness centre which only the really cool dudes knew how to use. Luckily the instructions screwed to the wall showed what to do: photographs of the four basic positions and two for the advanced class.

I phoned round the next morning and was delighted to find the right chain. Immediately I started Fred up I knew something was very wrong. This was not my normal paranoia. His engine sounded terrible. A harsh metallic clatter sounded like the tappets. A quick check revealed the inlet gaps had grown enormously in only two days. Normally they never changed in thousands of miles.

Suddenly the chain was the least of my worries. I needed a good KTM mechanic with a good supply of parts. There was no KTM dealer here and, even if there were, I'd probably spend weeks hanging around waiting for parts to arrive. I knew that if the country importer didn't have them in stock they could take two weeks to arrive. I crawled along, expecting the chain to snap at any moment. The first bike shop I found had no new parts at all and gave me directions to another nearby. It's always easy to find something if you know where it is. I wished I hadn't worn my motocross boots as if the chain snapped I'd have a lot of pushing to do. Three motorbikes parked on the street raised my hopes. A yellow 'Moto' sign and three friendly faces inside. Smiling, Ernesto, the owner, handed me a new chain. My heart sank. It looked too small.

'The size is the same but it is for a small bike so will only last 625 miles.'

Fred needed a hospital. He needed surgery. Would Ernesto recommend the KTM importer in Buenos Aires or São Paulo in Brazil? The two guys behind the counter debated a bit and two customers joined in. After a few minutes the consensus was 'São Paulo. São Paulo is very big.'

I called both importers. The advice was good. Even though the São Paulo importer was twice as far away he had much more stock. Would the chain last the 1,200 miles? Was this another sign? I'd always wanted to visit Brazil and now I could add Rio de Janeiro and the Pantanal – a vast floodplain the size of England and Scotland – on the way back.

Even better, my route went past Iguazú Falls. The coaches were a big giveaway that I was back on the tourist trail. From nothing but

230

a few trucks and cars, tourist buses came thick and fast. The Falls are close to where the River Iguazú joins the Paraná, and where Paraguay, Argentina and Brazil meet. At 270 feet high and nearly two miles wide they are three times the width of Niagara and much wider than Victoria Falls. The river plunges over the edge of a crescent, the aptly named Garganta del Diablo, the Devil's Throat, and thunders on to the rocks below. Hundreds of great dusky swifts zipped through the spray beneath me and disappeared into the cliffs. I leant over the railings to get a better view but it was hopeless in the oceans of spray.

A row of six swifts fought for position on a tiny bank of bright green moss inches from the chasm. They all faced upstream and jostled and twitched in the communal shower. The Falls were less tall and less concentrated than Victoria Falls but much lusher and greener. It seemed a huge waste of energy to let so much water fall in exchange for only photos. I was reminded of a biking couple I'd heard about. They took photos of themselves at every place on their must-see list holding a big white card with a big black tick on it.

Iguazú is on the Brazilian border. You can see the Falls from both sides, so getting into Brazil was easy. I felt fine going north when I'd planned to go south. Change was my only constant. The only things that didn't change were the changes themselves. Nothing stayed the same for long: people, places, sights, smells and sounds. I loved the unexpected. There was no familiarity. Everything was always different. I woke in a new town every day. The exception was Fred, my companion and friend, but now he was unwell I felt vulnerable. He was my freedom. He was my guide. Now I understood why people gave their bikes, bicycles and cars names. I relied on him to take me wherever I wanted. I was amazed at my luck that the engine problem happened in Argentina and not Bolivia. I could have been stranded there for months.

The same lucky vein ran through my route planning. I wanted to go to Ushuaia, the southernmost point of South America, but wasn't really sure. It was a long way to go just to be able to say 'Been there, done that'. My route was so flexible I didn't know where I was going on a daily basis. I had a running joke with Richard and Jane, the Brits I'd met in Quito, that my plans were pointless as they never materialised. My intentions were ephemeral and no indication of what I might actually do. Suddenly finding myself going north instead of south got me excited and looking forward to seeing places and things I would never otherwise have seen.

I left Guarapuava on the BR 373 to Curitiba, just the sort of road that's much more fun for two. Beautiful curves swayed gently from side to side down a tree-lined river valley. I imagined feeling the warmth of a girl's thighs behind me; but I was alone. I used the whole width of the road, carving an arc that sliced through the double white lines and kissed the apex. Perfect precision. Soft and sensuous. I was riding the euphoric wave of being in yet another new country. One final bend before the straight beside the river.

Someone stepped into the road ahead with his hand up. His police car was hidden behind a bank.

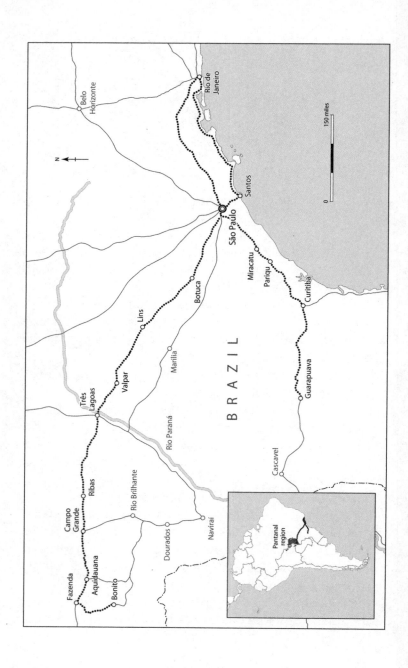

19

FEET NIBBLERS

I couldn't understand a word the policeman said. After a year of speaking Spanish my linguistic brain was locked out. His English was almost non-existent and I had no Portuguese. I had only been in Brazil for a few hours and was in the midst of my new-country ecstasy. It wasn't fair. It was only a little line on the road. I showed him my driving licence, my laminated colour photocopy. I couldn't care if he ate it.

'You cross the line. $100 fine. You pay reals.' He pointed back the way I had come. '30 miles.'

Here we were again. I slipped into 'all the time in the world' mode, kept smiling and kept the friendly but broken banter going even though I was annoyed. A truck hooted as it went past. I explained I didn't have any money at all and it was my first day in Brazil. It was a beautiful country and I was on my way to Curitaba.

'I am the nice one. My boss she not nice.'

He pointed to his shades-wearing female partner lurking behind the car. She walked slowly to show off her boots. They were polished a brilliant black. *CHiPs* (the 1970s US TV show about two motorcycle cops in the California Highway Patrol) was still popular here too.

'There is a cheaper way.'

I repeated I had no money, had only just come into the country and was going to get some cash in Curitaba. I hoped he didn't ask to see my wallet, which bulged with Brazilian reals. A few minutes later a car drove past honking madly as it straddled the double white lines but he didn't even look up. My resolve hardened as I recalled Peter Forwood's sage advice yet again. Never admit any error and waste as much of their time as possible. I carried on smiling, being frightfully pleasant and continually repeating that I had no money. I offered him a biscuit.

He nodded a 'Thank you' and helped himself.

'That is $500.'

He laughed. If I hadn't sent my cooking stuff home from Valle I could have brewed up a cup of tea to pass the time. Another car hooted as it crossed the lines. He sighed. After twenty minutes he handed me my licence and bade me farewell.

'Slowly!'

Two days later, the engine noisier than ever, Fred and I rattled into São Paulo, one of the largest cities in the world. It was even bigger than I'd feared. Like Mexico City, its population exceeds 20 million. London's is a paltry 12 million. Waldyr Siqueira, the owner of the KTM importer, advised me to find a hotel in Pinheiros, quite close to the shop. Luckily Waldyr's English was perfect as I still couldn't understand a word of Portuguese. My brain was lost in no man's land. My ears hadn't adjusted at all. The writing might well be very similar to Spanish but the pronunciation was completely different.

My hotel bathroom had two shower heads. One in the shower cubicle, and another at waist height between the basin and the loo, just underneath the hairdryer. Ah, it was for washing my hair. I noticed an on/off switch on the back. Or maybe it was for my feet? Its true function only dawned on me while sitting on the loo after breakfast the next day. It was for washing your bum. Too hot and it singed your balls, too cold wasn't so great either. Get it right and it was wonderful and totally eco-friendly – no trees required. It was so efficient I resolved to install one at home.

Fred was soon diagnosed with a failed inlet cam follower bearing and a slightly worn piston. Should I replace the piston? The engine had been professionally balanced and rebuilt by Swampy at home when it was new. If I replaced the piston it would probably be a different weight, so the engine would vibrate more. If the difference was significant the vibrations could get a lot worse. Memories of not being able to hold my teeth together because my first 640 Adventure vibrated so much sprang to mind. But then again the tyres hadn't lasted anywhere near their normal lifespan. Riding for several hours a day on a laden bike must greatly accelerate wear rates. It made sense to change things before they went wrong rather than wait for them to fail in the middle of nowhere. I decided to try preventive maintenance and hope the piston weighed the same as the old one.

While Waldyr's mechanic, Fabricio, fixed the engine I looked for other faults. The rear wheel rim was caked in dirt and oil from my automatic chain oiler. I noticed a large dent in the rim I hadn't seen before and then a crack in the rim beside one of the spokes. I cleaned the wheel and found another eight cracks, including one five-inch one that linked two spokes. The non-KTM wheel builder had relaced my wheel too tightly in Ecuador six months earlier.

'The KTM spokes are much thicker than normal ones so the wheel builder makes them too tight. We have seen this before,' said Waldyr.

Maybe the blessing in Copacabana had worked and prevented me from having an accident? Fabricio found a new smuggled rim at a discount and two days later Fred was ready to go. He needed a gentle 600 miles to run in the new piston, or about the distance to Rio de Janeiro and back.

Still chasing bicycle money, I called Rosa from my hotel the night before I left. Eduardo had given her $2,900, which she promised to send me. I could hardly believe it after all this time. I offered her $300 and asked her to send me the rest by Western Union. She refused to keep any of it and said she'd send it all to me.

'I will send you the money tomorrow. You will have it in two days.'

I woke in the middle of the night. A knock at the door? I ignored it. Maybe it wasn't my door. More knocks. Maybe it was another prostitute offering a special 3 a.m. rate. I wrapped a towel round my waist just in case. Instead of a beautiful buxom Brazilian I found a middle-aged man in a grey suit.

'Pardon, but are you using your telephone?'

I was taken aback by the question. He wasn't what I'd been hoping for.

'I am very sorry but your phone is not on the hook properly. I am very sorry.'

It looked fine to me, maybe he'd got the wrong room. I moved the handset and it slipped back into place. I had called Rosa's mobile in Mexico. It had been off the hook for seven hours.

'I am very sorry,' he said.

A ten-minute call to an English landline was $20. Mobiles always cost more. There was nothing I could do now. Trying to get the cost reduced with the night staff would be a waste of time. Negotiations on the hotel's huge mark-up would have to wait for the morning. I didn't sleep very well. How ironic to have blown my bicycle money on a phantom phone call. After breakfast I nervously asked the concierge what the cost of the call was, steeling myself for a little discussion. He entered my room number. The last entry was 1,650. At three reals to a dollar the call was $550. How much time did I spend on the call? I explained I'd been calling the same friend in Mexico but they were never there so I left a message. The previous three entries showed one-minute calls to the same number. We hadn't spoken for long, maybe three minutes.

'OK, we will charge you for three minutes.'

He swapped the 1,650 reals for 9. I was dumbfounded and thanked him. I'd just saved $547. Now I could spend $540 on something else and still be ahead.

I took the coastal road from Santos to Rio de Janeiro. Weaving around the coastline, I slipped from one bay to the next, the sea lapping at the sandy crescents and small fishing boats sitting fat in the water, waiting for action. Islands floated offshore and white houses with

238

terracotta tiles hid under the tropical trees and heavy haze. Even the locals sat under beach umbrellas.

The road was noticeably quieter at lunchtime. I came up behind a lone blue Toyota almost in the middle of the road. One man taking up all that space. One man hunting in his Messerschmitt. He never saw me coming out of the sun. In World War II British pilots were told not to stare at the pilot of the enemy aircraft but at a piece of the fuselage instead, in case he felt their stare and took evasive action.

Knowing that you're being stared at is a sixth sense, an intuition. That sense of imminent danger saved the famous British lion hunter Jim Corbett on many occasions. Animals have the same gift. It is better for birders, film-makers and hunters to think of anything but their prime purpose for the game can sense their intentions. I once met a professional photographer in Africa who'd spent days trying to photograph one particular bird. Eventually he gave up and went for a walk with no binoculars or camera, only to see the elusive birds all over the place.

Distance is no barrier. Sir Laurens van der Post relates how the Bushmen of the Kalahari (the San) could communicate over large distances just by thinking. Their range was far beyond sight or hearing. They could arrange a group meeting of several clans and they would all arrive at the same place at the same time. This sixth sense sends out a signal that is 'heard' by others. Rosa must have picked up my sadness when I abandoned my trip in Mexico.

Rio was a nightmare. Elevated motorways with many turnoffs to unrecognisable places snaked through favelas, past tower blocks and up steep slopes. The city sprawled across a series of coves hemmed in by high hills. I got lost several times before following a sign to Copacabana. Sweat dripped down my back in the rush-hour traffic. I got gridlocked on a one-way street too narrow to weave through with panniers. The streets felt like canyons between the tower blocks. It was claustrophobic. My backpacker room in Ipanema was $60 a night. I called a friend of a friend but only got his answer machine. I didn't like the heat, humidity or massive amount of posing going on.

As I headed out to visit Sugar Loaf Mountain and Cristo Redentor, the owner of my *hostal* advised me to take only $20 in cash, and to leave my camera and backpack in my room. Neither Fred nor my cameras were insured. That's why I never stayed anywhere that didn't have secure parking. I couldn't get a year's worldwide cover for my cameras so had no choice. Don't have an accident and keep everything as inconspicuous as possible. I covered the camera logos in black gaffer tape and justified a single hotel room as insurance that my bike and kit would be safe. If I did share a room in a backpackers I kept my stuff out of sight as much as possible. Until now other travellers had been my biggest risk as they knew the value of my toys. I decided not to risk my cameras on Sugar Loaf and then decided not to go at all.

What was the point in going to see something just because it was famous? I had to have an interest, a desire of my own. Why was I in an expensive city when I didn't really like cities at all? I couldn't relax. I wanted to keep going. Why did I go even further north when I wanted to head south? I felt uneasy and unsettled. A spur-of-the-moment idea to run in Fred's piston had made sense at the time, but after only two nights I beetled back to São Paulo. I wish I'd gone up Sugar Loaf Mountain now.

From São Paulo I headed for the Pantanal, a floodplain created by the River Paraguay flooding its banks in December. The joy of a fixed Fred, the vibrant green scenery, undulating hills, really good roads and millions of trees kept me going. There was no reason to stop. I loved Brazil. The sky was a blaze of orange and pinks on both sides of the road as Fred and I launched into the night. I abandoned any thoughts of a photo. It would never capture the breadth of the views and intensity of the colours, so I took a photo with my mind. If I continued I'd end up in Bolivia again. I'd stop if I got tired but it never happened. Adrenaline took over.

I rode for nine hours and rolled into the town of Campo Grande having broken my previous record. It must be a boy thing. I found a hotel at 998 km but continued past it, up and over an interchange, just to crack the pointless 1,000 km (625 miles) barrier. I was glad I wouldn't have to do it again. I can't see the point of doing a Nick Sanders. He has the world record for circumnavigating the globe on a motorbike – nineteen days. What a huge risk and a complete waste of time. What did he see? All to get an entry in the Guinness Book of Records and a huge amount of free publicity for his tour business. The record for eating live goldfish is over three hundred. Congratulations. What a useful social skill. It must be a great icebreaker at drinks parties. Well, now I had my own bit of uselessness. What a way to celebrate my first year on the road.

Another day and another destination. Cattle country. Miles and miles of hills, fields and trees. Sharper hills rose out of the ground in the distance. Even though it was cloudy it was 30°C and getting warmer as I descended into the Pantanal. I had no more clothes to take off and was drinking a lot of water.

While thinking about the exotic birds and animals that inhabited the Pantanal, a white line flashed against the grey clouds. Lightning. I was riding directly into a storm. But it was odd: the clouds didn't look black enough, the passing cars were all dry and none had their windscreen wipers on. The road continued straight towards the darkest cloud, but I couldn't tell how far away it was over the trees and surrounding low hills. I turned a corner and the road disappeared into a huge grey blanket. The hills had vanished. A wall of water raced towards Fred and me. Trees vanished as the blanket covered them. Mesmerised, I watched it swallow everything in its path. Behind lay blue sky and dry land, in front darkness and the sea. Suddenly I realised how fast it was moving and stopped to put my waterproofs on. Drops of rain spattered Fred while I struggled to get my waterproofs out of my panniers. I ran under a bush and while threading my motocross boots through my trousers looked up and fell over. The wall of water was only 200 yards away. Drops fell on me through the foliage. Fred was soaked. Sheets of rain crashed on to the

241

road. A lorry sped by in a fireball of spray. The rain was so heavy I was getting soaked through the bush. I was going to get drenched anyway and the sooner I rode, the sooner I'd be out the other side.

I'd never ridden in anything like it. At one point I slowed to 10 mph because I couldn't see anything. Lightning flashed on both sides and the thunder deafened me. Was this wise? Wouldn't it be safer to shelter? None of the locals took any notice. Balls of rain rebounded off the road and I shivered in the cold. The temperature had plummeted ten degrees. The road was awash with water. I was riding another river. Another flash. An instantaneous thunderclap. I thought of all the stories I'd read of people surviving lightning strikes. I couldn't remember one about a motorcyclist though. I glanced at my GPS. The screen was totally black. I turned it off and on again. Nothing, it was dead.

A few minutes later the rain eased, then stopped. The road dried out and the temperature soared. I stopped beside the road. Birds sang in the moist smell of fresh rain. A toucan, Brazil's national bird, flew across the road. The vivid yellow and orange of its beak shattered the forest around me. I felt a surge of joy. It was great to be alive, on my bike, soaked to the skin and bathing in Brazil.

The next day I continued down into the Pantanal, the world's largest wetland, the size of England and Scotland combined. Truly tropical, it got a little hotter with every mile. Most of the Pantanal lies in Brazil but it extends into northern Paraguay and eastern Bolivia. Every year the Paraguay river floods its banks in the rainy season and produces millions of islands out of the higher ground. The water dumps nutrients all over the basin and supports over six hundred species of birds and two hundred species of fish. I imagined it to be like the Okavango Delta in Botswana, where the rainy season produces similar swamps and islands, but the Fazenda San Francisco, the farm where I'd decided to stay for a few days, was lusher, more tropical and a lot noisier.

Two blue and yellow parrots watched me slurp runny chocolate from a forgotten pocket, then looked at each other and squawked.

Parrots can tell each other jokes. There was never a moment's silence from the constant cries and calls of birds, which rose to a crescendo at dusk before subsiding into the night.

Wanting to learn more, I walked to the top of the hill behind the farm each night and watched hundreds of ibis fly back to roost in a perfect V formation. Their black wings were silhouetted against billowing white clouds suffused with pink from the setting sun. The V shape reduces drag because each ibis flies in the upwash from the wingtip vortices of the bird in front. This can increase the flock's range by 71 per cent. In a variation of this theme jet airliners also have small vertical wings at the end of the main wings to reduce drag.

The farm teemed with life. Over 350 birds have been spotted on the ranch. During a night drive I saw my first giant anteater, capybara, ocelot and golden jackal. We didn't see a deadly fer-de-lance or any rattlesnakes though. The air was so warm and humid it was like sitting in a car in summer with the heater on. I woke dripping with sweat in the middle of the night, having cleverly left the window shut and the noisy air conditioning off.

The next morning we canoed down a lagoon. Brilliant red dragonflies flitted between the lily pads, monkeys crashed though the trees. The smell of wet mud and mouldy leaves filled the air. At dusk bats careered through the trees gorging on insects. Bats are fascinating. They have the largest testicular size variation for any mammal – up to 8.4 per cent of their body weight. Bats with bigger balls have smaller brains and vice versa. Big balls are needed to compete with other males, but males in monogamous relationships are able to put less energy into sex and more into developing mental skills. What a dilemma. Would I rather have a smaller brain and lots of sex with different partners or have a bigger brain and be monogamous? Do dimmer people have bigger balls? Oh dear. Time to head for Ushuaia before my head exploded.

The next morning I sweltered even just loading Fred, but once on the road to Bonito my speed created a cooling breeze. You feel the weather on a bike. The temperature suddenly dropped by five degrees in a few miles. I had ridden through the isobars, those lines on the weather maps, and the rain pissed down again. It drowned the sound of my engine and my visor misted up. Hailstones bounced off the road like marbles and melted almost as quickly. A big one stung my hand through my gloves. My feet swam in my boots and my gloves were sodden and heavy with water. The storm stopped as fast as it started and the sun burst out five minutes later.

Drenched but drying fast, I arrived in Bonito and headed for the municipal baths just out of town. The baths are actually a river, the Rio Formosa, and indeed warm enough to be a bath. You could almost see the humidity. Trees and reeds grew on the banks and branches hung over the water which flowed so swiftly it was hard to swim upstream. Several trout-sized fish fanned slowly around me as I bathed in the waist-high water. I lapsed into Jacques Cousteau mode again and started mumbling about the 'leetle feeshes.' A curious sensation made me look down. Several fish were nibbling my toes. Perhaps they had a unique flavour after a year inside my motocross boots.

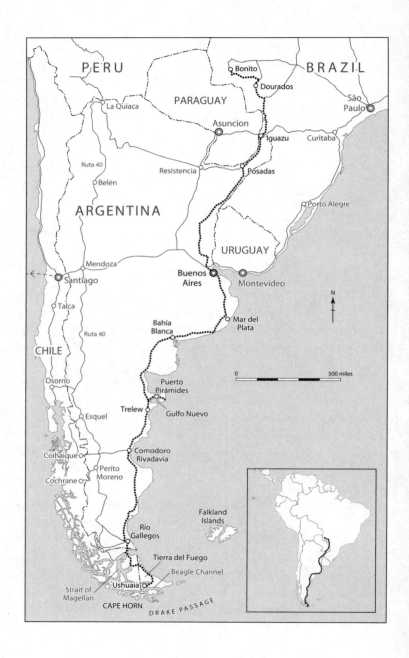

20

An Out-of-Body Experience in Patagonia

Richard and Jane were already in Buenos Aires, having finally got their bike out of Peru on a new *carnet de passage*, sent from Blighty by Paul Gowan at the RAC. Their bike's old *carnet* had expired and the Customs officials at Yunguyo on the Peru-Bolivia border had been adamant that they needed to return to Lima to sort things out. Even once in the capital it took them a month to organise, with a great deal of help from local people, not least Jorge Lira, the retired chief executive of Nestlé Peru and Horizons Unlimited's Lima Community.

I took them to Claridge, my favourite Buenos Aires restaurant, in the faded five-star hotel of the same name, where a liveried doorman stood beside the revolving mahogany door. The set dinner of a large glass of wine, a cold starter and my favourite rack of lamb – a row of seven lamb chops in one piece – a pudding and a coffee was only $10. Ever adventurous, I had been going there every night since I'd arrived in the city. It was a wonderful place to say farewell as Richard and Jane were nearing the end of their trip and were due to fly home from Santiago. I was sad to say goodbye.

While R & J planned their route south to see the whales at Puerto Pirámides, I called Rosa to chase my bicycle money. She said she'd sent it the week before. Western Union had no trace of any payment so I asked her for the reference number. She promised to email it to me. Another promise from ever further away.

Ushuaia beckoned. It is so far south the summers are very short. If I wanted to get there at all I had to make sure I didn't miss the weather window. I'd been advised to aim for January and February. March would be way too cold and the winds picked up then too. Time to head south.

I arrived in Bahía Blanca, a bay some 400 miles southwest of Buenos Aires, the next day. Darwin's *Beagle* anchored in Bahía Blanca in September 1832. He dined on such delicacies as rhea and arma-dillos, which he said tasted like 'beef' and 'duck'. His main role on the *Beagle* was to be a dining companion for Captain FitzRoy and he only assumed the job of naturalist over time. One of his key insights resulted from an excursion to Punta Alta, twenty-foot-high cliffs near Bahía Blanca, which Darwin wrote were 'very interesting from containing numerous shells and the bones of large animals'.

From these cliffs, Darwin excavated the bones of nine large mammals, none of which were known to science. They belonged to the Pleistocene and were over twelve thousand years old. The most unusual was *Megatherium*, a ground sloth the size of an elephant. He also found three other giant ground sloths and an extinct form of horse. Sloths are only found in Central and South America. He excavated two other sites, where he found more bones similar but not identical to living species, including something like an extinct camel. His finds were sent back to England for expert analysis. The extinc-tions played on his mind for years. He pondered their significance in *The Autobiography of Charles Darwin*:

> During the voyage of the *Beagle*, I had been deeply
> impressed by discovering in the Pampean formation great
> fossil animals covered in armour like that on the existing
> armadillos. It was evident that facts such as these, as well
> as many others, could be explained on the supposition

that species gradually become modified; and the subject haunted me.

The next morning, 60 miles south of Bahía Blanca, I crossed the Rio Colorado into Patagonia. It is vast. At 260,000 square miles it is 20 per cent larger than France but has a population of only 150,000. It stretches 1,000 miles to the Strait of Magellan in the south and 500 miles from the Andean lowlands in the west to the Atlantic coast in the east. A true steppe, it is a huge treeless void, a desert of stubble and stunted bushes. The undulating plains disappear to the horizon, continuously combed and cleansed by the ever present wind that drove settlers insane.

My plan was to ride south down to Ushuaia on Ruta 3, the easy tarred road on the Atlantic coast, then north into Chile on the legendary Ruta 40. Ruta 3 wasn't that easy as the westerly side winds never stopped. The average Patagonian wind is 30 mph and exceeds 70 mph every month. I had heard tales of cyclists trapped in cuttings for two days unable to pedal out under the onslaught. There are no trees to slow the wind down as it sweeps down from the Andes, flowing over the rolling hills and tufted grasses and blasting anything that tries to stand tall.

Bruce Chatwin helped put Patagonia on the map, both as a place and by defining a new genre of travel writing. In his book *In Patagonia* he set off on a quest to find another bit of Patagonian sloth skin to match the piece he had first seen as a child on his grandmother's bookcase. Patagonia was my bridge to Tierra del Fuego, the large island at the tip of South America. Ushuaia, my destination at the bottom of Tierra del Fuego, is the southernmost city in the world.

But there was a long way to go yet. Some 430 miles from Bahía Blanca I pulled into Puerto Pirámides, one of the best places in the world to watch southern right whales. Every year some four hundred migrate into the Gulfo Nuevo to mate and give birth and the next morning I joined a trip to try and spot some of them. We motored into the bay in a twenty-foot dinghy. Barely a ripple spoilt the sea until we darted across the glassy surface. Suddenly a yell went up and we stopped.

A huge black tail rose slowly out of the water, dripping with diamonds, before disappearing vertically into the depths. A blast from a blow hole shot a fountain of spray into the air as another surfaced nearby. A foul, sickly stench of rotten fish swept over us. Whale breath. Two people gagged and squealed. We drifted towards the whale, or did it swim towards us? The top of its head was covered in cream barnacles and studded with black rocks. I longed to swim with them but wasn't allowed to. They seemed to be inquisitive and friendly. One breached and landed back in the sea, creating an enormous wave of white water. A slight change of wind and another waft of whale breath. Perhaps they'd had enough of our smells too and they swam away.

Back in Puerto Pirámides I celebrated my birthday with dinner at the Las Restingas Hotel. I took a table on the first-floor veranda, which overlooked the whole cove and the sun sinking into the waves. I ordered the Patagonian lamb, but the wine list was pricey and the only half bottles were dumpy green things like genies' lamps. Half bottles of champagne cost $9. Too much, even on my birthday. I tried my usual ploy of asking for a discount and then, as an afterthought, added that it was my birthday. The waiter trotted off to ask the boss, then returned a few minutes later with a small bottle of champagne and removed the foil top before I could say anything. I panicked, thinking my dreadful Spanish had been misunderstood and I'd have to pay for it. He smiled and removed the wire cage holding the cork in.

'Nothing! It is a present from Madame.'

My anxiety turned into guilt as her kindness swept over me. The cork exploded from the bottle, flew over the railings and landed among some tourists below, who raised a cheer. I asked if Madame would like to join me but she was too busy and the waiter didn't like the stuff. I'd have to drink it all by myself. The first sip was heaven. My spirits soared as the bubbles danced and rose in the glass. I smiled. Why had I wasted all those years working so hard to end up in the loony bin? Why had it taken me so long to go on a big trip?

I smiled again. Those days were dead. All that mattered was now. That I was doing it and having the time of my life. Better late than never. I could worry about everything else when I got home. Enjoy the moment and savour every second. I sat back in my deckchair as the orange sun slid beneath the waves. I raised my glass and toasted the world. Perfectly pissed in Patagonia.

The next morning as a hangover cure I tried *maté*, the national drink made from the leaves of the *yerba maté* plant. I sucked on the metal straw sticking out of the wooden gourd. It had a strange mouldy taste – a cross between peat and grass cuttings. I couldn't feel any kick at all. Give me coffee any day. But the best buzz comes from riding quickly.

Soon I was balancing on adrenaline. My senses were wired, perfectly tuned to every nuance, every sign and sensation of danger. Riding on the edge but never crossing the line. The edge was control. A millimetre over and I was out. The edge was sharp and it cut. It was controlled risks. I went a bit faster. The euphoria of total control on the cliff. I felt alive. It was intoxicating. Fred and I were one. Adrenaline poured through me. We carved parabolic curves through a rare sequence of corners with mathematical precision. We were flowing in a dream. Time stood still. A little voice calmed me and I eased back, soaking up the moment and savouring the taste. It was far sweeter than coffee and far more addictive.

Trelew is a Welsh enclave, full of teashops like Casa de Te Gales Caerdyddd (Cardiff Welsh Tea Shop). Lewis Jones was one of the founders of the Welsh settlement in Patagonia and Trelew was named after him. He was born in Caernarfon, Wales and became one of the leaders of a movement to create a Welsh settlement where Welsh emigrants could preserve their language and way of life. In 1865 a group of 165 settlers landed near Puerto Madryn, midway between Puerto Pirámides and Trelew. Thirty-five miles south they discovered the Chubut river and survived by trading sheep and alfalfa with the indigenous Tehuelche Indians before expanding their territory west along the fertile valley. By 1915 a further 3,000 settlers joined them from Wales and the US. Soon they were exporting wheat to Buenos Aires and beyond. They still speak Welsh in Trelew.

I checked my email again but there was no news from Rosa. I called her office but she wasn't there and didn't answer her mobile. It was finally dawning on me that she'd stolen my money.

Back on the road I played good apples and bad apples. If the driver waved back he was a good apple, but it was a slow game as there were often many minutes between vehicles. Strange things started to happen. A speck of white morphed into view and slowly emerged from its chrysalis. It was a truck. High above, a lenticular cloud shaped like a perfect aerofoil chased the truck towards me. Perhaps some aliens wanted it? I expected the truck to suddenly vanish or rise into the cloud, but I was disappointed.

Clouds became art. They were far higher and like nothing I had seen before. Thin curves, scimitars and waves rolling through the skies. There was nothing beyond this land but the wild Southern Ocean and Antarctica. No wonder the weather was so extreme. Twenty minutes later another mirage appeared on the road. An island floated in the distance like a peak poking through the clouds. Senses got confused. My brain said one thing but my eyes said the opposite. After riding for three hours my brain told me my hands were gripping the handlebars from underneath with my palms facing the sky, but when I looked down but they were holding on from above as usual.

Everyone I met talked about the wind. It never stopped, even for one second. Constant and unrelenting, only the ferocity and direction changed. Ruta 3 is closed when coaches are blown over. I learnt to lean into sudden gusts, but trucks pulling trailers in the opposite direction were the worst. The first time it happened a wall of air broke over me like a wave and pushed me two yards to the edge of the road. Three feet from the centre line was too close. A bigger blast would have blown me off the road. I left as big a gap as possible and crouched down behind the fairing as the crosswind in front of the truck snapped into a vacuum when the truck passed by, followed by the turbulent wake that pummelled me back and forth.

The faster I went the less I moved. This made sense as I was 'in' the gust for a shorter time and the greater gyroscopic effect of the wheels made me more stable. The safest speed was as fast as possible so I accelerated towards trucks. It worked. A big push out from the bow wave and a suck back from the vacuum. Or was it just the delusions of a brain-dead biker?

Fred's fairing deflected the wind on to my chest, shoulders and head. My shoulders soon ached from hanging on so tightly, so I gaffer-taped an A4 plastic folder on to the fairing, reinforced with two bits of wood from the roadside, which extended it by six inches. My windless cocoon was complete bliss after days of holding on fast. After ten miles of dead-straight road across the steppe 15 mph fell off the speedo as I turned the corner. It felt like Bolivia again, where the combination of altitude and shitty Bolivian fuel had so strangled my motor that we couldn't overtake a lorry going uphill. But that was at 15,000 feet, not 1,000 feet. Here it was just the wind.

Big countries have big skies. The immense treeless Patagonian steppe made me feel tiny and insignificant, like a mosquito buzzing down a line of black silk. But the line was mine. I was painting a line around the world, leaving a thread that would last forever, a thread that lingered in the ether, a chain of anchored emotions that I dropped as I rode. Maybe strong emotions generate bubbles others can sense. Did that explain why I'd felt such sudden and intense sadness in Yungay, Peru, where thousands of people had died in the devastating landslide thirty years earlier? Was it riding into 'bubbles' left by others at places where they'd had sudden shocks that was keeping me safe on my trip?

The horizon had disappeared again. A mirage shimmered where the sky and land merged into the distance. Suddenly a surge of joy and pure happiness at being alive swept through me. I loved the excitement of being on my own miles from anywhere, not knowing what was going to happen. The thrill of an unexpected sight, the kindness of a stranger, being as far from a city as it was possible to be.

Another biker stopped at the side of the road interrupted my reveries. Rupert was on his way to Ushuaia. He was waiting for the engine of his blue Yamaha 49 cc Vino scooter to cool down.

Rupert looked tired. His face was red and he'd long given up shaving. He'd bought the scooter in Alaska and was riding to Ushuaia. After fifteen months he was nearly there. He'd planned to do the trip on a 100cc but hadn't been able to get hold of one. So here he was, on the fifth piston of the trip and having to stop every 20 miles for the engine to cool down. With a top speed of 30 mph, 125 miles was a big day for him.

We had almost crossed paths before. At high altitude in the Andes the scooter's engine had so little power he had to get off and push it. I had met his girlfriend Dorothée outside Cuzco several months earlier. She cycled while Rupert rode and they met up each night. He'd get food and lodging ready for her arrival so they could start again the next day. I was in awe of Rupert's perseverance and Dorothée's mental strength to grind out the miles for hour after hour, day after day.

I loved the wild emptiness of Patagonia. I loved plotting the smoothest line through the corners. The satisfaction of perfect parabolas linked together into a seamless, sinuous curve. Fluid precision. Every nerve, every fibre was bent to the task. My concentration was intense. The road led straight into the horizon. I went faster. The wind roared in my ears. Fred buzzed. Slowly, imperceptibly, my mind rose up and out of my body until I hovered just above and behind myself. I saw myself holding on to the bars. I had tunnel vision but sensed everything. The world was in slow motion. The suspension compressed in a dip in the road. My soul spread out over the land as I rode in total peace and tranquillity, a dreamtime oneness with Fred and the world. Suddenly I felt immensely powerful. Invincible. An addictive, intoxicating feeling flowed through me. I knew everything. This was now, this was life. Nothing could touch me. The ease of speed made me go even faster. It was so enticing, so easy. My little voice whispered 'This is not the place to crash'. Slow down and make it last. The thought broke the spell and I slipped back inside myself.

Maybe having so much time to think had awakened parts of my mind and allowed my sixth sense to filter through in Patagonia. There was no pressure to conform out here. You could be whoever you wanted to be. You became your own person. You were yourself. This was who I really was. Who I wanted to be. Free of the rat race. Free of possessions. Having so much time and space to think freed the spirit. I was retuned. Travel had cleansed my soul. I was happier and more relaxed than I had been for a long time. Perhaps that combined with intense concentration triggered my out-of-body experience and the strange messages from my hands. If I could do this now how far could I go? Maybe it had all started in the Priory, where I stripped away the damaged layers and rebuilt on pure foundations. Out here I was pushing my boundaries but had never felt outside my comfort zone. Maybe I could push a little more. I had so much to learn. I hoped the journey would never end.

I crouched a little more behind my fairing to get out of the wind. Only 60 miles to Río Gallegos. Suddenly, out the corner of my eye, the rev counter needle flashed to '8,000' and returned to '6,000' rpm. Had I imagined it? A few moments later it happened again. I throttled back immediately. The clutch was slipping. I was riding uphill into a very strong headwind at peak power. Only a few moments before I'd panicked when I'd opened the throttle and felt a sudden resistance. The throttle was against the stop again and a quick glance at my GPS showed a high vertical-climb rate up a slope I hadn't noticed. I changed down to maintain speed and make it easier on Fred's heart.

I had used car oil when I serviced Fred in Buenos Aires. Many motorbikes, including Fred, have wet clutches which run in the engine oil. Car oils have additives which make them more slippery and can reduce the friction between the clutch plates until they slip. That's what had happened.

I cruised into Río Gallegos and asked around for the best motor-cycle shop. Everyone agreed it was SM Motos. Marcos, Gustavo and Sebastian were saints. They helped me remove, clean, re-oil and replace the clutch plates. While I was refilling the engine with motorcycle oil, Gustavo noticed a hole in the carburettor inlet gaiter. That meant unfiltered dust and dirt-laden air could get directly into the engine and accelerate piston wear. He fixed it with special glue. Luckily the dirt roads were ahead rather than behind me so it was unlikely that any damage had been done. I checked the tyres and gasped at the state of the rear one. I'd fitted a new Pirelli MT90 in São Paulo, Brazil and it was knackered after only 3,750 miles in ten days' riding. They lasted 11,000 miles in the UK. The combination of high speed and constant use for several hours a day had reduced its normal life by two thirds. Was everything thing else wearing out at the same speed? To cap it all the SM boys wouldn't let me pay anything, so I gave them a pack of beers the next morning on my way south.

I was heading for the Strait of Magellan, across which lay Tierra del Fuego, 'the Land of Fire', the large island at the bottom of South America. When Magellan 'discovered' the island in 1520 he thought it was peppered with active volcanoes, but they were the campfires of the indigenous Fuegans who never let them go out. The Strait of Magellan is the safest of the three shipping routes round Cape Horn. Of the other two, the Drake Passage is the roughest as it takes in Cape Horn itself and is exposed to the full might of the Antarctic seas. The Beagle Channel is the next safest, an east-to-west route sheltered between the southern end of Tierra del Fuego and the many small islands off the foot of South America; it was discovered in 1830 by Captain FitzRoy.

Although it was only 70 miles as the crow flew from Río Gallegos to the Strait of Magellan, I had to first cross into Chile for 100 miles before re-entering Argentina. This diversion is a legacy of the 1881 border settlement, which saw Chile, desperate to avoid a war with Argentina as well as Bolivia and Peru (the War of the Pacific, 1879–83), agreeing to Argentina's terms. Thus a north–south border splits Tierra del Fuego into two, with Chile (to the west) having most of the land but no towns, and Argentina (to the east) having Rio Grande and Ushuaia.

Once across the three-mile Strait of Magellan, which was flat calm, and on to Tierra del Fuego it was another 300 miles to Ushuaia. I would be there that night. The closer I got the faster I went. I hoped it would not be an anticlimax. The dirt road swept across the pancake-flat island accompanied by the invisible wind. Tierra del Fuego was lusher and more vibrant than Patagonia. It was painted in inviting primary colours: a deep blue sky and perfectly clean clouds contrasted with the fresh green grass that surrounded me on all sides. Splashes of yellow appeared, the sweet scent of flowers filled the air, and then I rode through fields ablaze with millions of dandelions waving in the November summer. It was much warmer than I expected, just like a normal spring day at home. I imagined all their seeds taking to the air at once as I rode through a fog of tiny tickling parachutes.

A grey line broke the horizon. The first hills since leaving Buenos Aires. Black dots peppered the slopes. Trees. The first for 1,750 miles, since Rio Grande. Small, twisted and undersized, they clung to the ground, tormented by the wind and covered in lichen. It felt like Christmas and my spirits soared as I entered the stunted forest. Rounded hills grew into mountains. Snow garlanded the peaks. The trees became larger and more numerous. Proper forests. It was heart-warming after the relentlessly bleak and treeless plains. I was coming home. I meandered alongside Lake Escondido, gradually climbing through the forest on the flanks of the lake. I shivered as I crested Paso Garibaldi. Another, lower pass and I glimpsed the sea. The Beagle Channel. Ushuaia, the end of the world.

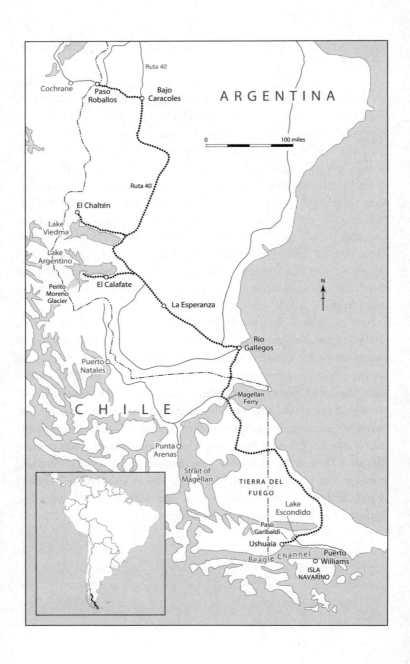

21

THE END OF THE WORLD

Ushuaia is the southernmost city in the world – if you live in Argentina. Puerto Williams, on Isla Navarino across the Beagle Channel, is actually further south but the Argentinians consider that irrelevant as it's a naval port, there is no road to it and it belongs to Chile. There is a long history of border disputes between the two countries, principally due to how the countries were explored: Argentina was explored westwards from Buenos Aires on the coast and Chile down from the north. They almost went to war in 1978 over three small uninhabited islands in the Beagle Channel. The dispute was settled by UK arbitration in favour of Chile, which upset the Argentinians and was a factor in the subsequent Argentinian invasion of Las Malvinas, the Falkland Islands.

Many years before any of these quarrels, Captain FitzRoy anchored in the Beagle Channel in 1833 for the second time, on this occasion with Darwin on board. His first visit had been on his first command, when he'd named the channel after his ship. He was only twenty-six when the Royal Navy sent him to survey Tierra del Fuego. When the indigenous *Yámana* Indians stole one of his boats he took hostages to try and secure its return. He took the Indians to the UK in 1830 and three of them were presented to King William IV and Queen Adelaide. On his second visit he returned the three hostages. It had been noted that there were no old Indians. The harsh climate and lack of food made survival difficult. Nor did it help that the Yámana tribe were cannibals, or that most ranchers regarded the Indians as 'pests' to be shot on sight. The last surviving pure-blood Indian, Virginia Choinquitel, died in 1999 aged fifty-six.

FitzRoy was a scientist and a man ahead of his time. He took a mercury barometer on his second voyage and it saved them many times by giving advance warning of storms when the mercury plummeted. After he left active duty he was appointed Meteorological Statistician in 1854 and created the first systematic weather forecasts from data transmitted by telegraph from far-flung weather stations. The organisation he created evolved into the Meteorological Office. He issued the first storm warnings and created the familiar shipping areas that include Rockall, Dogger and Finisterre. In 2002 Finisterre was renamed FitzRoy in recognition of his achievements.

All the Antarctic cruise boats are based in Ushuaia and the town fizzed with excited people: those just about to go to Antarctica and those who had just returned, who still pranced with the penguins. It was also the end point for many cyclists and bikers: the final destination. The main street was straight out of the Wild West. Each detached wooden building had its own raised wooden boards and saloon fronts. The only things missing were swinging doors, honky-tonk pianos and the occasional drunken tourist being thrown out through the window. Delicious aromas gusted on the wind as whole lambs sizzled on open wood fires. I ate lamb every day.

Inspired by all the Antarctica stories, I spent a lot of time canvassing other tourists' opinions on the best tour company and trying to decide whether, as a crap sailor, I'd be able to deal with the notoriously rough Drake Passage and the Southern Ocean. I'd felt queasy crossing the three-mile Strait of Magellan: how would I cope with twenty-one days in the roughest water on the planet? Everyone had stories of unseaworthy ships and of 'two days of hell' in the Drake Passage; stories of people being sick everywhere, and being repeatedly thrown out of their bunks throughout the night. One passenger had lost a finger and another had needed forty stitches on head and face wounds. Was it worth it to see millions of penguins?

My one common-sense cell squeaked into life and I decided not to go.

Instead, I left Ushuaia and headed north, winding my way back through the forests and over the two passes. The leaking gaiter fixed in Río Gallegos played on my mind. Was the engine noisier now? The clouds skimmed the tops of the mountains and promised rain, while the trees stood like silent sentinels watching over Fred and me. For the first time I wasn't in a rush. A new calmness and warmth flowed through me, my shoulders relaxed and I marvelled at the beauty of the mountains and pine forests rather than the curve of the road. I had been to the end of the world. I wondered if I would have enjoyed Ushuaia so much if I hadn't spent four days riding the 1,500 miles down the windy, barren and desolate steppes of Patagonia. A surge of elation swept over me. I was having the time of my life riding around the world with Fred. I turned a corner and the view took my breath away. I stopped and stared at the sunlight reflecting off Lake Escondido and the mirrored images of the mountains.

As I rode off the Strait of Magellan ferry in the late afternoon a familiar shape caught my eye. A dark blue scooter stood at the head of the queue on the slipway. The wind had really taken its toll on the rider. Rupert's face was redder than ever and he seemed even more tired. But his trip was nearly over.

In Río Gallegos I checked back into the same hotel. Walking to dinner that evening I saw a golden retriever, swishing his tail from side to side beside his owner. I had to stop and say hello, as all our family dogs have been retrievers. I am a doggy person and was soon patting, stroking and scratching his ears. Why do dogs like some people and not others, like we do? Is it an intuitive thing?

Dogs are far more perceptive than we are. In his book *Dogs That Know When Their Owners Are Coming Home*, Rupert Sheldrake

261

documents many examples of precisely that. Indeed, Liz and Brian Argent, the KTM dealer from whom I bought Fred had such a dog.

'When Liz's shopping in Kingston,' said Brian, 'the dog will suddenly wake up and go and lie by the front door. I know she'll walk through the door in exactly 15 minutes, so I go and get the tea ready. We worked out that he wakes up the moment she thinks "I've had enough I'm going home".' How could the dog know? There was no pattern to Liz's behaviour. The dog picked up her decision from three miles away. Perhaps another example of the sixth sense that the San people use in Africa to communicate over large distances. Maybe all this time to think was awakening my own dormant senses.

Ruta 40 ends at Río Gallegos. It starts more than 3,100 miles north at La Quiaca on the border with Bolivia and runs just east of the Andes; most of it is a dirt road. Che Guevara rode much of it in his famous *Motorcycle Diaries*. I'd be following in his wheel tracks. Not far from Río Gallegos, three rheas (ostrich-like birds the height of a small deer) ran across the road. They looked like brown roadrunners. Half an hour later a black dot appeared silhouetted on the horizon. Another cyclist. Ian Leitch was cycling from Ushuaia to Prudhoe Bay in Alaska. Brown stubble covered his face. His yellow and green bike pulled a one-wheeled trailer, containing a matching yellow kit bag and flag. He said that he sometimes cycled for twenty-four hours non-stop. I got the feeling riding the length of the Americas was just a training run. He was keen to get going. It was midday and his target was disappearing. He got out of the saddle and accelerated away.

Two days later I arrived at the Perito Moreno glacier, an immense juggernaut of ice 200 feet high and 20 miles long. It looked incongruous between the forested slopes. It moved and groaned and displayed a dazzling array of colours, from very pale blue to deep azure, from black through shades of grey to brilliant white. Other parts contained every variation of brown because of the soil and other debris picked up by the glacier on its way down. It was like the icing on a giant Christmas cake. The surface was sharp and jagged, riven by crevasses and sculpted by the wind and rain. I wanted to walk on the glacier but we weren't allowed within 200 yards of it and I soon found out why. Musical waterfalls dripped and splashed down the ice cliff when a sudden shotgun blast shattered the air. Huge chunks exploded out of the bottom of the wall of ice, creating tidal waves as they smashed into Lake Argentino. The glacier was calving. Exploding ice killed thirty-two people between 1966 and 1988, so now no one's allowed to get too close, not even the boats.

As I lay in my tent 40 miles away in El Calafate that night, a sudden pang of loneliness shot through me. If only I had someone to share things with. Why do the demons always come at night? What is it about the dark that makes everything so much worse? I remembered walking home from my neighbours' house in the dark when I was seven years old. There was a path, all of 30 yards long, between tall hedges but the only light was that from our gatepost just beyond a big oak tree. I always walked from our neighbours' humming and whistling, trying not to rush, but inevitably broke into a run near the oak tree. Maybe I was still running now.

The next morning I headed for El Chaltén, 100 miles away. As I rode across a stony plain a low line of skinny white clouds on the horizon showed how thin the atmosphere was. The earth's circumference is 24,900 miles but the world's breathable atmosphere would fit into a ball with a diameter of only 950 miles across and its oceans into a ball of just 850 miles in diameter, the distance from London to Rome. An image of both spheres astride Europe formed in my mind, tiny against the size of the planet. All life depends on these tiny balls of water and air, which we are polluting and destroying.

Ruta 40 rolled over undulating savannah whose brown grass stretched to the horizon. There were no towns, trees or people, only the wind. This was no place to crash. Sometimes an hour went past without encountering another vehicle. Every meeting was a small celebration. There was so little traffic I relaxed, my mind wandered. I could dream on the open road. Impossible in towns and cities, where cars constantly stop and turn and people cross without looking. Like in dreams, my subconscious made links, rekindled old memories.

There was no pressure. My spirit ran free. Habits leached away with every mile and intuition slipped in. Home was left far behind. The vast space heightened awareness and senses. I was pure and free. Free to move and free to think. There were no distractions, no radio, no music. Just pure thoughts inside my helmet.

At 50 mph I kept up with a cloud's shadow as it raced across the ground. The wind was far stronger here than on the way south. I hoped it wouldn't get worse in the high Andes. Another gust made me brush the edge of the rut. I wished I could see the gusts coming. This was the worst it had ever been. I screamed at the wind to 'fuck off' as another gust bashed Fred and me sideways. It made no difference at all but made me feel better. The edges of the deep gravel ruts tried to grab the tyres. Malign fingers, clawing at the rubber.

The surface of the *ripio* (gravel) road varied constantly. The newly graded parts were wonderfully smooth and fast but a slight colour change hinted of a sudden switch into deep ruts of loose stones and rocks. I kissed the side of the rut on another gust and fishtailed into a brief but scary moment. I could think only of the wind and how to fight it. My heart rejoiced at seeing another soul coming towards me, swiftly followed by dread they might be in my rut. I never overtook a single car in three days on Ruta 40. Normally it was the other way round. A grey saloon lay abandoned on its roof in the middle of a vast plain with no corner in sight.

I was spending so much time on my own, thoughts and memories buried deep floated to the surface of my mind. Nothing escaped. My subconscious floated free. People, places and faces came back. Once I thought I saw my father walking down Piccadilly, London near where he used to work. The memories bubbled up and flew away on the wind. It made me calm and deeply relaxed. I dwelt for days on everything I'd ever done.

We discussed ways to manage stress and anger when I was in the Priory. One method is to write your feelings down. The mere act of writing them down gets them out of your system. Another way is to put your feelings in a bubble and watch them float away on the breeze. Perhaps this was what was happening to me now. I examined each memory and let the feelings expand over the hills into infinite space, dissipating and draining away as they spread out. Such thoughts only arose when my mind was free to wander, like on huge plains under huge skies. Patagonia. That was surely why I'd had my out-of-body experience here.

A strange movement to one side and I used the back brake. A common rhea whizzed across the road in front of me. Its light brown feathers blended perfectly with the dried grasses. An unpredictable, fifty-pound, four-foot-high torpedo. There was no sign of any human habitation at all: no houses, farms, telegraph poles. Nothing but Ruta 40 and the wind. The sense of space and desolation was immense. Pure Patagonia. Treeless plains and a low horizon of snow-capped mountains. At last I turned west off Ruta 40 towards Chile. I stopped for a wee in the middle of nowhere beneath clouds of thin alien space-ships and ate biscuits for lunch. A tornado appeared in the distance and grew ever larger. It was chasing a vehicle. As the tornado stopped the dust engulfed the green pickup. Fred and I were coated in grit and fine sand. The driver got out and, smiling, asked if he could help me. He had bushy black eyebrows, a grey Zapata moustache and a black beret. Atilio Mendes was on his way home for lunch.

'My farm is just over there.' He waved his arm down the road but I could see nothing but miles of windswept Patagonia. 'Ten miles.'

The Andes looked like hills from here. There was no visible sign of life anywhere but this was his home, his garden. He had been born here. He invited me home to lunch but I was anxious to get into Chile before darkness fell.

Two turns in one minute signalled the end of the steppe and the start of the Andean foothills. The mountain peaks glistened white and the *ripio* road wove through the dry brown scrub. The tallest bush didn't even reach my knees. A cool wind blew off the top of a green lake. At the far side spindly bushes reached above my head, their fingers catching the air scented by a herb I did not know. A small herd of Friesian cows grazed on patches of rough grass in a valley tucked between two hills. V-shaped funnels of grass revealed hidden watercourses on the hillsides. Around a bluff a secret valley of fields, fences and poplar trees burst into view. Two red roofs stood silently in a green oasis.

At a paltry 1,700 feet there was no altiplano at Paso Roballos. The Argentinian border guards were just as friendly as those at La Balsa on the Ecuador-Peru frontier. I drank their coffee and they ate my biscuits. Grass grew out the centre of the single-track *ripio* road as it inched across no-man's land. I hummed, happy to leave Ruta 40 behind and almost on a new-country high. The Andean lowlands appeared as a myriad of convoluted hills folded into each other like a giant profiterole. A few yards ahead a big sign faced the other way. Intrigued as to whether it said 'Welcome to Argentina' or 'Goodbye from Chile', I slowed. As I turned my head to read it, the front wheel crashed down in a massive jolt.

22

THE MOST BEAUTIFUL ROAD
IN THE WORLD

I snapped the throttle wide open. The front reared up, the back dropped and Fred stopped dead, smashing my balls on the tank. Chilean cattle grids are cheaper than Argentinian ones. They don't span the whole width of the road. I'd ridden into the three-foot-wide gap in the middle. The two panniers stopped Fred's rear end falling deeper into the hole and left the back wheel dangling in space. As usual I looked around to see if anyone was watching. There was not a soul within miles.

The sign said 'Chilean Army. Military Area "The Baker".'

Chile was green. Guanacos (South American members of the camel family that are related to alpacas and llamas) grazed in the distance. I followed a river that was more wash bed than watercourse for the winter snow had long gone. A lone poplar tree stood beside a small brook that tumbled beneath the road. Green fields and forests clung to the fertile edges of the flat valley. Lower down more poplar trees protected Estancia Chacabuco, a huge farm. It was bought in 2004 by conservationist Kris Tompkins, the former CEO of the outdoor clothing company Patagonia Inc., who plans to give it back to Chile as part of a 750,000-acre Patagonia National Park.

Chile was different. The *ripio* road couldn't stay straight for long. Fred and I constantly twisted and turned deeper into the Andes through a pine-forested valley. A sharp intake of breath and I stopped beside a glacial river. Río Baker sparkled a vibrant greeny-blue, the same colour as that childhood crayon, but here the colour came from suspended minerals. It completely filled the bottom of the valley and looked deep. Ever down and ever greener, the first grassy field brought joy to my heart. This was like England. Forests covered entire hillsides down to the river's edge. The water writhed in swirls and eddies in the strong current and had a menacing power. Elated, I camped in Cochrane in an orchard after waiting for the owner to put the pigs to bed.

This region is so sparsely populated that Cochrane is the only village between Coihaique 190 miles to the north and Puerto Natales 400 miles south. The next morning I started the famed Carretera Austral, the Southern Hemisphere Road, which runs 500 miles south from Puerto Montt to Cochrane, and continues 125 miles further south to Villa O'Higgins. It is the only road in this part of Chile. The government built it to increase settlement and prevent Argentinian encroachment. The population barely passes 100,000 along the entire length of the road. The landscape is so mountainous and so riddled with lakes, fjords and glaciers that in some places it was impossible to build a road at all. Ferries link these sections but they stop running in winter, cutting off some places for months. The first part of the route between Puerto Aisén and Coihaique was only completed in 1936.

Thirty-five miles north of Cochrane I rounded a corner to yet another sharp intake of breath and stopped. A land bridge separated two lakes. Several houses stood back from the small bay where a jetty and a lone pleasure boat bobbed lazily under the morning sun. Huge hunks of mountains tumbled into the farther lake and several small forested islands broke its surface. I'd been here before. A distant memory, a familiar feeling, twinkled at the back of my mind, but every time I tried to coax it out it sank back into the depths.

I followed Río Baker north to Lake Bertrand, where more poplars beside the lake hinted at houses nearby. The first wire fences. A wooden summer house stood barely ten feet above the icy water. Only four miles later the *ripio* road stopped at the edge of another lake, beyond which two glaciers drooped over the top of the mountain like a fried egg. I waited as the ferry chugged across the narrow inlet, the diesel engine shattering the silence and fighting the fast-flowing current that links Lake Bertrand to Lake General Carrera, the largest lake in Chile. One hundred yards away a new suspension bridge neared completion. I was the only passenger on the *Dr Hans Steffen*, which could only take two cars at a time. Victor was the captain and Juan and Irwin his crew. We chatted about the beauty of the lakes and mountains over biscuits. Locals manned the ferry on a rota, as volunteers, so they'd actually get more free time when the bridge opened. They hated the idea of going to Santiago. Why would anyone want to live in a city?

Chile is the oddest shaped country in the world – just look at a map. It is 2,600 miles long and averages only 110 miles wide. It's only when you see it for yourself that it makes perfect sense. Dr Hans Steffen was a geographer who worked on the Chile and Argentina border commission during the 1890s, and his reputation and writing inspired others to leave Germany for a new life in Chile. The Chile-Argentina Boundary Treaty of 1881 stated: 'The boundary-line shall run in that extent over the highest summits of the said Cordilleras which divide the waters, and shall pass between the sources [of streams] flowing down to either side.' The highest peaks favoured Argentina and the continental divide favoured Chile. However some large lakes that were on the Argentinian side drained into the Pacific. Unsurprisingly, the Chileans argued these should be theirs and the Argentinians likewise. Unable to agree, they accepted UK arbitration in 1902. The UK ignored the geological arguments – that a Chilean catchment area meant the whole lake should be Chilean when the largest part was on the Argentinean side – and instead divided each lake in half and apportioned them equally to both countries.

After 55 miles I entered the Ibáñez valley and rode alongside the Hudson river. The flooded gravel beds were filled with dead grey trees that clawed at the sky. Grey glacial water flowed fast around the trunks, roots and stumps and past the occasional green island. It felt sinister, like a graveyard from a nuclear blast, for only the trees in the floodplain were dead. Those on the slopes were untouched. It reminded me of photos of Mount St. Helens in Washington, USA, where the volcanic eruption flattened millions of trees like matchsticks, leaving not a leaf, only bare dead trunks. Cerro Hudson, the southernmost volcano in the Chilean Andes, erupted twice in August 1991. The first, smaller eruption on 8 August produced an ash column six miles high. Between 12 and 15 August it erupted again, creating an ash column 11 miles high which reached the Falkland Islands 625 miles away. Tephra (rock fragments spewed into the air by an eruption) covered an area of 31,000 square miles, or about twice the size of Switzerland. Interestingly, when tephra is ejected it has an electrical charge and often produces lightning. The tephra clogged the Hudson river, causing it to flood out over one mile wide, and the toxic ash killed the trees.

Half an hour later the *ripio* changed colour and I instinctively throttled back. It had turned black. A beautiful two-lane tarred road soon flowed beneath Fred's wheels. Why have a tarred road here? What was so special about Villa Cerro Castillo? I stopped for biscuits. Fred's motor sounded noisier as it ticked over. I blipped the throttle and listened carefully. Was it worse or just my usual paranoia? The tarmac relaxed me. I hoped it would last the 50 miles to Coihaique. I slalomed up the Cuesta del Diablo, a series of switchbacks like a giant game of snakes and ladders, clipping the apexes and using the whole width of the road, my own personal racetrack. But the tar ended all too soon and it was back to *ripio* again.

Why sandwich a section of tarmac between two lengths of *ripio*? A long line of poplars glowing and glistening a brilliant green beside the road transported me back to my childhood and the daily school run. Mrs Bates had been an ambulance driver in the Second World War and liked to put her Triumph Vitesse through its paces. Her favourite overtaking spot was past the poplars on the Leatherhead bypass. I'm sure she was always trying to break her record as we overtook at every opportunity. Another link to my past was forged and a deep comfort and peacefulness flowed through me.

One flashback sparked another. Suddenly the distant memory triggered by the twin forested islands in the lake earlier that day popped back into my mind and burst into life. The beautiful bay, islands and impossibly blue water reminded me of a poster I'd had on my bedroom wall. I was seven and Saturday shopping with my father when a huge poster caught my eye in an ironmongers. It was bigger than my bed. I begged my father to buy it. It stayed on my bedroom wall for years. Pine-forested hills surrounded a blue lake with a small island in it. Mist clung to the tops of the trees. I spent many hours camping on the island, cooking sausages on my fire, fishing in the lake, walking in the woods and having many adventures.

I was having those adventures now.

Memories of my father floated to the surface. Fishing off Brighton pier and the elation of catching whiting which we ate at home. The photo was fresh in my mind. The beautiful island rekindled images of my bedroom and my orange wallpaper as Mike Rutherford's song played in my mind.

> *I know that I'm a prisoner*
> *To all my father held so dear*
> *I know that I'm a hostage*
> *To all his hopes and fears*
> *I just wish I could have told him in the living years.*

Gigantic rhubarb leaves with thorny stems squeezed the road. The deep red trumpet-shaped flowers of copihues (Chilean bellflowers), the national flower of Chile, flamed the semi-tropical forest. Shrubs and trees pressed in on both sides of the narrow *ripio* road and brushed both sides of a passing truck. It was like riding through a greenhouse. Fred and I zigzagged up the 1,500-foot Portezuelo Queulat, a steep valley wall, and immediately zigzagged down the other side. The track had a big camber and deep powder feathered the edges. Parque Nacional Queulat was only 90 miles north from Coihaique, where I'd spent the previous night.

I'd already dropped Fred twice that day, turning around to take photos. Riding was scary because the Chileans drove so fast and the thick forest gave no warning of where the road went or what might be coming. With no passing places I knew I'd have take to the soft stuff to get out of the way, so I crawled around the blind corners, ready to jump. Nevertheless, one madman appeared in a ball of dust. I slowed, ready to bail out but he saw me at the last moment, flicked right and sprayed me with gravel; his flat-bed lorry with a JCB digger high on its back passed in a flash. The JCB swayed violently in my mirrors as the driver fought to stay on the road. I shuddered. I loved the scenery, remoteness and thrill of riding such a magical road, but the local loonies scared me.

Half an hour later I threaded through the forest around another lake. As I crested a ridge the view stopped me short again. Puyuhuapi, a tiny hamlet, lay on a beach at the head of a fjord. A voice invited me to stay a while, just like it had in Vilcabamba, Ecuador. A peaceful serenity, a timeless enchantment like a lullaby invited me in. The air tasted soft and pure. Puyuhuapi means 'Sweet Island' in Chono, the language of the local indigenous people. It looked like Switzerland or Austria. Several large wooden houses with pointed roofs seemed too big for such a tiny place, as did Casa Ludwig, a five-storey chalet. Casa Ludwig was built by four Sudeten Germans from Rossbach who had been inspired to emigrate to Chile by Dr Steffen's books. The place he described was just like their home town but with more rain. Otto Uebel, Carlos Ludwig, Ernesto Ludwig and Helmuth Hopperdietzel arrived in 1935 and founded Puyuhuapi. The fjord was uninhabited and as the forest grew right to the shoreline they had to first clear the land and then use the abundant reeds to build their first shelters.

I filled up with petrol at the wooden hut by the stream. It was so rustic I was surprised the pump used electricity. The owner pointed to the smoke rising lazily from a wooden house across the road. The café in the front room was the only place to eat. Two tables and a counter displayed cakes and pastries. They had no savouries, only delicious cakes and coffee. I asked where I could stay but the señorita told me everywhere in the hamlet was full. It was the busiest time of year. Helga had lived there all her life. Her grandfather had emigrated from Germany in the 1930s to escape the Depression and start a new life.

The Carretera Austral was the most beautiful road I'd ever ridden. It changed continuously, a tiny lifeline threaded through forested

274

canyons. Rustic, remote and resolute. The huge scale of the scenery dwarfed and cradled me at the same time. It could take an hour to reach the opposite side of a valley. Mountain fortresses towered in the distance and pines filled the crisp clean air. It was how I imagined Norway to be, sprinkled with a little summer Switzerland. I kept checking the impossible greeny-blue colour of the lakes against the sky to make sure my eyes weren't deceiving me.

Actors are taught to be 'in the moment' so when they play the same part over and over again it never stales and always comes across as fresh as the first time. That's how I felt riding the Carretera Austral. I saw many mountains, rivers and lakes but every one was different. Every mile was new and exciting. Sometimes the view was so breathtaking I just stopped and stared, speechless and overwhelmed. Rather than the steep-sided, claustrophobic and almost menacing presence of the Peruvian Andes, the valleys here were more rounded, open and welcoming. Huge snow-capped mountains and vast forests engulfed tiny hamlets on a scale I'd never seen before. The scenery was so achingly beautiful I felt I could die there.

My thoughts turned to my father again. He killed himself because he was deeply depressed, a condition brought about by the deteriorating economic climate of the early seventies. He owned a successful firm of London quantity surveyors but the oil crisis of 1973, the subsequent London Stock Market crash, the long miners' strike, very high inflation and the eventual downfall of the Heath government all took their toll. In 1974 the new Labour government introduced a punitive 83 per cent income tax rate and a big project he'd been working on for a long time – the Thorpe Park Adventure development in Surrey – was shelved. We'd had a model of the site showing the rides and buildings on our dining room table until it disappeared one day. All these factors made him fear that his business and income would collapse. He lost weight. Everything he'd worked so hard to create would be destroyed. Unable to see shades of grey between the black and white of his predicament, he became depressed. At that time depression was not widely recognised as an illness that could affect otherwise quite healthy people. There were not the support services we have now, nor the private facilities that I was able to make use of. In the calm and logical note he left behind, he said how sad he was that he would not see us 'married and have grandchildren' – something I've failed to do so far. For many years I was angry with my father for taking his own life, but it was an incredibly brave and selfless thing to do. He thought his life insurance policies would pay up; however, they do not in the case of suicide. But time heals, and here, on the Carretera Austral, I was not angry any more, only sad, very sad. We can only do what we think is right at the time. Fred's blessing made me realise how much I missed and loved him.

At Futaleufú I headed east back into Argentina and on to Ruta 40. It was tarred and the 230 miles north to Bariloche on the southern shore of Lake Nahuel Huapi didn't take long. I camped in a pine forest. Was Fred's engine getting noisier?

Two days later I rode north and turned into Parque Nacional Lanín towards Paso Tromen. A volcano appeared on the skyline between two forested hills. Volcán Lanín was a perfect cone. Patches of snow rimmed the crater. The ripio road arrowed across a plain and disappeared into a haze. The haze deepened. It grew and came straight for me at speed. I stopped and it broke over me in a cascade of grit and dirt. I couldn't see anything and shut my eyes, trying to hold Fred upright in the buffeting wind, which disappeared as fast as it arrived. We were both still standing.

Large monkey puzzle trees, Chile's national tree, grew beside the road and soon gathered into troupes. Once over Paso Tromen I descended through an entire forest of them, like riding through botanical gardens. The mature trees were 120-foot-high monster gherkins, full of dense spiky branches but devoid of monkeys. Chile has no native monkeys so how did the tree get its name?

Archibald Menzies was a Scottish plant-collector and naval surgeon on Captain George Vancouver's 1791–5 circumnavigation of the globe. A suitable combination of talents as at that time medicines were primarily derived from plants. Menzies attended a dinner hosted by the Governor of Chile and was served the seeds of the conifer as dessert. He put them in his pocket rather than eat them, germinated the seeds on the return voyage and gave them to Sir Joseph Banks at Kew Gardens in London. The tree was initially known as 'Sir Joseph Banks' Pine' until one visitor to the Gardens apparently quipped that it would 'puzzle any monkey to climb', and so the nickname was born.

In its native habitat the lower half of the trunk was bare. Branches drooped from the upper half so it looked like a big arrow pointing into the sky. One tree grew out of the middle of the road. In true useless British Health and Safety style the trunk displayed a large sign pointing drivers to the right.

That night I camped under a big coihue tree in Pucón. As I snuggled into my sleeping bag the heavens opened in a roar. My pillow was my sweater stuffed into a soft draw-string nylon bag, a good example of my 'have more than one purpose' rule for kit. Feeling smug I'd got the timing right, I smiled. My tent was my home. There was nowhere I'd rather be. In two weeks I'd be on Easter Island, basking in the sun. The constant chatter of the rain lulled me to sleep and I dreamt of palm trees and fabulous food.

The next morning I was riding through postcards. Fred's wheels crunched the *ripio* road beneath snow-capped mountains and through cool, crisp, clean air. The rough terrain was Fred's natural home but we were caught in a paradox of beauty. It felt like my home too, but I'd never felt so vulnerable before, nor so worried about having an accident. The many-thousand-foot drops off the Chachapoyas to Celendín road in Peru had been easy compared to this. This was like riding along the top of a tube. The soft edges sloped steeply into bushes, trees or scree. I couldn't see far ahead through the almost continuous tunnel of trees. Vehicles suddenly appeared without warning and they went too fast. I was scared. There were no passing places. The *ripio* turned constantly and distant dust was the only warning of an approaching vehicle. I repeatedly scanned the bushes looking for an easy escape. I didn't want to end up like Matt Pope, the biker I'd met near El Chaltén, whose encounter with a Toyota pickup on the Austral had put him and his Africa Twin off the road for a month. I wanted to get off the Austral as soon as possible.

In many valleys bare trunks stood silhouetted against the sky. They littered the barren hillsides too, like discarded matches. The sight of them made me angry. They were the legacy of a promise the government made in 1937. In order to populate the Austral region it offered settlers ownership of any land they cleared of trees. Some of those trees have relations in unexpected places. Several species, including the southern beech (*Nothofagus*), share affinities with flora found in Australia and New Zealand. This is a legacy from some 120 million years ago, before the great landmass Gondwanaland broke up into the continents of South America, Africa, Arabia, Madagascar, India, Australia and Antarctica. Indeed, fossils from Chile are also found in Antarctica. Settlers came and started hundreds of forest fires to stake their claims. The subsequent soil erosion silted up rivers and stopped ships reaching Puerto Aisén, a superb natural harbour at the end of a 30-mile fjord from where cattle and sheep were exported.

That night I pulled into Hotel Libertador in Chillán, having left the Austral far behind. The next morning I met Simon and Jane, a British couple on their way south. I hadn't spoken English since leaving Ushuaia three weeks earlier and was struck by an old ailment – traveller's diarrhoea. Words tumbled from my mouth in a continuous stream so fast it had no substance, just a watery wordy mess. I'd been on my own too long. Simon's friendly eyes panicked. I noticed but I was in full flow. They began edging away. I should have stopped before they ran but I couldn't.

'Sorry, but we have to catch a bus,' and they left. I couldn't help myself. It was good to talk. So nice to speak English to English people. A bit of England in a foreign land.

Chillán was only one day from Santiago and the end of my road through South America. But first I decided to check Fred in at Chillán's KTM workshop. I feared the engine was noisier because one of the main bearings was failing. I'd caned Fred's motor ever since I started my trip and especially since Brazil. Perhaps doing 3,750 miles from São Paulo to Río Gallegos in ten days had been too much. Or was it 'Just My Imagination', my paranoia? Pablo, the KTM mechanic, thought the bearings were noisy. I totally relied on Fred. Without him I was nothing and went nowhere. My theory of preventive maintenance kicked in. Better spend now to save a major breakdown on the next leg of my trip, in Australasia or Africa. And Chilean wage rates were 25 per cent of those in New Zealand. Fred would go into hospital in Chile. Pablo stripped and rebuilt the engine in three days, after which Fred was quieter and happier. Did he vibrate more? No. Relieved, I rushed back to my hotel, checked out and set off, determined to get in a few hours' riding before nightfall.

I rode the 250 motorway miles to Santiago before dark. I found a cheap hotel in Las Condes and tried Rosa one last time. She didn't answer her mobile but I got through to her office in Valle. Her colleague told me Rosa wasn't working there any more. She'd left two weeks ago and they had no idea where she was.

I finally accepted Rosa had stolen my money. The thought had gnawed away at the back of my mind, taking the edge off my trip. She'd probably used it to fund her father's farm, growing mushrooms, orchids and pork for Mexico City. She loved that farm. At least the money would be put to good use.

I had been madly in love with her and had asked her to ride south with me. It would not have taken her long to size up all my possessions. I could have asked her to marry me.

'Consider it a cheap divorce,' advised my good friend Caroline. I had spent $150 on phone calls and had lost $3000 on the bicycle. I had got off lightly. My spirits rose as I let the money float away. Besides, my next stop was Easter Island, the most exciting place on my list. I couldn't wait to wander among the stone giants.

I would fly from Santiago to Easter Island, then on to Tahiti and Auckland, where Fred would join me again. The Santiago office of LAN Chile Airlines had offered to store Fred for free until I asked for him to be shipped to New Zealand. Our road trip across the Americas together was now over. We'd covered 33,000 miles between New York and Santiago and would do another 30,000 before we returned to London. But that's another story. Right now I had some giants to meet.

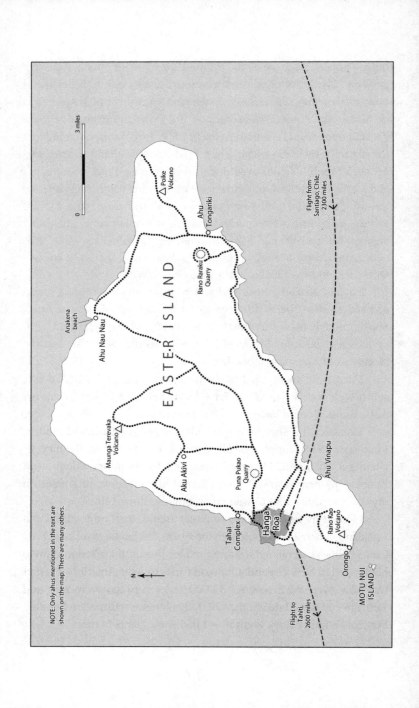

NOTE: Only ahus mentioned in the text are shown on the map. There are many others.

N

EASTER ISLAND

Poike Volcano

Ahu Tongariki

Rano Raraku Quarry

Anakena beach

Ahu Nau Nau

Maunga Terevaka Volcano

Aku Akivi

Puna Pukao Quarry

Tahai Complex

Hanga Roa

Ahu Vinapu

Rano Kao Volcano

Orongo

MOTU NUI ISLAND

Flight to Tahiti, 2600 miles

Flight from Santiago, Chile, 2300 miles

0   3 miles

23

MOAI MOAI EVERYWHERE

'Hotel? You need hotel?' said the smiling faces at Arrivals, but ever the experienced traveller I breezed through the wave of heat and herds of tourists and took the first taxi into Hanga Roa, the only village on Easter Island and home to about 90 per cent of the island's 3,500 inhabitants.

The door to the El Tauke guest house lay wide open but no one came when I called. I went inside but there was no one home. I walked to the next nearest *hostal*, past palms and banana trees, my bag feeling increasingly heavy. Sweat dripped down my chest. The windows and doors were all open at that *hostal* too, but it was also empty. As there were only two flights a week everyone went to the airport to tout for custom. I'd cleverly walked straight past all of them. I wandered down the hill along a leafy street of whitewashed wooden buildings towards the sea and hoped the *hostal* wouldn't be full when I returned. Superior life forms booked ahead. Dusk was settling over the island. Birds screeched from the bushes, hidden among the tropical leaves. I clambered over a stile into a field which sloped gently to the shore. Rough tufted grass brushed against my legs.

I froze at my first sight of a *moai* (stone statue). Five giant *moai* stood silently on a grassy ledge with their backs to the sea. They stared majestically over the T-shirted tourist, who barely reached their navels, and projected an aura of extraordinary calm as the setting sun haloed them in a vast cloak of orange. This was the Ahu Vai Uri grouping, part of the so-called Tahai Complex, which comprises three *moai* groups in all. The other two are Ahu Tahai and Ahu Ko Te Riku, both with one *moai* apiece. An *ahu* is the platform upon which the *moai* sit and these are the oldest *ahu* on Easter Island, dating from AD 690. There are 887 *moai* on the island in an area of just 66 square miles. If England had the same *moai* density there would be over 3.3 million of them, in the US that would be 124 million, or one *moai* for every two US citizens.

I sat on the warm grass and gazed up at the angular faces of *Ahu Vai Uri*. Surprisingly they all faced inland (as all *moai* do except for those on *Ahu Akivi*). Oversized heads sat on broad shoulders and both arms were folded on top of a slightly paunchy stomach. They had no legs. The tallest *moai* had half of his head and one shoulder missing, as if sliced off by a giant sword. The smallest was a mere stump and unrecognisable as a human form. An empty base hinted at a sixth *moai*. I drank in the sheer size of the giants.

Easter Island first came to the attention of the West when the Dutch explorer Jacob Roggeveen arrived there on Easter Day 1722. He noticed that the islanders' canoes leaked badly and were poorly made. How could they have survived weeks at sea in such vessels? The world's most isolated island is a tiny spec in the Pacific Ocean, 2,300 miles from the South American mainland and 2,700 miles from Tahiti. Even Pitcairn, the nearest inhabited island (of mutiny on the *Bounty* fame) is 1,300 miles away. The mystery deepened when Roggeveen saw the giant stone statues and realised there were only a few hundred people on the island. How could they have created and moved so many statues, many of which were over 30 feet high?

The next morning I rented a 125 cc Yamaha motorbike.

'Begin at the quarry,' said the landlady of my guest house. 'Everything started there.'

I rode out of town past the runway that NASA lengthened so the Shuttle could use it in an emergency. The road snaked between rolling grass fields high above the sea. As there's no protecting coral atoll, the waves have carved precipitous cliffs around the island and there are only three beaches. The strong wind, treeless horizon and heat made it feel like a tropical Patagonia. A hill like a blunt sawtooth rose in the distance but was overshadowed by Poike, the volcano that anchors the eastern end of the island. Easter Island is an isosceles triangle with two sides of 9 miles and the other of 11 miles and a volcano at each apex. Having grown from the junction of three tectonic plates, the island is a mountain that rises precipitously from the sea floor, which explains why there are so few beaches. The sawtooth hill was Rano Raraku, a caldera whose central cone collapsed and left a lake. The islanders – the Rapanui – excavated the stone in the caldera for their statues. It was the quarry where it all began.

When Captain Cook arrived in 1774 he realised that the Rapanui were Polynesians because Mahine, the Tahitian man he had with him, was able to converse with them. The spread of the Polynesians across the Pacific is the farthest migration of any race in history. By around AD 1200 they had colonised every habitable island between Hawaii, New Zealand and Easter Island. They sailed in twin-masted ocean-going canoe catamarans, against prevailing winds to make it easier to find their way home. All they needed was an island with large hardwood trees. Scouts left on two-way exploration trips to greatly reduce the risks. Sailing close to the wind on the outward leg, they then turned back once half the food was eaten and if no land had been found. The return journey was much swifter and safer, sailing with the wind. In 1999 a traditional Hawaiian sailing canoe travelled 1,600 miles eastwards from Mangareva (the largest of the Gambier islands) to Easter Island in just seventeen and a half days.

Even so, it was still an achievement to have found a tiny island only 11 miles across in thousands of miles of ocean.

In 1947 Thor Heyerdahl, in his famous Kon-Tiki expedition, travelled 4,300 miles in three and half months on a balsa raft west across the Pacific from Peru to Polynesia to prove that the original Polynesians could have come from South America rather than

Southeast Asia. He and his five-man crew survived by catching sharks by hand. Although he showed it could be done he found neither evidence nor scholars to support his claim.

Undaunted, Heyerdahl mounted an archaeological expedition to Easter Island in 1955, and in his book *Aku-Aku: The Secret of Easter Island* sought to prove that the original settlers came from South America and that the Ahu Vinapu stonework was of Inca quality. But this didn't convince the academics either.

However, a 2008 genetic study by Erik Thorsby of the University of Oslo in Norway shows that while most of the colonisation came from the west, people also arrived from the Americas in the east, so Heyerdahl has been partially vindicated. Historians think the Polynesians were led there by seabirds. Easter Island originally had the densest seabird population in Polynesia. The birds would have roamed far and wide looking for food, returning home at dusk. When the Rapanui arrived on Easter Island, from Polynesia, they discovered a forested, semi-tropical island inhabited by millions of birds but no land mammals.

The forests are long gone. They were felled for fuel, presaging the ecological catastrophe that was already hitting the island by the seventeenth century. As I neared the old quarry black dots peppered its external grassy slopes. The pinpricks grew into blackened stumps. The *moai* are so large they can be seen from a mile away. My heart quickened. The shapes became ever larger until I discerned those famous faces. Oval and imposing. Thirty or forty of them stared out with their backs to the Rano Rakuru crater, poking out of the ground at every conceivable angle, like giant drunken Woodentops. *Moai, moai* everywhere. Despite their size, I was surprised how thin the heads were. Even the ones buried beyond their chins towered over me. Every single one was male. Almost half (397) of the island's *moai* are in and around the quarry. The outside of the quarry was the nursery where masons completed the face, ears and back designs and carved the arms and hands before the statues were moved to their final resting place. I walked up to one and just stared at it, marvelling at the distinctive face, the very long and very strong nose and elongated ears.

The path steepened towards the crater rim. It was so hot I walked slowly to keep cool. Water and bright green reeds filled the 400-yard-wide crater, in complete contrast to the bare slopes outside. One side of the crater had been worn away and the crater lake drained through a small V-shaped cut in the rim. Inside the crater many *moai* lay around in all stages of production, from barely recognisable human blocks, through rough-hewn faces to the finished article. All the *moai* carved inside the crater passed over this stream on their way down to the nursery on the lower slopes. There were even more up on the outside ridge, including two completed *moai* that had been abandoned face down, with spectacular southerly views. It looked like the masons had only just put down their tools and walked away, but archaeological evidence indicates that the last *moai* and *ahu* were built in about 1620.

The Rapanui carved their statues with obsidian (volcanic glass) tools, since they had no metal ones. They decided on the site and positioning for each new *moai* according to how easy it would be to drag the rough-cut block down the slope from the quarry. The furthest point on the island is only ten miles away. It is estimated it took six men with obsidian tools twelve to fifteen months to make a small fifteen-foot *moai*. All the *moai* had the same form except one, Tukuturi, a kneeling Buddha-like figure with a lifelike head at the eastern end of the quarry. El Gigante is the biggest *moai* of all at 68 feet tall, estimated to weigh about 270 tons and considered far too large to be movable.

The Rapanui stone-carvers believed the *moai* had *mana* or power. The population was once divided into ten clans, each with its own tribal lands. Legends told of many wars between the two main factions. Opposing clans pulled down each other's *moai* to break the statues' necks and deprive them of their *mana*. It was not enough just to push a *moai* over. The power of the *moai* depended on it being able to 'see'. That was why so many were toppled forwards on to carefully placed boulders that would both hide the eyes and break the neck.

As dusk approached I sat at the top of the hill above several *moai* and stared out over them just as they stared out silently below me.

There was not a sound but the soft whisper of the wind. The fields slid away and flowed out over the island, punctuated by two dormant volcanic cones. A dry stone wall meandered over the open grassland from Hanga Roa, split at the bottom of the hill below and encircled the quarry, hemming us in. A few miles away replanted eucalyptus trees darkened the crest of a hill. The eerie presence of the huge stone statues transcended anything I had experienced before. I shivered as darkness fell. The Rapanui never visited the quarry at night. They didn't believe the *moai* were dead.

The quarry's 'Golden Age' was during the fourteenth and fifteenth centuries when the island's population peaked at about 12,000, but it was all downhill after that. By 1650 the combined effects of deforestation and overpopulation made decline inevitable, but it was the appearance of white men that triggered the final collapse. The nadir occurred in 1876 when the population crashed to just over a hundred. In his book *Collapse*, Jared Diamond argues that Easter Island 'is the closest approximation that we have to a complete disaster unfolding in complete isolation', and that the deforestation of Easter Island was 'amongst the most extreme in the world'.

The population grew quickly in the fourteenth and fifteenth centuries and the Rapanui fanned out across the island, chopping trees and feasting on the birds as they went. Naturally, the easiest sources of food didn't last long. Islands are especially vulnerable to deforestation but many different factors combined to cause Easter Island's calamity. In his study of deforestation on eighty-one Pacific islands, Diamond identified nine potential contributory factors. Easter Island had all nine. A key factor was the introduction by the Rapanui of alien species like rats, sheep, sparrows, hawks and partridges. The extinction of the giant palm, for example, was probably down to the rats the settlers brought with them. The rats ate the palm-tree nuts and prevented the tree regenerating. Together, the new creatures so devastated the island's ecology that by the early 1600s the whole forest had gone and all the tree species were extinct. No forests meant no clouds, and no rain meant no streams.

With too little food for too many people, the *moai*-building society collapsed into civil war around 1680. The obsidian tools morphed into spear points for killing not carving. When Captain Cook anchored off Hanga Roa in 1774 he sought provisions. The islanders were willing to trade but there was little food to acquire. In his book *Island at the End of the World,* Steven Roger Fischer states that Cook was convinced some dreadful event had occurred because there were few women and the population was in a wretched condition. Indeed, the Easter Island women were 'neither reserved nor chaste, and for the trifling consideration of a small piece of cloth, some of our sailors obtained the gratification of their desires'. (Today all islanders have European ancestry.) Some of the statues had fallen down or lay broken, but others were still standing. The population was thought to be about 2,000, but Cook realised the 'fertile land could support many more'.

In the 1860s 'blackbird' ships despatched from Peru kidnapped islanders for the Peruvian domestic labour market. After the abolition of slavery the Peruvians had exhausted the local supply of indigenous Quecha and Aymara workers, which led to serious labour shortages. In 1861 Dubliner Joseph Charles Byrne arrived in Peru and proposed the government trade in 'indentures instead of people' (as Steven Roger Fischer explains in *Island at the End of the World*) from a pool of cheap labour in the Pacific Islands. These contracts would be sold to the highest bidder at public auctions. Easter Island was the nearest source and in December 1862 about eight 'blackbird' ships anchored off Hanga Roa to collect 'immigrants'. They abducted about half the population but, having no resistance to tuberculosis, smallpox or dysentery, the captive labourers died in their hundreds. When the French minister in Lima complained, a number were returned home, but some had smallpox. Only four hundred islanders survived: 94 per cent of the population had died or been forcibly relocated in only nine years.

Missionaries arrived and further threatened the health of Rapanui culture by banning nudity, tattooing, traditional signing and dancing, as well as most sexual practices. By 1868 not one *moai* was left standing. French Catholic missionaries had baptised all the islanders and also quashed the Birdman cult, the islanders' method of determining a leader for the next year. A French sea captain, Jean-Baptiste Dutrou-Bornier, exploited the power vacuum. He acquired land and planned to send the Rapanui to Tahiti as indentured servants, so clearing the island for his sheep farm. Thanks to his ruthlessness and firearms he soon 'owned' some 80 per cent of the island. He confined the Rapanui to Hanga Roa and forced them to work on his farm. The situation became so desperate for the Rapanui that in 1871 the whole island of 505 tried to emigrate on one ship, but it could only take 275 people. Dutrou-Bornier's end finally came when three Rapanui murdered him in 1876. At that point there were just over a hundred Rapanui left on the island.

The next day I rode past the quarry and turned away from Poike volcano to Anakena beach. The sandy track threaded through a small grove of coconut palms behind the beach. Their shade made it the best picnic spot on the island. The midday sun burnt the air. Four picnic tables were already occupied and three children played football while the grownups unpacked. Five *moai* stared through the trees from Ahu Nau Nau's ten-foot-high platform, which extended halfway across the beach. Wandering beneath the palms, which swayed in the cool breeze, I emerged into the sun. The remains of two more *moai* – a small stump and a headless corpse – completed the *ahu*. Four of the *moai* sported *pukaos*, huge red stone cylinders like massive Christmas cakes on their heads. The *pukao* were made from scoria from a different quarry and averaged five tons each. Spaces at either end of the *ahu* suggested missing *moai*.

The *moai* had their backs to the sea. The ceremonial area in front of them felt like a stage with an enormous, imposing audience staring down from on high. I gazed up into the huge eyeless faces while the *moai* sniffed the sizzling lamb drifting through the trees.

Like all the *moai* on the island, the Nau Nau were the colour of an old waxed yellow crayon. They all had different swirly tattoos on their backs – unique designs since each was carved to represent a person. Each was a 'memorial to great chiefs', as British archaeologist Katherine Routledge discovered, whose 'living face' kept the memory of the ancestor alive. This was just one of many groundbreaking discoveries that Routledge made on the island during her sixteen-month stay there with her husband, in 1914–15, as related in her book *The Mystery of Easter Island*.

The noses of the Nau Nau *moai* were very long, often more than half the length of the head but all different shapes. One turned upwards, pig-like, at the end. The ears were as long as the noses. The head jutted forward slightly which accentuated the chiselled chin. The arms hung down on each side and met in the middle. The five fingers, impossibly long and slender, met over the navel. A light collar of contrasting cement revealed repaired necks. The *pukaos* were a deep, dirty scarlet. When they were new, *moais* were yellow, *pukaos* red and *ahus* white. Apparently the *moai* are modelled on a penis. Perhaps this explains why they got larger over time. But why create so many? Was there a 'mine is bigger than yours' rivalry between clan chiefs, stimulated by not much else to do on such an isolated and once fertile island? The relatively flat island and homogenous society meant all the clans could use the same quarry and drag their *moai* to wherever they were needed.

The *moai* remained blind until placed on an *ahu*. They only came alive when the eyes and *pukao* topknots were added. The eyes always looked slightly upwards rather than down and the opening of the eyes activated the power and *mana* of the statue. From then on certain activities were banned if the *moai* could see you. All the Nau Nau *moai* were blind. The existence of the eyes was only discovered in the 1980s when Sergio Rapu Haoa, a Rapanui, discovered an eyeball at Anakena. The eyes were made of white coral and the pupil of red scoria, the same material as the *pukao*. Carbon-dating Nau Nau's coral put the oldest *moai* at AD 1100 and the most recent to around AD 1600.

It was impossible to ride any distance without seeing an *ahu* or *moai*. The size and number of them was overwhelming. Extraordinary statues invite extraordinary explanations. Erich von Däniken visited Easter Island for his book *Chariots of the Gods?* 'The usual explanation, that the stone giants were moved to their present sites on wooden rollers, is not feasible in this case,' he asserted, since 'no trees grow on the island'. Also 'the rock is too hard to cut with modern tools'. Von Däniken never let the facts get in the way of a good story. There could be only one explanation. Aliens.

The next day I rode to the quarry again but turned right towards the water. Flat fields sloped gently towards the sea. The breaking waves formed a white backdrop to the largest *ahu* on the island. Ahu Tongariki was my favourite simply because of its size: fifteen standing *moai* filled a platform that is over 100 yards long, but it may have had as many as thirty *moai* in its heyday. They ranged between 18 and 46 feet in height and weighed an average of forty tons; the heaviest was eighty-seven tons. In May 1960 a tsunami destroyed the *ahu*, hurling *moai* up to 700 yards inland. It took Claudio Cristino, a Chilean archaeologist, four years to re-erect them. Only one *moai* has a *pukao*. These *moai* are 15 of the 313 on the coastline – an average of one every three quarters of a mile. Imagine England with 14,500 Stonehenges around the coast. I sat on the ground and stared up at them, marvelling at their long fingernails and paunchy stomachs. I never got over the sheer size of the *moai*.

Heading back, I took the red-dirt road between the western edge of the runway and the cliffs to Rano Kao, the caldera at the southernmost end of the island. The green slopes dropped down to the round lake filled with totora reeds. On the other side the lip plunged 1,000 feet to the sea below, creating the feeling of an impregnable fortress. It is no wonder the Rapanui felt they were the only people on earth. Three small islands jutted out of the sea about a mile away, where water foamed against the rocks.

After the internecine wars, population decline and devastation from deforestation, the Rapanui created a new social order: the Birdman cult. It started here at Orongo on the top of the cliff. The cliff was still strung with some fifty grassed-over platforms atop stone walls that blended into the top of the crater. All faced the islands.

Mata Ngarau is the highest point on the rim and was the most sacred place at Orongo. Hundreds of petroglyphs cover the rocks: arms with extraordinarily long fingers, strange faces with big bulbous eyes, frog-like animals and numerous otherworldly designs. Many of the images are Birdmen, with the body of a man and the head of a frigate bird. The long straight nose and bulbous base is extremely phallic.

The old systems of ancestor worship and rites had failed to stop catastrophic deforestation, famine, tribal wars and rapacious foreign interest. So the commoners overthrew the old order and merged the original deities into one god, the creator, Makemake ('Of the phallus'). They proclaimed Makemake as the new source of the island's *mana*. He created the earth, sun, stars and people, rewarded the good and punished the bad. He used thunder to say when he was angry. Every year Makemake brought the sooty terns and frigate birds to Motu Nui, the furthest of the three offshore islands. The arrival of the birds became the core of the new Birdman cult.

This cult centred around a race between the clans. The leader of the clan that obtained the first unbroken sooty tern's egg of the year became the Birdman for the next twelve months. The tricky bit was that sooty terns only nested on Motu Nui, the most distant island, one mile away across shark-infested waters. Contestants, *hopu manu,* represented the clan leaders. Each *hopu manu* climbed down the thousand-foot cliff, swam to the island using a float of totora reeds and stayed there until he found an egg. He then swam back with it attached to his forehead, scaled the cliff and presented it unbroken to his clan chief.

Many died in the attempt – either by falling down the cliff, being eaten by sharks or in fights with rivals. The successful *hopu manu's* chief became the Birdman and the sole representative of Makemake and ruler of the island for the following year. The losers had to ritually lacerate themselves with spears tipped with large flakes of volcanic glass, or *mata'a*. The Birdman shaved his head, eyebrows and eyelashes and spent the year being waited on. He was not allowed to wash or cut his nails for the whole period. During his reign the

Birdman's clan was powerful and protected by his *mana*. His followers roamed the island and burnt the huts and toppled the *moai* of those who crossed them. The following year the new Birdman took revenge in a downward spiral of destruction. By 1840 there were no *moai* left standing. The last Birdman competition occurred in 1878, after which they were stopped by the missionaries, who were hell-bent on destroying an indigenous culture that they did not understand.

Erich von Däniken came to Orongo too, and in *Chariots of the Gods?* states 'orally transmitted legend tells us that flying men landed and lit fires in ancient times. The legend is confirmed by sculptures of flying creatures with big staring eyes.' Clearly aliens landed here too.

That evening, after a dinner of tuna ceviche, salad and *camote* (sweet potato) at the Merahi Ra'a Restaurant in Hanga Roa, I wandered down the main street looking at souvenirs. There were plenty of wooden carvings of half-man half-bird creatures as well as tablets with strange inscriptions – replicas of *rongorongo*, the Rapanui 'writing'. *Rongorongo* was only deciphered in 1997, by Steven Fischer, Director of the Institute of Polynesian Languages and Literature in Auckland, New Zealand, an expert in linguistics and epigraphy. He interpreted the meaning of the 2,300 characters carved into the four-foot hardwood pole known as the Santiago Staff, which had been acquired by the French colonist Dutrou-Bornier and swapped for a keg of Chilean gunpowder in 1870. In his book, *Glyphbreaker: A Decipherer's Story*, Fischer concludes that the Staff detailed a series of chants that explained the creation of the world. He was only able to decipher one of the twenty-five other *rongorongo* scripts so the secrets of *rongorongo* remain locked away.

24

LIFE ON THE LINE

And so ended my eighteen-month, 33,000-mile ride from New York to Easter Island.

The southern half of South America is so sparsely populated it was often a joy just to see another human being beneath the huge skies and treeless plains of the Patagonian steppe. My mind wandered on the empty roads and reconnected to hidden memories. Time to think made me reassess my life and re-evaluate the dreams I'd had when I left university. Back then I'd wanted to opt out, be green and live in the countryside. Instead I got caught in the rat race, hooked on consumerism and lived in London. At my nadir, just before I admitted myself to the Priory, I owned seven motorbikes and two cars. It took my breakdown to shake me out of the rat race but it took longer to escape consumerism. I'd been chasing money and possessions but became much happier and more relaxed without them.

I doubt I'd ever have gone on a big trip if it hadn't been for the Priory. I got a huge kick when Fred and I rode off each morning: the joy of being outside, on the road and travelling at speed. Riding the line became my job, and I relished the 'how great it is to be alive' feeling that I'd never had on my commute back in the UK. I wondered if my life would ever be the same again.

Time to think also helped me come to terms with the many mistakes I'd made in my life. In the same way that my breakdown made me reset my mind so my trip reset my life. Instead of dwelling on regrets I became more accepting. I began to want to move on rather than wonder what might have been. I came to recognise the natural rhythm of good and bad days, good and bad weeks. Everything cycles up and down, and the worst moments always come at night. I came to see that as normal.

Indeed, on my trip the best things happened when things went wrong. The extraordinary kindness of strangers who went out of their way to assist yet wanted nothing in return. People wanted to help. Spending so much time in my helmet stripped away some of my ego and enabled me to approach people in a more friendly, more open way. I became more receptive and tolerant.

I loved everything about my trip but the loneliness followed me like a dark shadow. I knew I wouldn't have rushed if I hadn't been on my own. I kept telling myself it was better to travel alone than not at all, better to regret the things I'd done rather than those I never did. I worried that I was still single because I'd learnt a wrong behaviour. For, once a behaviour has been learnt it becomes ingrained and difficult to change. Perhaps my trip really has changed the way I think.

Time to think re-awoke senses swamped by the noise and pace of daily life. I learnt to trust my instincts, intuition, and act without a second thought, which saved me from accidents – like 'seeing' the reflection of the white truck in the leaves on the Blue Ridge Parkway in Virginia – and helped me understand how Rosa 'knew' I was upset from hundreds of miles away in Mexico. As I relaxed I listened to myself. I came to know how fast was safe because my intuition told me so. Accelerate up to the line, feel and ride the edge of adrenaline but never cross it. I developed those skills and emerged feeling more in tune with myself. The culmination of that new power was my out-of-body experience in Patagonia. Maybe I had to be on my own to make the connections. You need time to think.

My other big worry was my mortgage. It made me rush and kept me moving. I rarely stayed in one place for long. It sat at the back of my mind sniping in the dark. I was brought up not to borrow money and my values didn't change despite the miles and what I kept telling myself; I was spending tomorrow for fun today.

But the most important moment occurred when I named my bike Fred after the blessing in Copacabana. On the Carretera Austral in Chile, a forested mountain beside a lake dotted with islands reminded me of the poster which had once hung on the wall of my childhood bedroom. I had persuaded my father to buy it for me when I was seven. Fred and I rode through the poster. Fred opened my mind. Fred made me realise I'd never grieved for my father, that I'd shut him out and locked him away. I came to understand how much I missed my father and how much I wished I had known him. My journey brought his memory alive and that wouldn't have happened without Fred. Fred is my friend, he harbours my memories and is a part of me.

I am a long-distance rider. This is my job. This is what I do. Every day I wake up somewhere new, get on Fred and ride. The former loneliness of the long-distance rider has gone. I am no longer alone, because Fred is here.

Appendix I
WHERE ARE THEY NOW?

Though most of my encounters on the road were fleeting, I have kept in touch with some of the people I met; others, sadly, have slipped through the net.

US

Ara Gureghian   The motorcycling chef I met at the campsite in Suches, GA has his own website (http://theoasisofmysoul.com) and is working on his first book. 'After almost 5 years on the road we are in Cody, Wyoming, US, on our way to colder temperatures in Canada with my buddy Spirit (American Pit Bull) on "Old Faithful", my 1996 BMW GS motorbike (252,000 miles on the clock) with a Ural sidecar!'

Sue Galpin   The crazy racer I met in Suches, Georgia is still 'riding BMWs, teaching sport-riding and safe techniques. I have ridden over 750,000 miles on motorbikes and still ride every day. I'm racing again at Suches next year, and even though I'm in my sixties, still ride like I stole it!'

Mexico

Catalina Del Castillo   Catalina invited me to the 'best disco in Mexico' in Acapulco. She now lives in Sao Paulo, Brazil, happily married to a Swiss guy. 'I switched from motorcycle horses to real horses as Brazil made it very difficult for us by not giving us driving licences. So I only ride every time I go to Valle de Bravo, our favourite place in the world, where we hope to retire one day!'

Jan Marc Staelens   The dancing professor lives in Thailand with his wife and baby daughter and still rides motocross bikes whenever and wherever he can.

Juan Balam Ibarra   Juan, who let me stay in his house in Valle de Bravo, still lives in Valle, where he now has a young son and manufactures yurts (http://mexyurts.com). He also does consulting work in community development all over Mexico. He rides his Africa Twin every day and twice a week takes his Husky 510 on hardcore enduro rides on the very technical trails of Valle.

Leah and Dom Breen   The Ozzie-Irish couple got married and now 'live on a 160-acre farm near Adelaide in Australia with two gorgeous sons and a baby on the way! We have a small earthworks business that Dom operates and it's doing well.'

Guatemala

Jodie Miner   I overtook Jodie three times on her bicycle: in Guatemala, Costa Rica and Ecuador, but she still got to Ushuaia before I did. She currently 'lives in Seattle, Washington, US with my husband and two daughters, where I spend as much time as possible hiking, kayaking, and skiing. I haven't ridden much since Ushuaia, but my two-year-old took her first kayak ride at 5 months and is showing worrying signs of loving a good adventure as much as I do.'

Sergio Conte   The guitar-playing traveller from Ischia, Italy, is currently 'cruising the North Tyrrhenian Sea on a 22-metre motor yacht. I will be the captain until next November then I will move to Hawaii for my holidays.'

Ecuador

Brian Coles   A regular at the Turtle's Head, Quito, Colesy is 'now happily married in Denmark. I found treasures here – my son and daughter – and reflect daily on "that year away", these memories are life's nectar. We have a plan in about five years to go to South America for a year or three.'

Dan Walsh The *Bike* magazine journalist I met in Quito published a collection of his *Bike* articles in *These Are The Days That Must Happen To You*. After 2005 'I spent another year in Buenos Aires, living in the faded Ritz, then another year in Panama, Costa Rica and Nicaragua. Now based in Manchester. Still riding, still writing, still travelling, still searching. Still rarely still...'

Mariano Gon The export manager of Santa Cruz Bicycles in California (www.santacruzmtb.com), who helped me try and recover my money, is 'now Global Sales Manager at Santa Cruz and riding whenever I can. I just got married to my high-school sweetheart and I'm planning to cycle to La Paz, Baja California, just as soon as I have a slot in my diary.'

Mike and Marci Cohen Mike, the US advertising exec who knew that 'the secret is to be happy on your own lawn' reports that 'since meeting you in the Galápagos, my wife and I have retired. You'll find us cruising the New England coast in summer, skiing Jackson Hole the winter, and travelling to the far corners of our remarkable planet in between.'

Richard and Jane Heaphy The British couple with whom I shared pisco sours and a silly sense of humour in several different places in South America now live in London with their two lovely girls. They say they 'can't wait to go travelling again, but next time it will be family adventures in a camper van'.

Trys Menhinick The artist I met in the Turtle's Head in Quito is 'currently living in Salford, Manchester. Painting pictures and constructing an exhibition of works relating to life here.'

Peru

Nelson The charismatic muleteer on my donkey trek in northern Peru, who I'm sure can boil an egg, is now a local guide for the Gran Vilaya expeditions organised by Chachapoyas Tours.

Tina Motley The Gran Vilaya expedition, which became my Indiana Jones chapter, was one of the highlights of my trip. Tina owns Chachapoyas Tours (www.kuelapperu.com and www.kuelap. org), which has grown considerably and now also runs 'tours to the Lake of the Condors and Tajopampa ruins'.

Bolivia

Ian Reeves I met Ian pushing his blue trolley somewhere beyond Lake Poopó. He's hoping to complete his epic walk from Ushuaia to Alaska, and writes about it at http://ianwalk.com – I hope he too brings out a book. These days he is: 'ecstatically married, one foot on a plane to India to walk from the south to as far north as we can get on our visas, teaching and tutoring Spanish in the meantime. life. is. wonderful.'

Brazil

Waldyr Siqueira The owner of the KTM importer in São Paulo where Fred got his engine fixed up will by late 2011 have relocated to new premises nearby, at Rua Francisco Leitão 653, Pinheiros, São Paulo (www.ktmbikes.com.br and www.husaberg.com.br). He still imports Husaberg motorcycles, now also sells KTM bicycles, and has a service shop for KTM bikes and motorcycles and Husabergs.

Argentina

Rupert Wilson-Young When I encountered Rupert he was riding from Alaska to Ushuaia on a 49cc moped which got so hot that he had to stop for a cool-down every 20 miles. He now lives in Montreal, Canada with his wife, Dorothée (who cycled with him), and their son and daughter.

Matt Pope I met Matt on the road to El Chaltén with Mount Fitzroy towering in the background. 'I was still recovering from my accident on the Careterra Austral and was unsure about my crudely repaired Africa Twin. I completed my circuit of South America without further mishap and returned to Guildford, from where my work with scientific instruments has kept me travelling the world, albeit mostly without the motorcycle. I now ride a KTM 990 and talk a good bike trip'.

UK

Austen Fairbairn Austen, who inspired me to go on my trip in the first place, lives in rural Lincolnshire 'writing and ranting about world events.'

Liz and Brian Argent The couple who sold me Fred still run Motorite, their motocross shop in Surbiton, London and are 'looking forward to retiring to the countryside.'

Fred Fred is still with me. After doing so many miles together, and sharing such a profound journey, I cannot bear even to remodel him, let alone part with him. As for me, I'm assimilating the lessons I learnt on the road, contemplating a move out of London to greener pastures, and steering myself in a new direction.

Appendix II
TRIP FAQS

The most common questions I'm asked about my trip are:

What was your favourite place?

Any day spent not working, but my answer usually depends on the mood I'm in when asked. If I could go anywhere right now it would be Easter Island – because of the size and number of the *moai*, and the Polynesians.

How much did you spend?

I budgeted on $50 a day (excluding fuel), as this is what everyone else seemed to do, but the daily outlay depends entirely on which country you are in. First World countries are always expensive. It also makes a difference whether you are moving or not, cooking your own food or eating in restaurants, and sleeping in a tent or a hotel. Some days I spent less, others more.

Most cyclists I met budgeted on $5 a day.

My largest costs were the tourist trips, like the Galápagos cruise, and flying Fred from place to place. Planning helps with the latter but not the former. You get the best tourist deals by turning up on the day. It also helps if you don't buy too many bicycles.

What went wrong with your bike?

I had only one major engine problem: the inlet cam follower that failed in Argentina, which was fixed in São Paulo, Brazil.

Most other issues were caused by my modifications (I made over fifty to the standard bike) and wear and tear. Doing high mileages in a short space of time greatly accelerates normal deterioration rates. I wore out a brand new rear tyre in 4,000 miles by riding from Rio de Janeiro, Brazil to Ushuaia at the bottom of South America in ten days. They usually lasted 12,000 miles.

I used preventative maintenance to replace things before they wore out on the basis that it was cheaper to fix a problem before it occurred. It works well on helicopters.

The other cause was pilot error – such as my using the wrong engine oil in Buenos Aires, Argentina, which led to the clutch slipping in Patagonia.

How did you ship your bike?

I flew it everywhere. It flew as cargo – either in a custom-made crate or strapped to a pallet. I prefer air freight to sea freight because it is much quicker. Sea freight can take months as the ship can be diverted en route. Although the sea leg costs less, port storage and handling charges and the cost of board and lodging while waiting for it to arrive can erode or negate the savings.

On the London to New York flight at the start of my trip, I landed three hours after my bike, walked round to the Newark cargo terminal, cleared my crate through Customs, borrowed a crowbar, put the wheels on, connected the battery and rode away three hours after I landed.

Appendix III
KIT LIST

Items were in seven colour-coded drawstring bags – e.g. '(navy)' – for easy identification. I started with cooking gear (a stove, fuel bottle, and small nestled pans) but sent that home from Lima.

Tank Bag

Cameras	Digital SLR + 20-200 f2.8	Digital SLR 28-80 f2.8	Flash
(custom-fitted foam)	Lens cloth	Polarising filter	Remote control

Top Box

Documents	*Carnet de Passage*	Bike Registration (V5)	Bike invoice
(A4 zipper)	International Driving Permit	UK Driving Licence	
	Vaccination certificates	Health insurance	Passport photos
Computer	Laptop	Charger	Mains cable
(laptop bag)	Cloned drive	Backup photo drive	Flash card reader
	Mouse	Security lock	
Overnight	Razor + blades	Universal Sink Plug	Deodorant
(small zipper)	Toothbrush	Toothpaste	Dental floss
	Airline eye mask	Ear plugs	Paracetamol
	Head torch	Loo roll	
Books	Current book	Guidebook	Notebook
Health	Mosquito repellent	Sun cream	
Other	Phone charger	Toolbox spanner	

Pannier 1

Riding Gear (brown)	Winter gloves	Silk gloves	Neck warmer
Clothes 1	Down jacket (compression sack)	Sweater (navy) – doubles as pillow	
Camping	Tent	Tent poles & pegs	Groundsheet
Navigating	Maps	Compass	
Feet	Hiking boots	Sandals	
Health	First-aid kit (red)	Mosquito net (red)	Water filter (blue)
Other	Binoculars		

Pannier 2

Clothes 2	Quick-dry shirt (1)	t-shirt (1)	Handkerchief (1)
(green)	Pants (1)	Socks (2)	Warm socks (1)
Clothes 3	Quick-dry convertible trousers (1)	Quick-dry shorts (1)	
(blue)			
Camping	Sleeping bag	Silk liner	Thermarest
Camera	Camera chargers (mauve)	Camera tripod (black)	
Library	Guidebooks	Other books	

Appendix IV
Useful Links

Adventure Rider www.advrider.com
Very active thumper forum.

Book Updates, Talks and Upcoming eBook and iPad/Android App
www.jeremybullard.com

Foreign & Commonwealth Office
www.fco.gov.uk/en/travel-and-living-abroad/travel-advice-by-country/Travel advice
The latest reasons not to go anywhere.

Horizons Unlimited www.horizonsunlimited.com The overlanders'
biking site with a huge breadth of information, forums and advice.

Scotts Performance Products www.scottsonline.com If I could
have only one extra on my bike it would be the Scotts stabilizer; it
saved me from a high-speed crash when a kangaroo torpedoed me
in Australia. They are a standard fitment on the KTM 640 Rallyes –
the factory Paris–Dakar bikes.

Touratech www.touratech.com
All the toys you could ever want.

Appendix V
Selected Reading

General

Bruce Chatwin, *In Patagonia*

Ed Culberson, *Obsessions Die Hard: Motorcycling the Pan American Highway's Jungle Gap*

Richard Feynman, *The Pleasure of Finding Things Out*

Hergé, *The Adventures of Tintin: Tintin and the Picaros*

Alexandra Horowitz, *Inside of a Dog: What Dogs See, Smell, and Know*

Nigel Marven, *Incredible Journeys*

Andrew Parker, *Seven Deadly Colours*

Mark Prendergast, *Uncommon Grounds: A History of Coffee*

Jim Rogers, *Investment Biker*

Rupert Sheldrake, *Dogs That Know When Their Owners Are Coming Home*

Dick Teresi, *Lost Discoveries*

Matt Walker, *Moths that Drink Elephants' Tears*

Galápagos

Antonio Adrian, *The Galápagos Phat Guide*

Johanna Angermeyer, *My Father's Island*

Charles Darwin, *On the Origin of Species*

Michael D'Orso, *Plundering Paradise*

John Hickman, *The Enchanted Islands*

John Kricher, *Galápagos*

Jonathan Weiner, *The Beak of the Finch*

Peru and Machu Picchu

Hiram Bingham, *Lost City of the Incas*

Erich von Däniken, *Chariots of the Gods?: Was God an Astronaut?*

Hergé, *The Adventures of Tintin: The Seven Crystal Balls*

Johan Reinhard, *Machu Picchu: The Sacred Centre*

Gene Savoy, *Vilcabamba: Last City of the Incas*

Hugh Thomson, *The White Rock*

Easter Island

Jared Diamond, *Collapse*
Steven Roger Fischer, *Glyphbreaker: A Decipherer's Story*
Steven Roger Fischer, *Island at the End of the World*
Thor Heyerdahl, *Aku-Aku: The Secret of Easter Island*
Katherine Routledge, *The Mystery of Easter Island*
Jo Anne Van Tilburg, *Among Stone Giants*
Shawn McLaughlin, *The Complete Guide to Easter Island*

Thanks

Inspiration

Austen Fairbairn for inspiring me to ride to Cape Town in the first place.

Liz Argent for telling me to 'just go, and worry about the money later'.

Fred

KTM for making such a wonderful machine that can go anywhere and do anything despite the rider.

Swampy Marsh of Marsh Performance, Portsmouth, UK for building a fantastic engine.

All the KTM dealers I visited who helped me keep Fred in fine fettle, especially Oliver Nix at KTM Sommer (now KTM Team West) in Oberhausen, Germany (www.ktm-sommer.de), for his efficient service; Brian Argent at Motorite, Surbiton, UK, for telephone support; and Waldyr Siqueira in São Paulo, Brazil.

Kit

Andy Goldfine at Aerostich in Duluth, MN, US (www.aerostich.com) for making such a great jacket (with 14 fabulous pockets) that is still in daily use.

Scotts of Montrose, CA, US (www.scottsonline.com) for making the steering damper that saved me from several major crashes. If I could have only one toy it would be this.

On the Road

Thanks to all those mentioned in the book, and especially those unfortunately omitted, for their kindness and generosity. I wish I'd asked for and written down your names.

Caroline Cuffe for her wise advice and for sending my cleverly left-behind cooking gear to Texas.

Juan Balam Ibarra for letting me stay in his house in Valle rent-free.

Richard and Jane Heaphy for bringing balance to a barking biker and making me feel quite decisive.

My mother, Shirley, for sending and receiving various packages. I couldn't have managed without Mission Control.

The Book

I would like to thank all those who have helped me publish this book, especially my editor, Lucy Ridout, who has totally transformed my scribblings into the book you hold in your hands. Thanks also to Nick Hill for the excellent maps, Anthony Stileman for the photos, Julia, Winston and Mark for the cover and John Button and Mike Kirby for their printing patience. To my mother and my sisters, Caroline, Philippa and Katy, for their love, support and bossiness. And to Simon, Phillip and Kevin and of course to George, Tori, Morty, Tabitha, Seb, Nick and Abi.

I also owe special thanks to Liz Kendall for her patience, advice and understanding, Louise Down for her help on the title, and a great debt to my friends who soldiered through the early drafts: Caroline Cuffe, Charles and Mandy Irving, Deborah Goring-Morris, Olwen Griffith, Nick Harper, Nevile and Lesley Player, Roger Burt and Sam Manicom.

Obviously after all this help the remaining errors and omissions are entirely their fault.